Women's Liberation

Women's Liberation

The Arya Samaj Movement in India

Sangeeta Sharma

RAWAT PUBLICATIONS

Jaipur • New Delhi • Bangalore • Hyderabad • Guwahati

ISBN 81-316-0376-8

Published by
Prem Rawat for **Rawat Publications**
Satyam Apts, Sector 3, Jawahar Nagar, Jaipur 302 004 (India)
Phone: 0141 265 1748/7006 Fax: 0141 265 1748
E-mail: info@rawatbooks.com
Website: www.rawatbooks.com

New Delhi Office
4858/24, Ansari Road, Daryaganj, New Delhi 110 002
Phone: 011 2326 3290

Also at *Bangalore, Hyderabad* and *Guwahati*

Typeset by Rawat Computers, Jaipur
Printed at Chaman Enterprises, New Delhi

Because he only gave to the world,
Dedicated to the revered memory of
Shri R.S. Jain

Contents

Preface

The present work explores the decisive and unique contribution of Dayanand Saraswati and Arya Samaj in the realm of social reform, particularly the comprehensive, structured and multi-layered programme that they initiated for women's liberation. The indisputable contribution of Arya Samaj towards betterment in women's status in the early decades of the twentieth century needs to be particularly commended on account of the fact that the main focus during these years had shifted to the agitation against the British leading to the hegemony of the nationalist struggle. Numerous organizations which had been striving for social reform in the nineteenth century, due to the irresistible pull of the political agitation, had become involved in the political processes. Consequently, the quest for social reform got considerably subdued and the urgency and enthusiasm that had defined women's issues in the nineteenth century was palpably missing in the twentieth century. Arya Samaj, however, assiduously remained engaged in its efforts to bring about progressive changes in the social fabric and herein lay the historic role of the movement. Moreover, the Samaj was able to impart critical importance and urgency to women's issues which no earlier or contemporary movement could accomplish. This work is an attempt to highlight the ceaseless campaigns of the Arya Samaj for betterment in women's conditions.

Ironically, the dominant image of the Samaj that has survived in popular memory, British official records and even in historical writings is one of communal organization and a movement that has been often held responsible for worsening of inter-communal relations. This overriding discourse regarding the Samaj has eclipsed a significant strand of the movement, i.e., its persevering endeavours for social and religious reform. In this work an attempt has been made to project Arya Samaj as a vibrant movement combatting superstition, challenging the caste system, championing the cause of women's education, striving for rehabilitation of widows and pleading for liberalization of marriage.

The primary campaigns of the Arya Samaj were in the realm of women's education wherein they were able to translate the theoretical debates of the nineteenth century into concrete programmes. Their dogged perseverance produced widespread social sanction for women's education. The success of Arya Samaj in this particular direction was ensured by the numerous dimensions they imparted to women's education. It is rarely recognized that Arya Samaj's Herculean efforts to diffuse education amongst women prepared the ground for women's participation in the freedom struggle and the emergence of the women's movement.

The Samajist success was most noteworthy in the sphere of rehabilitation of widows wherein they displayed exceptional commitment in formulating strategies and programmes for amelioration of their deplorable lot. These exertions deserve appreciation particularly when they are adjudged in the backdrop of the failure of the earlier movements. The meaningful, structured and concerted programme of the Samaj that strove for dignity and self-sufficiency for the widows has been discussed in detail.

Studies on Indian Renaissance and social reform in the nineteenth and twentieth centuries have dealt with the progressive role of Arya Samaj very perfunctorily. This work is therefore focused on the holistic perspective, multi-pronged strategies and whole hearted enthusiasm of the movement on issues like women's education and widow remarriage. Despite the fact that the movement derived inspiration from ancient tradition, their perspective and efforts with regard to women's education and widow remarriage was clearly a sincere struggle for gender equality and social resurgence.

The present work is the revised edition of my Ph.D. thesis conducted under the supervision of Dr Pratibha Jain. The thematic content of the book was conceived by her and thereafter she followed the writing of the book with unfailing interest. It was her constant urging and keen desire that the Ph.D. thesis is finally being published. I have no words to express my gratitude to her not only for being an ideal teacher but for being that inspirational figure who has all through been a beacon of light and a pillar of strength for me.

The study has been based on wide-ranging sources that had been lying untapped in numerous libraries. In this context I would like to acknowledge the facilities and rare source material provided by numerous libraries, institutions and distinguished individuals. I remember with particular gratitude the magnanimity of noted Arya Samajist scholars Dr Bhavani Lal Bhartiya, Dr K.S. Arya, Principal DAV College, Chandigarh and Dr Rasa Singh Rawat, Principal, DAV School, Ajmer who provided me access to the immensely prized personal collection and archives. The invaluable cooperation extended by the staff of Nehru Memorial Museum and Library, New Delhi, National Archives of India, New Delhi, Sarvadeshik Arya Pratinidhi Sabha, Delhi, Arya Samaj, Adarsh Nagar, Jaipur, Panini Kanya Mahavidyalaya, Varanasi and Central Library, University of Rajasthan, Jaipur is duly acknowledged.

I dedicate this book to Shri R.S. Jain, an exceptional human being, who actually lived the values that he professed. He combined in himself amazing qualities of head and heart, personifying honesty, generosity, humility and simplicity. A truly versatile personality, he had the phenomenal capacity to give love unconditionally. It was undeniably God's greatest blessing that I received the affection and concern of such a noble soul. It is a privilege to dedicate the book to him.

I owe the completion of the work to the unstinted cooperation of my mother, Anil and Anushruti who form the most reassuring presence in my life. I would like to thank Mr Pranit Rawat of Rawat Publications for speedy publication of the work.

‖Chapter 1‖

Women in the Nineteenth Century

Context and Perspective

Indian sub-continent has been known for wide diversity in cultural practices and multiplicity of social orders. Consequently, social conditions, particularly the status and position of women, in the sub-continent are defined by wide divergence across castes, classes and regions. Peculiar political circumstances, environmental factors and regional traits are some of the factors that engendered plurality in women's situation. Therefore, earlier centuries were defined by multiple images of women. For example, some communities observed strict *purda* for women whereas others had matrilineal family structures in which women exercised a great deal of freedom and social clout. Some disapproved of widow remarriage, while others attached no stigma to widowhood and allowed women recourse to easy divorce and remarriage. The fact is that Indian society in the pre-colonial era was not uniformly governed by a singular set of laws and diversity in customary practices across regions resulted in heterogeneous nature of women's rights. However, the dominant discourse on women that surfaced in the colonial critique as well the Indian responses in the nineteenth century focused on the concerns, values and norms of middle class women in the Indian society.[1] The contemporary social reform movement also articulated the issues and evils that were pertinent to the women of the middle classes. The forthcoming discussion, therefore, deals largely with the trajectory of changing attitudes towards their status and condition in society.

The historical reconstruction of the status and condition of women in the Indian society has underscored a course of gradual deterioration since the post-Vedic period. The subsequent epochs witnessed the subordination of women within the family and exclusion from the spheres of power, resources and education. The low status of women was particularly signified by the emergence of specific social practices like *sati*, prohibition of widow remarriage, preference for child marriage etc. Significantly, these practices continued unabated till the nineteenth century. These practices that largely revolved around the institution of marriage and women's exclusion from formal system of education remained the focus of the reformers in the social reform movement of the nineteenth century.

The decline in women's status from one of equality and self-reliance to sheer dependence and curtailment of freedom was a historical process that commenced from the post-Vedic period onwards. The Vedic period, roughly extending from 2500 BC to 1000 BC, has been often recorded in historical writings and deeply embedded in popular perception as the glorious epoch of Indian womanhood.[2] The period was marked by equality of men and women in the spheres of marriage, religion and in terms of their access to productive resources and education privileges. Despite the patriarchal structure of society, women as real companions of men actively participated in mainstream societal activities. Women of this era were equal and independent members of the society, whose cooperation was valuable in securing prosperity in peace and victory in war. More importantly, in the absence of differential moral codes for men and women, the concepts of honour, chastity and purity associated with women were unknown which ensured for them a large measure of freedom. Women, therefore, were not burdened by the dead weight of stereotyped images of women – a good wife, the weaker sex, the loving mother, a temptress etc. This 'Golden Age' theory in Indian history has been perceived as an outcome of the historical reconstruction that took place during the nineteenth century as a result of the cultural and political encounter between the Europeans and the Indian intelligentsia. According to Uma Chakravarti, the European Orientalists initially articulated this perception of the past. Colebrook had advanced the Golden Age theory as early as 1805 and later with extensive Indological research it received approval from Orientalists like Max Muller, Speier and Clarisse Bader.[3] This exaltation of the ancient period as the golden epoch of Indian womanhood was accompanied by a contrarian trend defined by onslaughts on Hindu civilization, social practices and religious beliefs, especially the low status of Indian women, by English Utilitarians, Anglicists and Christian missionaries in order to uphold their moral superiority over their colonized subjects. These attacks, while generating a fierce debate over the respective superiority of the oriental and the occidental culture, led to the reconstruction of Indian history that reinforced the Golden Age theory advanced by the European Orientalists.

The high status occupied by women in the early Vedic period, however, did not last long and from 1000 BC onwards one can observe the intensification of tendencies that accelerated women's subordination. The subjugation of the non-Aryans led to the introduction of slavery, which in turn diminished the importance of women as productive members of the society. This period (1000 BC to 500 BC) also witnessed the erosion of women's educational privileges, since the Vedic studies were now made a long and complicated process, covering a period of 12 years. Henceforth, *Upanayana* became a mere formality for women. Some of the reasons for the worsening position of women were the introduction of non-Aryan wife into the Aryan household, the evolution of the theory of transmigration and the increasing religious significance of the male child. As far back as the *Vedas*, there have been instances of gloomy responses to the birth of the girl child. In *Atharva Veda*, the birth of a girl child is distinctly denigrated and prayers and ceremonies to prevent it had come into vogue.[4]

The subsequent period, from 500 BC to 100 AD, popularly known as the age of the *Sutras*, witnessed the entrenchment of patriarchy as an ideology and gradually institutionalized the deprivation of women. Till about 400 BC the general trend as evidenced by the *Grihasutras* and the contemporary Buddhist literature was towards grown-up marriages. The writers of the *Dharmasutras* (400 BC to 100 AD), however, insisted on pre-puberty marriages and deprecated widow remarriages. Even amongst them, Vashishtha and Baudhayan hastened to add that marriages could be delayed for a period of three years after puberty, if suitable matches were not available. This period further led to denigration of the girl child and preference for sons.

Therefore, in the later Vedic and post-Vedic periods, the girl child became increasingly unwanted and there are many passages in the *Brahmana* and epic literature that reflect an unfavourable outlook towards the daughters. In addition to the inevitability of the son for performance of the last rites for attainment of salvation, social exigencies of the period also led to deprecation of the birth of daughters. One of the reasons was the evolution of the custom of hypergamous marriages wherein the marriage of the girl in a family of equal or higher status was considered integral to the honour of the family. In the arrangement of such marriages, the groom's family has traditionally been considered as the dominant and superior party while daughter's father was considered inferior in status. Moreover, the rigidity of the caste rules led to further complications in the settlement of marriages. Social vulnerability of the girls coupled with a steady decline in the status and position of women as a result of inhibitive social practices made the arrival of the girl child not as agreeable as the son.

New social norms codified in books called *Smritis* from 200 AD to 500 AD legitimated a pattern of norms and restrictions that transformed women from equal and independent members into dependent and subordinate members of the society. The codification of the social order in the *Manu Smriti* has deeply influenced the model of womanhood that continued for centuries. The period from 500 AD to 1800 AD was one of rapid decline in women's status and completed the process of women's subordination. Widow remarriage, even of child widows, became strictly prohibited and the custom of *sati* acquired legitimacy. Despite the overall subordination of women, the law-givers recognized women's right to property in the form of *streedhan*, the scope of which was further enhanced by the seventh century AD.

However, it needs to be emphasized that, in addition to the codes of social behaviour as defined in scriptural authorities like the *Smritis*, *Dharmashastras* and *Dharmasutras*, customary law was an important source of law, ethics and social codes governing marriage and women's rights. The widely used terms for custom were *achara*, *sadachara*, *shishtachar*, *loksanghraha* etc. In fact, *Smriti* writers – Gautama, Manu and Brihaspati – granted special recognition to custom. Narada even proclaimed that custom overrides the sacred law. The local customs varied from region to region with southern states granting more rights to women.[5] In fact, the liberal attitudes of Yajnavalkya and Vijneshwar, as far as women's property rights were concerned, have been attributed to their origin from southern region.

In studying the decline in the status of Indian women, historians have identified close linkages between economic development of society and position of women. Women's retreat into the household and their withdrawal from participation in productive activities of society, as it evolved from pastoral and nomadic existence to a more sedentary one based on agriculture, have been considered as key factors which led to women's subordination especially in the core Indo-Aryan kinship region. Some specific factors for subordination of women and their marginalization from the public sphere in these regions were cultivation of wheat which did not require any significant contribution of labour from women, use of the iron plough and horse riding as an essential requisite of war expertise. Moreover, in conditions of war, women came to be viewed as a liability to be protected.[6]

Apart from the multitudinous factors responsible for the gradual deterioration in women's status, the primary factors, which are being increasingly highlighted by historians and social scientists, are the role of caste system and the joint family system. The authoritarian role of caste structures and the way they perceive women as custodians of ritual purity and social honour is the starkest reminder of the conservative attitudes. The interface between caste and gender reveals the way in which the latter impinged on the lives of women. The rigidity of the caste system that dates back to the post-Vedic period led to a hierarchy between the sexes, emphasizing the superiority of males at the expense of females. Many scholars have supported the thesis that growth in caste orthodoxy also led to strict sex orthodoxy.[7] The caste system is premised on the cultural perception of a fundamental difference in male and female sexuality. The contrast has been expressed culturally by likening a woman to an earthen pot which is easily and permanently defiled if used by a person of a lower caste or one of a different religion, and a man on the other hand, to a brass pot which is not easily polluted and can be restored to purity by rubbing, scrubbing and if necessary by putting it through fire. Veena Das has put forward the view that women were literally regarded as 'points of entrance' to the caste system.[8] If women indulged in behaviour, especially in the arena of marriage and sexual relationships, that violated the rules, norms and values of a particular caste then not only the purity of women but ritual purity and honour of the entire group was endangered. Multifarious control mechanisms were devised to control and contain female sexuality resulting in child marriage, marriage within sub-caste, prohibition of widow remarriage, permanence of marriage tie and curtailment of freedom of women. These differing perceptions regarding male and female sexuality naturally meant that while caste rules controlled and regulated lives of both men and women but the latter were punished frequently and severely and at times much more brutally for their transgression.

Marriage and sexual relations formed the key area in which caste rules adversely impacted women's lives. Significantly, the caste rules acquired precedence over *shastric* injunctions, so much so that for doing a deed forbidden by caste, even though it was sanctioned by *shastra*, a person could be excommunicated. Kamaladevi Chattopadhyaya has cited the famous case of the late nineteenth century when Parshuram Patwardhan, the General Commander of the then Peshwa wanted to delay his daughter's marriage to save her from the misery of early widowhood. While the *pundits*, after deliberations, approved of a later marriage on the basis of *shastras* but the father could not act on this opinion, fearful of caste tyranny and possibility of ostracism.[9] Even in the 1920s, a hapless victim of caste tyranny would exclaim, "... the greatest hindrance to social reforms is caste. If I want to educate my girl, the caste would step in and say you should not do it. If I wish to postpone my children's marriage ... the caste raises its hand and forbid me. If a widow chooses to marry again and settle respectably in her home, the caste would threaten to ostracize her."[10] Women were constrained from exercising choices especially in the realm of marriage, sexual relationships, dress, mobility, education etc. By the twentieth century, social reformers like Vivekananda, Jyotiba Phule, N.G. Chandavarkar and Pt Ramabai looked upon caste as the greatest hurdle to the betterment in the condition of women.

The caste system emerged as the basic organizing principle of the Hindu society by second century AD. A distinctive feature of the caste system was a definite scheme of social precedence amongst the castes with the *Brahmin* at the head of the hierarchy followed by *Kshatriyas*, *Vaishyas* and *Sudras*. The four *varnas* representing dimensions of knowledge, power, wealth and labour and the castes and sub-castes were entitled to varying degrees of respectability, privileges and circle of social intercourse. The rigidity of caste system dates back to the post-Vedic period when the *Brahmin* was becoming the sole guardian of knowledge and as such claimed supreme honour from all the lower castes. According to G.S. Ghurye, by the third period of Indian history, i.e., the period of *Dharmashastras* from second century AD to eighth century AD, the *Brahmins* had emerged as the most exalted group. Apart from spiritual matters, their advice was sought on all mundane matters. S. Das has put forward the thesis that subjugation of women was an outcome of the deliberate strategy on the part of *Brahmins* during this period. When the laws which minutely regulated the rights and duties of the numerous sub-castes, as well as their interrelations with other castes were being formulated, the *Brahmins* realized that there still remained one group which retained tremendous influence and spiritual power on account of its reproductive power which was further enhanced and sanctified by the ancient worship of female deity. There could be "no uncontested or secure supremacy for *Brahmins* until woman lost her high estate, stood degraded and branded as an inferior in the eyes of men and moulded into a mindless slave to religious dictation".[11] Henceforth, women came to be grouped with the *Sudras* and were regarded as private property of men.

The crystallization of the caste system followed by supremacy of the Brahmins and the notions of ritual purity in the post-Vedic period, thus, had serious implications with regard to the position of women. Any caste, which wished to raise itself, found it necessary to conform to the marriage of girls before they reached the age of puberty and prohibition of their remarriage, even if widowed in infancy. Any rise in caste hierarchy entailed numerous hardships to women. Several writers have observed a direct relationship between a rise in caste status and increasing constraints on women. M.N. Srinivas has described this change of lifestyle required of any upwardly mobile caste as "Sanskritization".[12] According to him, this process resulted in regressive attitudes towards women in the form of prohibition of remarriage, pre-puberty marriages and several other constraints. Quite significantly, these restrictions were more widespread amongst the upper castes while amongst the lower ranked castes control over women's sexuality was not so stringent. Therefore, any caste that aspired to rise in caste hierarchy viewed curtailment of women's freedom and strict control over their sexuality as necessary attributes to be practised by them in order to raise their ritual status.

However, it has been argued by some scholars that women from lower castes as well as women from the Dravadian regions were relatively free from such strict control over sexuality as compared to the women of the upper castes in the Northern India who followed the Brahmanical-Aryan customs derived from scriptural authority. Women from lower castes or *Shudras* were considered out of the *varna* system and hence they were not governed by the code of the *Smritis*. A scrutiny of the contemporary customs of various castes and regions reveals the different forms of divorce and remarriage prevailing among communities. Similarly, among various castes and tribes, along the Malabar coast, there were female-headed joint family households and matrilineal inheritance patterns.[13] The above discussion makes it evidently clear that there were caste groups, communities and regions wherein a strict sexual code did not govern women's lives and they had greater rights as far as remarriage, divorce and property ownership are concerned.

Status and Position of Women in the Nineteenth Century

Position of women in the medieval period has been a subject of debate. Some historians subscribe to the view that owing to political exigencies and cultural factors brought by the establishment of Muslim rule, downfall of Hindu kingdoms and the advent of Islam, there was a marked decline in the status and condition of women signified by the increased prevalence of *sati*, *purda,* polygamy and constriction, of educational opportunities. While scarcity of information renders it difficult to ascertain the factual conditions, it is being increasingly asserted that women were not victimized by restrictions and inhuman practices, as has been generally assumed. As far as incidence of *sati* is concerned, the number of widows immolating themselves with their dead husbands, though on the increase, was never high, since in majority of the castes it was not a common occurrence. Although there are no statistics, the cases of *sati* in the medieval period were about one to five per cent of the total number of widows. Similarly, the practice of *purda* was not a common practice among

Hindu women. In the medieval period, even the use of *chadar* was confined to those Hindu women who belonged to families that had come in close contact with the Muslim society and Muslim official class, such as *Khatris* and *Kayasthas*. Similarly, even amongst the Muslim women there were class variations. While the poor women covered themselves with *chadar*, the ladies from elite families began to use *burqa*. It, however, appears unlikely that women from poor Muslim families of weavers, craftsmen, dyers or cultivators wore a *burqa* since they had to work like labourers. Similarly, even some kind of instruction was imparted to women as *Vikramankavdevacharita* corroborates. For instance, *Brahmin pandits* were usually employed to teach reading and writing to women of well to do families. There are also numerous examples of women who were qualified to govern. There are also instances of creative and literary feats by women. Jain *sadhvis* were also highly literate and moved about preaching the doctrines of Jainism.[14] Moreover, even prior to the advent of Islam, as has already been discussed, the growth of strict sex orthodoxy around the second century AD had led to the gradual entrenchment of patriarchy in the subsequent centuries resulting in severely disadvantaged conditions for women. *Smriti* writers, especially Manu, reinforced the basic theme of women being unfit for independence. The curtailment of freedom adversely impacted women's access to education and resources as also their participation in productive and political spheres. These restrictions withdrew women from the public sphere and precluded them from involvement in any meaningful social endeavour and the incidence of regressive customs further aggravated their oppression and victimization. While there has been a debate over the spatial spread of these customs and practices, extent of their rigidity as well as variations across class and caste in the nineteenth century, it is nonetheless certain that the prevalence of these evils did inhibit and stifle women's lives within the family and adversely affected their access to educational opportunities and economic resources.

Prevalence of child marriages was a common social practice that severely retarded women's physical, biological, and mental development. Innumerable reasons have been adduced to explain the widespread phenomenon of child marriages in the Hindu society. Coupled with the *Shastric* injunctions that enjoined parents to marry off the girls before they attained puberty to escape the horrors of hell, was the Brahmanical tyranny that was too willing to bolster up such extraneous religious practices. Caste and clan prejudices were, in part responsible for this social practice. Conventions and customs that accompanied the caste system made it obligatory for the parents to settle the matches for their children at the earliest within the same caste and of equal or superior status. To the Hindus, the rules of caste rendered marriage beyond the sub-caste almost a social sin. Along with this factors of family connection, pedigree, religion and customs were also taken into consideration. Care was taken to marry into the families of the same status. An added impetus was given to the practice of child marriages when it acted as an indicator of family honour. This led to the paucity of matches, making the field of selection narrower and thereby encouraging a keener competition resulting in child marriages. The anxiety to get the best matches left the parents no option but to "marry off their daughters at the age of three, four and five years or even younger". The severe standards of morality and chastity further lowered the age of marriage. It was beneficial for the parents who thought it advisable to hand over their daughter to her husband before she blossomed into her youth. Virginity and modesty of the girl were deemed to be her inalienable virtues. "The Hindus are so scrupulous with regard to the virginity of their wives that they [try to] marry extremely young ... nor will they marry a person with whom these virtues have already appeared to which sex is subject."[15]

Even in a comparatively advanced province like Punjab, girls were married off before there was any chance of losing virginity. In Punjab, infant marriages owed their origin to the force of circumstances created by repeated invasions, exposing the fair sex to growing insecurity. Under the operation of these forces, child marriages became a common practice and non-conformity to it came to be regarded a matter of social disapprobation.

Some scholars, however, contend that child marriage did not imply consummation of marriage. According to them, as a general rule, the first marriage ceremony was performed at quite a premature age but the consummation of marriage took place only after active symptoms of puberty appeared. This was the general trend in northern and southern India in the eighteenth and the nineteenth centuries. The ceremony gone through was nothing more than a 'betrothal'.[16] However, in the province of Bengal, the girl bride had to accompany her husband immediately after the marriage ceremony in most of the cases.[17]

The miserable condition of widows formed a key component in the colonial as well as reformist discourse on the condition of women in the nineteenth century. A widow's life was devoid of all comforts, pleasures, luxuries and any hope for the future. She was allowed only one meal in a day and often expected to observe fasts. Since her presence was considered inauspicious, she was shunned from all joyous and auspicious occasions like marriages being held in the family. In fact such an austere lifestyle often drove the widows to prostitution. It was found that in the latter half of the nineteenth century, 90 per cent of the prostitutes in Bengal were widows, a fact accepted in Rabindranath Tagore's novel *Chokher Bali* and Bankimchandra's *Krishnakanter Will*. In the whole of India the number of widows was approximately 11 per cent of the females aged between 15 and 40 and among the Hindus the proportion was 12 per cent.[18]

Some contemporary voices have challenged the commonly held views and emphasized the need to deconstruct the stereotypes that have characterized these descriptions regarding the miserable condition of widows. In this context, Lal Behari Dey remarked, "English people have somehow or the other got the idea that a Hindu widow receives a harsh treatment from the relations of her husband. This is not true. There are, no doubt, exceptional cases, but as a general rule, Hindu widows are not only not ill-treated but they meet with a vast deal of sympathy."[19] Pratap Chandra Mazumdar also felt that the widows were often not persecuted, at least in Bengal. The miseries from which they suffered were willingly courted by them.[20] The rigours of widowhood also lessened as one went down the caste hierarchy, the widows of the lower castes and the agricultural castes in Punjab, Rajputana and other provinces could contract second marriages, which were variously called *Natra*, *Karewa* or *Karas*.[21] The custom of remarriage was prevalent among Lingayats of Karnataka, Kapus of Telangana, the Jats of Punjab and Ajmer, certain castes among the Maravars, Namosudras of Bengal and the Banias of Bihar. In northern India, all castes except Brahmins, Kayasthas, Banias and Rajputs permitted remarriage. It was also accepted as a universal custom in the Darjeeling and Manipur regions.[22] Prohibition of remarriage was perceived as a badge of high ritual status.

However, it was the melancholic condition of child widows that received widespread sympathy and attention. The number of such widows was unusually high and according to one survey in Calcutta in 1891 there were 10,000 widows below the age of four in and around the city which then had a population of only four lakhs.[23] Even those reformers, who were otherwise known for their regressive stance on the issue of widow remarriage, lent support to the cause of the remarriage of child widows. Pandita Ramabai, while giving a graphic picture of the life of child widow in the nineteenth century wrote "... destitute as it is of the least literary knowledge, void of all hope, empty of every pleasure and social advantage, (child widowhood) becomes a curse to herself and to society, at large."[24]

The social evil of polygamy was not a very widespread custom, being practicable only among the aristocracy and *kulins* in Bengal. Polygamy was neither enjoined by the Hindu *shastras* nor was it considered socially respectable. The *shastras* enjoined upon a Hindu to take a second wife only in cases where the first wife did not bear a son. Despite this, the permission and approval of his first wife was essential. The restrictions and conditions that governed second marriage of men were seldom observed and Hindu men often contracted second marriages even when they had one or more children by the first wife. Law afforded no protection against such irregularities. Such marriages were, nevertheless, not popular in the Hindu society. As Dubois says, "Society on the whole viewed plurality of wives even among the great, as an infraction of law and custom."[25] Moreover, for the common man, polygamy could neither be advantageous nor very fascinating, particularly in the lower classes where the major part of marriage expenses was borne by the bridegroom. The presence of two wives added to dissensions within the family and disturbed the peace and harmony of the entire household.

The most outrageous form of polygamy was prevalent in the province of Bengal among the *kulin* Brahmins, who were considered as the most honoured among the numerous sub-castes of the Brahmins. Moreover, one of the reasons for the persistence of the evil custom was that *kulin* girls could not be given in marriage to anyone of lower castes. The *kulin* Brahmin men often married an indefinite number of wives in order to satisfy the desire of the brides' families (who often paid large sums for these alliances) to get their daughter married to one of the highest of Brahmin castes. This intense keenness of the families to raise themselves up in the caste hierarchy led them to arrange highly mismatched and unequal marriages. Contemporary Bengali literature is replete with instances relating to the evil of *kulinism*. From a tract published by Ishwarachandra Vidyasagar, it came to be known that in less than 100 villages in Hughli district, 133 *kulin* Brahmins had more than five wives each.[26] The lot of women married to Kulins was lamentable. The latter were not expected to maintain their numerous wives. The ill-fated girl with no property rights, hence, with little authority in the parental home was reduced to the life of a slave, especially after the death of her parents. In many cases, she was driven to the extent of seeking shelter in prostitution.[27] Ishwarchandra Vidyasagar expressed his deep anguish over their condition thus, "With the *kulin* Brahmins the sacred rite of matrimony had been notoriously degraded to a system of shameful traffic. These men ... are accepting the hands of crores of maidens, the great majority of whom were never destined to enjoy the blessings of a wedded life."[28] Effectively, however, polygamy was a vice of an infinitesimal part of the populace, the larger sections of society refraining from the practice.

If inevitability of marriage, incidence of child marriages, ill-treatment of widows and *purda* were some of the factors that effectively controlled women's sexuality and checked the development of individuality of a woman, then the extremely brutal custom of *sati* challenged her right to existence as a human being. "Victims of *sati* were punished for no offence, but the physical weakness, which had placed them at man's mercy."[29] *Sati* has been defined as 'outright cruelty [against women] masquerading as religion'.[30] Originally, a custom of the *Kshatriyas*, it gradually came to be acknowledged by several castes, particularly, the upper castes. The reasons adduced for its gradual legitimization are misinterpretation of some vague references to *sati* in the *Vedas* by the Brahmins, the difficulty of protecting women in times of war, decline of Buddhism, contagion with tribal and other cognate cultures who believed that comforts of the dead in the after-life could be ensured by burning with him his wives, jewellery, slaves, and other favourite possessions. Brahmins took to the practice to excel the *Kshatriyas* in the pursuit of ascetic practices.[31] Hindu women resorted to *sati* as a means of securing social status and renown for virtue in a stagnant society which otherwise held no promise of breaking the 'routine banality' of their lives as widows.

The incidence of *sati*, however, remains a contentious issue. While it has not been feasible to establish the exact incidence of the practice in the pre-British period, due to the lack of statistical data, it was certainly higher in the warrior families of Rajputana. However, even in the eighteenth and the nineteenth centuries, the incidence of *sati* was not very common. There were regional variations as well as caste-wise differentiations as far as occurrence of *sati* was concerned. In Bombay and Madras, the practice of this rite was very restricted. Government records in the first quarter of the century show that in these two provinces, annual average from the period 1800 to 1812 was only 12 *satis*. Tanjore district recorded the highest number of 24 *satis*, during the 18 months preceding 1817. In Central India, only 3 or 4 cases of performance of *sati* used to take place annually.[32] The above-mentioned figures substantiate the fact that the practice of widows immolating themselves on the funeral pyres of their husbands in the general Hindu population was not high. In Bengal, the custom was more widely spread. In 1803, William Carey, the Baptist missionary in Serampore in Bengal took a census of *satis* in an area extending 30 miles of Calcutta and found that 438 widows had been burnt during that year. Calcutta and regions around it – the districts of Burdwan, Hoogly, Nadia and 24 Parganas provided 57 per cent of the 'virtuous wives' or '*satis*'. However, the figures pertaining to the incidence of *sati* raise serious doubts over the real agenda of the Christian missionaries and the British Government when they unduly overstated the prevalence of the practice. The Government record of the period reveals that even in Bengal, *sati* was not accorded any recognition in the area of Vishnupur.[33]

The evil of *kulinism* rampant in the province of Bengal has at times been considered as one of the reasons for the greater number of *satis*.[34] Yet others have identified a relation between inheritance rights of the widows and the practice of *sati*. According to the *Dayabhaga* school of law, a widow was entitled to inherit the property of her deceased husband. The greedy and rapacious relatives naturally had an interest in eliminating her from the scene.[35] Some writers have explained the phenomenon of *sati* in Bengal differently. While treating it as an offshoot of British colonial administration in India, they believe that the induction of Brahmins in the British administration exposed them to liberal influence of the west, leading to a fear psychosis among them of losing their position as leaders of society and religion and led them to uphold *sati* more fervently. Kamaladevi Chattopadhyaya has defined *sati* in its 'recrudescent form' 'a bastard product' "of crude colonial penetration"[36]. According to Radha Kumar, 'the Bengali epidemic of *sati* was as assertive-defensive reaction to colonial rule'[37]. Krishna Basu writes, "It was the *babu* culture which made a sadistic sport out of *sati* to demonstrate their ritual purity and allegiance to traditional high culture and, to this extent, this culture was itself a product of western and modern encroachments upon traditional lifestyle. *Sati* was the weirdest response to new cultural inputs and traditional innovations."[38] It has been contended that the anti-*sati* regulations introduced by the British in Bengal also proved to be counter-productive and had adverse repercussions as far as incidence of *sati* was concerned. These legislations, enacted on the basis of shastric interpretations between 1812 and 1818 made a distinction between legal and illegal *satis*. These laws led to an actual increase in the incidents of *sati* for they were widely interpreted as a sign of government approval of widow immolation.

Strict control over women's sexuality, on the one hand, resulted in child marriages and prevalence of *sati* while at the same time leading to severe curtailment of women's freedom of movement. It is, however, not clear as to when the concept of seclusion of women came to be regarded as the means to uphold their dignity and femininity. There are no statistics or historical material to determine the incidence or extent of its prevalence at various points of history. In popular consciousness as well in historical writings, *purda* is associated with the advent of Muslims, some even going to the extent that the Muslims introduced the practice. Imitation of invaders and protection of women are commonly held as the contributory factors for prevalence of *purda*. However, a consensus has now emerged that seclusion of women certainly predated the advent of Muslims. References to some form of *purda* and seclusion are found in the epics. The royal families secluded their women after the beginning of Christian era when the notion began to prevail that "royal ladies should not come within public gaze".[39] A distrust of women's character and fear of their uncontrolled sexuality is perceptible in the *Smritis*, particularly the

Manu Smriti. "If my mother going astray and unfaithfully conceived illicit desires, may my father keep that seed from me."[40] Manu allotted to women a love of bed, seat and ornaments, impure desires, wrath and dishonesty. These perceptions regarding women's sexual behaviour probably led to restrictions on women's mobility.

It would be, however, wrong to presuppose the presence of absolute seclusion and strict veiling of women in all the regions. Women in Maharashtra, where Mohammedan influence was never very strong, did not observe *purda*. Similarly, in Punjab, only married women observed *purda* while growing girls roamed about freely.[41] In Bengal too, *purda* was necessitated due to the joint family system.[42] It should be added that women of lower classes did not observe *purda* for they had to assist their male relations in agricultural work. A rise in social status was, often, accompanied by seclusion of women. The practice was, however, largely limited to the cities, the women of the villages being free to move about.[43] Hindu society did not encourage free association and familiarity between the opposite sexes, but at the same time, it did not impose a curtain over women's appearance in public. "A woman could go anywhere alone, even in the most crowded places, and she need never fear the impertinent looks and jokes of idle loungers."[44]

Lack of formal education in the eighteenth and the nineteenth centuries emerges as the single most important factor for the perpetuation of the existing social order and the inherent evils. The concept of female education was laden with multifarious prejudices, the popular one being the incurrence of the curse of widowhood on educated girls. Moreover, reading and writing came to be associated with prostitutes and dancing girls and, hence, considered derogatory for respectable women. It required much effort to bring girls to school. A district officer in Assam wrote: "It is very difficult in Muffasil to get parents educate their girls. They are too useful in the houses and parents think they will forget and despise household duties if they learn how to read and write. Girls thus qualified are said to become *Dushts*, which means they are less likely to submit to their parents' choice of husband."[45] In his report on education in Bombay 1865–1866, the Director expressed his deep regret, "Looking at the question, broadly, I am afraid, it must be asserted that public education of course is incompatible with the system of infant marriages and with so many existing prejudices of the people on the most delicate subjects, I am humbly of the opinion that private and missionary exertion may do much to help the cause but the government is precluded from taking any prominent steps to accelerate the movement." In 1866, there were in Bombay 33 government schools for females and the number of pupils was 1,036, while the private female schools were 32 in number with 1,400 pupils.[46] The government schools were, however, unsatisfactory in nature. The Director of Education in his remarks commented adversely, "The first characteristic of our girl schools is extreme irregularity of attendance; the second is that they are in reality infant schools, in which, it appears to me that the great bulk of the children being very young, sit, looking on, while a few girls at the top of the school receive a little instruction."

Even in South India, the idea that woman should receive education outside their own homes did not receive enough sustenance in the eighteenth and nineteenth centuries. It was considered fit only for public dancers. Female children devoted to the profession of dancing at the Hindu temples were educated. In Madras, an enquiry conducted by Sir Thomas Munro in 1826 stated that there were 11,758 indigenous schools and 740 colleges giving instruction to 1, 57,664 boys and 4,023 girls; most of them were dancing girls.[47] Even in the third quarter of the nineteenth century, when other provinces were making some headway in the area of female literacy, South India presented a dismal picture. In the absence of any special interest and effort on the part of educational authorities in Madras, there were no government female schools and most of the 139 female schools sponsored by private enterprise were meant for children of European descent. Similarly, in Mysore, there were no government female schools and of the seven female schools under private management, two were designed for European and Eurasian girls and four were for Hindu girls. In Berar, there were no female schools till 1865 or 1866. Due to social prejudices and numerous obstacles, women's education did not receive adequate attention. The following statement reflects the government's reluctance to promote it at the cost of boys' education. "The movement in favour of educating girls is interesting and should be encouraged to a certain extent to show that female education is one of the things government aims at, but I believe that most certain, and the speediest way of educating the women of India is to educate the men."[48]

The province of Punjab, as compared to other provinces, was fairly advanced. The response of Punjabi populace to female education was, therefore, distinctive. The first Administration Report of the Board of Education pointed out that it was remarkable that female education, which was still almost unknown in other parts of India was to be found in Punjab.[49] There were female teachers and pupils drawn from all the communities – Hindu, Muslims and Sikhs. There were schools run by Sikhs and Mohammedans for girls. The Hindu girls, however, received most of their education by means of instruction at homes. The efforts of the government coupled with those of natives produced satisfactory results in the province. In 1866, the Punjab stood foremost of all other provinces in the realm of female education. In Punjab, in 1865 and 1866, there were 1,029 female schools composed of 333 government schools and 696 private schools with 19,561 pupils.[50] However, these figures also do not reflect a very encouraging picture. The majority continued to view public instruction for women as taboo. Even as late as the 1820s, Sir Malcolm Hailey, Governor of the province, was to observe that hardly one Punjabi among a hundred could expect to have an educated wife.

Absence of formal education should not, however, be construed as "lack of education" among women. Dubois' testimony that Hindu housewives showed "a shrewdness, a savingness and intelligence which would do honour to the best housewives of Europe", implies that some kind of training was imparted to women. In fact, the above-mentioned statistics on educational institutions for girls have totally ignored the traditional systems of dissemination of knowledge through which women received education in areas pertinent to their social and economic needs. It is true that formal educational institutions that are integral to the modern system of education were not the standard methods of imparting education to women but diffusion of knowledge and requisite skills was given adequate attention. William Adam's report on education in 1835 refers to *pathshalas* in Bengal and Bihar for boys prior to British intervention in the realm of education. According to him, these *pathshalas* were open for girls as well. Although the number of girls attending these *pathshalas* was minuscule and those who attended could pursue the same for only a few years because of early marriage.[51] Thomas Munroe's report on education around the same period testifies that although formal system of education was not in place but they received education in homes. Moreover, girls of the royal families, particularly in the Rajput and Maratha royal households, in addition to conventional instruction in feminine spheres, received military training which included horse riding, use of weapons and even hunting expeditions.[52] According to Altekar, every village had its own religious teacher (*puranika*), who gave lectures on religion, philosophy and culture to womenfolk. He comments, "Though unlettered, they thus became better and more faithful custodians of ancient traditions and culture than even literate men."[53]

In the aforesaid discussion while one can locate certain universal features regarding the condition of women in Indian society yet it defies any linear narrative. The forms of patriarchy and incidence of numerous evils varied not only across regions but factors of caste and class remained pertinent to their occurrence. These factors determined the extent and harshness of their prevalence across the sub-continent. Whether it was the condition of widows, incidence of child marriage, polygamy and *sati*, observance of *purda* or lack of access to education, the social scenario is defined by multiple situations. However, the women's question of the nineteenth and twentieth centuries focused primarily on the women of the middle classes and privileged sections or the *bhadralok* homes of Indian society who bore the maximum impact of these practices. The imperial critique of Indian society and the contemporary indigenous responses continued to be highly selective descriptions of Indian women. As Kumkum Sangari and Sudesh Vaid have contended that the dominant cultural critique effectively excluded the concerns of the women who enjoyed some measure of independence like women of lower strata, Vaishnavnite women and courtesans and prostitutes. These were women who had access to the public sphere of 'street, marketplace, fair and festival' and were not particularly oppressed by social practices from which the *bhadramahila* suffered. According to them, "the question of how many groups were actually touched by 'reform' issues such as *sati*, widow remarriage, child marriage, female education, eradication of *kulin* polygamy remains".[54] They further argue that the model of womanhood that emerged from historical reconstruction of the past, the colonial accounts as well as the social reform movement focused on issues that were not affecting a sizable number of women. The women's discourse in the nineteenth and twentieth centuries sought to articulate and universalize exclusive and homogenized versions of a particular class of women. Paucity of adequate and authentic data has also has been another limitation in the historical construction of the social history. It has not been possible to assess the real extent of women's education as women were instructed within the private realms of the *zenana* or within the four walls of the house. Moreover, the critique of child marriage has to be seen in the context that it did not necessarily lead to the consummation of marriage. In view of these factors it has not been possible to reconstruct a comprehensive and accurate account of women in the nineteenth and twentieth centuries.

Genesis of the Social Reform Movement

The advent of the nineteenth century marks a watershed in the social, religious and political history of India. This period is generally called the period of Indian Renaissance. The intellectual ferment generated during the period also provoked eager questions regarding the foundations of religious and social life. The social reform movement in India that originated in the early decades of the nineteenth century was an outcome of the process of self-exploration and self-definition engendered by the encounter between the imperialists and their colonized subjects. The movement constituted the first all-India response to the cultural and moral challenge posed by the colonial rule. Since its initial stages, the movement was largely concerned with changes affecting the structure of Indian society and family. The specific causes that engrossed the attention of the reformers were evils and malpractices that affected women's status and position in society. Roy's incessant campaign, coupled with the initiatives of the Christian missionaries and the British government against *sati,* marked the beginning of a movement that subsequently dealt with ill-treatment of widows, ban on remarriage of widows, child marriages, polygamy and absence of educational opportunities for women. Disabilities associated with the caste system also attracted the attention of the nineteenth century reformers.

The social reform movement has been often traced to the exposure to the modernizing forces of the West, the social conditions shaped as a result of British interventions and the challenge posed by the stringent critique articulated by different imperial agencies – the

British officials, particularly the Liberals and Utilitarians amongst them, and the Christian missionaries. However, there has been a school of thought that traces the urge for reform to indigenous sources of inspiration, particularly the age of the *Vedas* and the *Upanishads*. At the same time, there is the totally divergent view that has questioned the historical construction that traces the emergence of women's issues to the western influence. Instead they seek to emphasize a consistent tradition of reform in the sub-continent that has time and again questioned the nature of inequalities and hegemonies inherent in gender and caste.

The origin of social reform endeavours has been often attributed to the impact created by the ideas, unleashed by the British rule, through administration, English education and Christian missionaries. Neera Desai has designated this body of ideas as 'liberalism'. The main tenets of this thought were social utility, equality of individuals, rationalism and respect for human personality.[55] The impact created by the liberal ideology of J.S. Mill was perceptible to some extent in the writings of the reformers. Spencer's theory of evolution was yet another major influence on the Indian reformers. His ideas of evolution proved that "change in social institution was a natural process, that it could be guided by men, that no violent breaks with the past were called for and that ultimate progress was certainty". The theory helped the reformers in convincing the masses of the inevitability of change, often warning the latter that "unless Indian society improved its 'efficiency', its survival might be in danger".[56] Spencer's works were translated into major Indian languages.

The challenge posed by Christian missionaries in the nineteenth century helped the cause of social reform in two ways – constructive and competitive. On the one hand, the direct influence of the Christian doctrines in creating awareness regarding the numerous social and religious evils prevalent in the Indian society has been widely acknowledged. "If today there is an awakening among us", spoke N.G. Chandavarkar, "on the subject of religion that is a great deal due to the light brought by him. To the Christian missionary, is due to a great extent, the credit of religious and social awakening of which the school Hindu Protestantism is the fruit".[57] The competitive aspect was stirred by the highly unfavourable and negative perception of the missionaries regarding the people and culture of India. It is now generally agreed that the strident and comprehensive civilizational critique articulated by the missionaries was not stimulated by purely altruistic motives. In fact selective and highly prejudiced portrayals of Indian society and religion as barbaric, primitive, superstitious and irrational were ill-motivated campaigns to demonstrate the superiority of Christianity so as to enable mass conversions. The vehement propaganda of the missionaries coupled with fears regarding their agenda for mass conversions to Christianity stimulated an enquiry into the society, history and culture of India. The threat from Christian missionaries also motivated indigenous efforts to reform the social and religious practices of Indian society. According to K. Natarajan, "the fear of Christian missionaries has been the beginning of much wisdom among us".[58]

Some scholars, while denying the superiority of the western sources of inspiration, have attributed the emergence of the movement to India's glorious past in the Vedic and epic days when women enjoyed high status. According to V.R. Mehta, "Researches by Jones and Max Muller had already created a profound sense of admiration for the cultural traditions of the country … . The Renaissance thinkers generally turned to the thinkers of the Vedic and classical periods for inspiration." He contends that a major source of influence was the ideas of German philosophers like Schelling, Fichte, Kant and Herder. He has argued that when a reaction started against the British Raj there was revulsion for some of their ideas like individualism, materialism, and *laissez faire*. To counteract some of these concepts they sought philosophical justification in German philosophy and their ideas of *volk*, community, duty and nation. According to Mehta, "Some of the thinkers and social reformers of this period in India also thought that the only way to expose the weaknesses of utilitarianism which lay at the roots of the thinking of English administrators in India was to exalt the notion of community, *volk* and obligations."[59]

The social reform movement has been perceived by Veena Mazumdar as an attempt on the part of the reformers to preserve the family. According to her, men who settled down in metropolitan cities to work and to pursue higher education left their womenfolk behind in the villages. This common practice coupled with modern education created "barriers between men and women of such families. Close companionship between husbands and wives became impossible in the face of this tremendous gap of experience".[60] The only class of women that could fulfil this role in urban settlements was that of the courtesans and prostitutes who were accomplished women, trained in the arts of social intercourse. With increasing urbanization, prostitution became more commercialized and the demand for new recruits to the profession could no longer be met by traditional courtesans. Therefore, the large number of high caste widows, "helpless victims of family neglect and even torture" became an "obvious recruiting ground".[61] These developments naturally threatened the integrity of the family structure, its economy and the health of the male members of the family, instigating the reformers to do away with evils like permanent widowhood, child marriages and polygamy. Even women's education was advocated to bridge the mental gap between husbands and wives. It was argued that their empty minds made them indulge in quarrels, which destroyed the harmony of the family and compelled men to seek their relaxation outside.

However, it would be fallacious to presume that reform movements were an offshoot of the numerous developments in the nineteenth century. Some scholars claim that throughout Indian history efforts had been made to reform society and religion. The saint philosophers of the thirteenth century like Ramanuja and Madhava signified the emergence of liberal attitudes as far as ritual status of the *Shudras* was concerned since they advocated temple entry for the lower castes and the removal of other caste-related disabilities. The Bhakti movement in the sixteenth century was also an attempt to liberalize the orthodox conception of religion by rendering the ritual-ridden religious beliefs into simple idioms imbued with humanistic values. Most of the Bhakti saints were in favour of abolition of the social disabilities based on caste and gender.[62] Similarly, the Mughal emperors Akbar, Shah Jehan and Aurangzeb had made serious efforts to check the incidence of *sati*, at times by making it a punishable crime.[63] There were also totally indigenous movements in the eighteenth and the nineteenth centuries that came forward with a radical social programme. Abolition of the inequalities inherent in the caste system and a fierce attack on the privileged position of Brahmins formed their principal agenda of reform. The most important of these sects were Charan Dasis of Delhi, Haryana and Rajasthan, Kartabhajas of Nadiya, Spashadayakas, Sakhibhavakas and Haribolas of West Bengal, Satnamis of Northern India and Central Provinces and Paltudasis and Apapanthis of Oudh. The sects were mostly founded by low caste men with a desire for social betterment. Guru worship was one of the most conspicuous features of these religious sects. They preached equality of mankind. Followers of these sects held women in high esteem. Women were eligible to become Gurus. Charan Dasi's first disciple was his sister Sahajibai who later on became the Guru of the Charan Dasis. Aule Chand's wife succeeded him as Guru of the Kartabhajas. Similarly, the widow of the founder of Balrami sect succeeded to the gurudom of her husband. The Sakhibhavaka sect of Calcutta eulogized Radha as the personification of the Sakti of Krishna. Their extreme devotion to this female divinity not only led them to assume female garb, dress and ornaments but also manners and occupations of women.[64] They condemned infanticide, *sati*, enforced widowhood and pleaded for equality of men and women, but they did not evolve any clear ideology or programme for their upliftment. It has been argued that the eighteenth century was a period of instability when the old political order crumbled leaving spaces for new movements to develop. The anti-caste movement in Maharashtra during this period is said to have originated during the disintegration of Peshwa rule leading to the decline in Brahmanic hegemony in the region.[65] It is true that unlike the later reform movements they were essentially localized efforts and did not become widespread campaigns equipped with organizational strength and a strategy for social legislation. It was the imperialist critique of the Indian society and religion, especially the visibly low status of Indian women in the nineteenth century that formed a veritable challenge that provoked the exponents of Indian Renaissance to launch campaigns against inhuman practices and emphasize the urgent need for women's access to education.

Social Reform Movement: Approaches and Issues

The social reform movement of the nineteenth and twentieth centuries was initiated by the educated middle classes in the backdrop of an ideological and cultural conflict between the British imperialists and the Indian intelligentsia. The cultural confrontation was provoked and preceded by an unabashed indictment of the Indian social and cultural practices, especially the low status of women, by the Christian missionaries and English Utilitarians. The western critique evoked two types of distinctive responses from the native intelligentsia. At one level, they sought to assert the cultural superiority of the Indian heritage and constructed the theory of a Vedic Age to counteract the colonial critique. On the other hand, they sought to accept the assessment as a valid and justified criticism of the degenerating state of the Indian society and religion. Consequently, several aspects of Hindu social order and religious practices were re-examined from different perspectives. Both the responses led to a critical revaluation of Indian life, social institutions and religious tradition.

The social reformers, like the imperial critics, had constructed a model of womanhood that was an elitist concept in terms of class and caste. They had derived and formulated the programme of reform from this dominant discourse on Indian womanhood. Nevertheless, the movement incorporated numerous strands and strategies. The nature of the movement has been characterized by multiplicity of approaches. Similarly, the nature of issues has revealed regional and ideological variations. Moreover, the social reformers were sharply divided over some issues like widow remarriage, women's education and the recourse to social legislation. Significantly, the strategy for reform also differed in different regions, and varied with the passage of time. The initial emphasis on recourse to *shastric* or scriptural authority was also accompanied by a class of reformers who rejected tradition as the basis of reform and instead adopted rational approach to understand and resolve social issues. In the later stages, the movement became more focused on issues like women's access to education and betterment in the condition of widows. Reformers' perspectives on the content and objective of women's education and the options for widows, however, remained far from homogeneous and showed different trajectories of development. In fact these issues involved the larger question of control over female sexuality and the threat to the institution of family. Consequently, the twin issues of women's education and widow remarriage generated some of the most engrossing debates of the social reform movement in the nineteenth and early twentieth centuries.

The followers of the Young Bengal Movement epitomized the rational approach to social reform. They were followers of Henry

Derozio and David Hare, the founder of the Hindu College and were called Derozians. Their rational perspective and progressive ideology on social and religious issues led them to question some of the integral features of Hinduism, particularly the caste system and the low status of women. They scandalized Hindu orthodoxy beyond measure and became objects of scathing criticism and disapprobation by all sections of the Hindu society. In popular perception, the Young Bengal movement is associated with offensive activities like drinking to excess and throwing beef into a Brahmin's house. Quite pertinently, the Derozians in fact pioneered the cause of social reform, particularly issues related to tyranny of the caste and subjugation of women. The young Bengal radicals lent unequivocal support to the cause of widow remarriage as early as the 1830s. Their commitment to the cause was reflected in their unrelenting campaign in its favour through the columns of their journals *Enquirer, Spectator* and *Gyananveshan.*[66] It is seldom pointed out that Indian Law Commission had taken into serious consideration their proposal for widow remarriage.[67]

When the Widow Remarriage Act was enacted in 1856 they suggested concrete amendments in the law to render it more practical and progressive. For instance, they keenly felt that there should be clarity regarding the definition of widow remarriage and the mode of its solemnization. They also pleaded for inclusion of the Marriage Registration Clause, under which the contractual agreement between the two parties concerned was to be registered within six months from the date of solemnization before officials appointed by the Government for this specific purpose. Perhaps, the most significant suggestion put forth by the young radicals was that a widow, who had not attained puberty, should not marry. Arabinda Poddar has rightly remarked in this regard, "Viewed in retrospect, however, it appears that the Young Bengal intellectuals like Kishore Chand Mitra, Pearyachand Mitra, Rasik Krishna Mullik and Radhanath Sikdar had a clearer grasp of the issue in question than Vidyasagar … . Vidyasagar's petition was silent on these points … . The Young Bengal Intellectuals, on the other hand, by focusing attention on them did not only anticipate the Civil Marriage Act of 1872 but indirectly pleaded for legislation to abolish the superstitious practice of child marriage."[68] In the petition filed by leading Derozions some wide gaps in the Widow Remarriage Act of 1856 came to light. Young Bengal intellectuals expressed keen interest in women's education too. Ram Gopal Ghosh, a leading Derozion, was referred to by Bethune in his letter to Dalhousie as his "chief adviser".

Despite their perceptive and progressive understanding of women's issues and the perseverance that was exemplified in their endeavours, the Derozions utterly failed to make any impact on the Hindu society. The flagrant ways of its exponents, their agnostic attitudes in an age of religiosity and traditionalism, their inability to gather support and the want of a stable organization stifled the Young Bengal Movement in its infancy. Significantly, the outrageous behaviour of the Derozians was perceived as a serious threat from within the Hindu society. Nevertheless, the latter's rational critique of decadent social institutions and cultural practices was a vital factor in triggering off the early efforts to reform the Hindu society without engendering a break with Hindu society.

The second response to the colonial critique was characterized by caution and moderation. While championing the cause of social reform, they emphasized continuity of social order and religious tradition. The reform measures were justified by deriving support from *shastric* authority. The subsequent phase of the reform movement was defined by multiple strands as new issues, approaches and campaigns emerged that broadened the movement and at the same time deepened the contradictions within it. The reformers like Jyotiba Phule, Keshab Chandra Sen, N.G. Chandavarkar, Pandita Ramabai, D.K. Karve, Vivekanand and Dwarkanath Ganguli signify the evolution of significant trends within the existing movement.

The dominant approach towards reform in the nineteenth century was characterized by continuity of tradition wherein scriptural authority was invoked by exponents of Indian Renaissance to vindicate their stand on eradication of social evils, especially the sensitive issues pertaining to women's situation. Roy, in his tracts against *sati*, pleaded for its abolition by drawing upon the *Vedas, Smritis* and the *Bhagwat Gita*.[69] Ishwarchandra Vidyasagar's booklet 'Marriage of Hindu Widows' cited scriptural evidence in support of widow remarriage. Although the reformers believed in rational and humanitarian principles yet they took recourse to *shastric* authority as a matter of expediency is adequately substantiated by the great reformer in the preface.[70] Similarly Roy, in one of his tracts against *sati*, demonstrated a rational-humanitarian approach when he recounted with rare sensitivity the deprivations and sufferings of women in a patriarchal society. He rejected the notion of women's intellectual inferiority as compared to men. He felt that since women have been deprived of educational opportunities to demonstrate and develop their natural talents, it was unjust to consider them as deficient in learning. Roy felt that while women of lower classes have to undergo tremendous physical stress due to demanding housework, those belonging to the upper classes suffered mental anguish because of their husband's infidelity, polygamous marriages and neglect. He even expressed deep distress over the fact that women were legally obligated to continue in unhappy marriages. Thus, the manner in which Roy empathized with women's victimization in day-to-day life, irrespective of their class or caste, was indeed incredible as he questioned practices that were considered extremely normal and acceptable in those times. The use of scriptures was, thus, a strategic move to seek popular support for reformist measures since break with tradition failed to reform the community as a whole. Moreover, some reformers like Ranade were of the conviction that 'continuity of creed, of traditions, of philosophy, of modes of life and thought' has been an intrinsic trait of the Indian culture. "Change is sought not as an innovation but as a return and restoration to the days of our past history."[71]

The nineteenth century reform movement, therefore, emphasized continuity of tradition and social structure and in Ranade's view was in the great Hindu tradition of reform – reform which always sought out the ancient principles in order to restate them. This particular approach to social reform characterized by caution, deference to tradition and emphasis on historical continuity rather than purely rational and humanitarian interpretation of social issues was embraced by like reformers like Ishwarchandra Vidyasagar, Rammohan Roy, Dayanand Saraswati and Ranade.

However, as the movement progressed, the method of tradition practiced by reinterpretation of ancient texts was increasingly being questioned by reformers. N.G. Chandavarkar remained highly skeptical regarding reliance on *shastric* texts as the basis of reform. He adopted the more generous view that after all it was the man who made the *Shastras* and he was not made for *Shastras*.[72] "If the *Shastras* themselves say that we can make new customs, I do not see why the social reformer should confine himself to the *Shastras* alone."[73] He brushed aside the protagonists of blind allegiance to the past and their apprehensions by telling them that, "Human nature is so full and so fond of the past, at least in India, so inert and supine, that there is no danger of any reformer running headlong and revolutionizing society."[74] The futility of relying on *shastric* basis for reform dawned upon the new intelligentsia. Satyendra Nath Tagore, ICS, wrote to N.G. Chandavarkar, "It is a wise policy to give *shastric* basis to the movement but with us the voice of *shastras* has ceased and, indeed, the *shastras* may be made to speak anything you choose for, anything you may do in support of your position, and an orthodox *pandit* will cite the same texts against it."[75] The reliance on scriptural authority not only tremendously hindered the manoeuvrability of the reformer but also forced him to meet the orthodoxy on its own ground.

The most significant realization among some of the leading reformers was that caste was the crucial factor in the determination of customs and not the *shastras.* The later reformers looked upon caste as the 'greatest monster' that they had to kill.[76] Vivekananda, while acknowledging the impact of caste system remarked, "So what is the basis of India's social order. It is the caste law. It is the caste that determines all .... We are married sometimes when children. Why? Because the caste says, if they have to be married anyway without their consent, it is better that they are married early ... ." He further said, "Daughter and caste combined ruin the poor Hindu, because, you see, she must marry in the same caste and even inside the caste, exactly, in the same order, and so the poor man may sometimes has to make himself a beggar to get his daughter married."[77] Ramabai voiced the same opinion. She opined that the strictures of modern caste system were responsible for the misfortune of Hindu women.[78] Jyotiba Rao Phule linked the subordination of women to Brahmanical domination. Phule viewed the prevalence of evil customs that resulted in oppression of women and Shudras as the impact of Brahmanism. To combat the same he gave a call for the unity of *Strishudratishudra* in which women as a class of Shudras were included and appealed to the oppressed to reject Brahmanism. His anti-Brahmin movement was specifically motivated for the liberation and education of women who, he felt, had been kept 'unenlightened' by Brahmins, who wanted to preserve their superiority.[79] As leader of the Brahmo Samaj,

Dwarkanath Ganguli and his associates Sibanath Shastri and Manmohan Ghosh had repudiated all taboos and restrictions prescribed by caste.

Despite increasing realization on the part of the reformers of the tyranny of caste system and its impact on the status of women, the movement never assumed the form of a full-fledged attack on the existing social structure and the rigidity of the caste system. Even in the 1920s, a helpless victim of caste system would exclaim, "... the greatest hindrance to social reforms is caste. If I want to educate my daughter, the caste would step in and say you should not do it. If I wish to postpone my children's marriage, till they are sufficiently grown up, the caste would raise its hand and forbid me. If a widow chooses to marry again and settle respectably in her home, the caste would threaten to ostracize her".[80]

Only a handful of reformers contested and confronted the issue of women's subordination and strict control over their sexuality. Pandita Ramabai, Jyotiba Phule and Agarkar challenged the traditional socio-cultural pattern of unequal relations between the genders. Ramabai severely condemned marital rights of men over their wives. Quoting from Manu, she showed how the wife is classed with cows, mares, female camels, slave girls, buffalo-cows, she-goats and ewes. The rights of a husband over a wife are so complete that yearly epidemics that carry away women are not unwelcome to women who are persecuted by social, religious and state laws. Ramabai was deeply agitated over the Rukmabai case when the British court had ordered the latter to live with her husband against her wishes. She articulated her anger over the combined strength of patriarchal forces represented by the British imperialism and Indian men. According to her, "Taught by experience of the past, we are not at all surprised at this decision of the Bombay court. Our only wonder is that a helpless woman like Rukmabai dared to raise her voice in the face of the powerful Hindu law, the mighty British government the one hundred and twenty nine million men and three hundred and thirty million gods of the Hindus, all ... having conspired together to crush her to nothingness. We cannot blame the English government for not defending a helpless woman; it is only fulfilling its agreement made with the male population of India."[81]

Phule's radical and progressive posturing over women's issues was revealed as early as 1850 when he had set up schools for girls. He even started a home where unmarried girls and widows could give birth to 'illegitimate' children without disclosing their identity and later he managed to get these children adopted. According to Radha Kumar, "this was especially radical as the codes repressing women's sexuality were most strictly administered by the upper castes, so such a home would have been used by upper caste women".[82] In 1882, Phule extended his whole-hearted support to Tarabai Shinde whose booklet *Stri Purush Tulana*, published in Poona had invited fierce hostility even from the progressive members of his organization, Satyashodhak Samaj. Phule accused these individuals of defending the traditional family structure which allowed men to enjoy whatever pleased them while women were helplessly tied to their homes. According to Gail Omvedt, for Phule "the issue was the formation of a new and egalitarian husband-wife relationship; the goal was the breakdown of the old authority structure within the family".[83] Quite significantly, such radical perspectives were not acceptable in the highly conservative Brahmin stronghold in Poona.

Gopal Ganesh Agarkar also dealt with women's issues in a rational manner and upheld equality of access to education and health. Agarkar questioned the rigid sexual division of labour and argued how it was inimical to the healthy development of both, men and women. In his essay on common curriculum for boys and girls he remarked, "It is feared that if co-education became a reality then many men might have to do domestic chores like minding the babies, washing clothes, cleaning utensils, cooking, grinding grain, etc. So what? Women are not predestined to such chores. Again, no one can prove that the nurture of children is exclusively a woman's job simply because she gives birth to them .... There is no inevitable link between bearing children and undertaking the burden of domestic chores." While pleading for women's reproductive rights and control over their bodies he remarked, "... why women have to bear ten or twelve children? We feel strongly that they do not do this of their own volition. We are convinced that men force women into repeated pregnancies. Had men themselves experienced even a small bit of the pangs of childbirth, they would have controlled their sexual predispositions .... It is important to note that *conjugal relationship requires the consent of both partners in all matters*"[84] (emphasis added). Significantly,

Agarkar was much ahead of his times when he raised precisely the same issues that the women's movement addressed in the 1980s and the 1990s. His insistence on equal and consensual nature of sexual relationship, compatibility between husband and wife and above all, advocacy of women's rights over her body reflect a stance that was unthinkable during those times. Thus, even in the nineteenth century there were some voices that sought to treat women as individuals entitled to the same rights as men. They questioned physically debilitating practices like forced pregnancies and innumerable household chores that were considered extremely normal in those times. The manner in which Phule, Ramabai and Agarkar empathized with women's privations and suffering was indeed commendable. However, the fundamental changes that they aspired for in man-woman relationship have yet to find social acceptance even in the twenty-first century.

The regressive nature of women's discourse in the nineteenth century is exemplified in the debates on women's education and the alternatives that were put forth for widows. The miserable condition of widows aroused some of the most graphic responses in the social reform movement. However, the option of remarriage remained a sensitive issue and characterized by considerable reluctance and confusion even among the reformers. Similarly, education was espoused not because of its liberatory content but to confer dignity on women within the family and also to improve efficiency in their traditional roles as mothers, wives and homemakers. Only a few reformers like Agarkar, Ramabai, Phule and Dwarkanath Ganguly conceived of new social roles for women and, therefore, advocated a curriculum that would equip them for these extra-familial roles.

Notes

1. Several scholars have drawn attention to the class orientation of the women's discourse as it shaped in the nineteenth century. During the later stages of the movement, exponents like Vivekanand realized the futility of the social reform programme that focused only on the concerns of the upper castes. He remarked, "Most of the reforms that have been agitated for during the past century have been ornamental. Every one of these reforms only touches the first two castes and no other. The question of widow remarriage could not touch 70 per cent of Indian women ..." For details refer, Amiya P. Sen (ed.), *Social and Religious Reform: The Hindus of*

British India, pp. 68–69; Kumkum Sangari and Sudesh Vaid (eds.), *Recasting Women: Essays in Colonial History*, 'Introduction', pp. 9–10.

2. For a historical overview of the women's status and position in Indian society refer, A.S. Altekar, *The Position of Women in Hindu Civilization*. For a more in-depth understanding of the historical context, perceptions, and ideas about Indian women, also see, Pratibha Jain and Rajan Mahan (eds.), *Women Images*.
3. Uma Chakravarti, 'Whatever Happened to the Vedic *Dasi*? Orientalism, Nationalism and a Script for the Past', in Kumkum Sangari and Sudesh Vaid (eds.), op. cit., pp. 29–60. Also, Uma Chakravarti, 'Beyond the Altekarian Paradigm: Towards a New Understanding of Gender Relations in Early Indian History', in Kumkum Roy (ed.), *Women in Early Indian Societies*, pp. 72–81.
4. Shakuntala Rao Shastri, *Women in the Vedic Age*, pp. 43–44.
5. Flavia Agnes, 'Plurality of Hindu Law and Women's Rights Under it', in Flavia Agnes (ed.), *Women and Law in India*, pp. 18–19.
6. Satish Balram Agnihotri, *Sex Ratio Patterns in the Indian Population: A Fresh Exploration*, pp. 339–340. He has argued how ecological, technological and historical factors reinforced each other in the north-western region to create a strong ethos of female subordination, the effects of which are still being felt.
7. For linkages between caste and gender refer, Leela Dube, 'Caste and Women', in M.N. Srinivas (ed.), *Caste: Its Twentieth Century Avatar*; M.N. Srinivas, *Social Change in Modern India*; S. Das, *Pardah: The Status of Indian Women*; Prabhati Mukherjee, *Hindu Women: Normative Models*; Joanne Liddle and Rama Joshi, *Daughters of Independence: Gender, Class and Caste in India*; Pt Rama Bai, *The High Caste Hindu Woman*; Veena Das, 'Indian Women: Work, Power and Status', in B.R. Nanda (ed.), *Indian Women: From Purdah to Modernity*.
8. Veena Das, 'Indian Women: Work, Power and Status', in B.R. Nanda (ed.), op. cit., pp. 134–135.
9. Kamaladevi Chattopadhyaya, *Indian Women's Battle for Freedom*, p. 57.
10. G.S. Ghurye, *Caste and Race in India*, p. 161.
11. S. Das, op. cit., pp. 52–53.
12. M.N. Srinivas, *Social Change in Modern India*, p. 1.
13. Flavia Agnes, 'Plurality of Hindu Law and Women's Rights Under it', in *Women and Law*, pp. 18–19.
14. A.S. Altekar, op. cit., p. 24.
15. V.P.S. Raghuvanshi, *Indian Society in the Eighteenth Century*, pp. 96–97.
16. Pandita Ramabai, *The High Caste Hindu Woman*, p. 22.
17. M.L. Sircar had explained this practice to be a recent development of the nineteenth century. According to him, "with the progress of enlightenment this rigid grandmother discipline has begun to be disregarded and

we have now true physiological marriage almost immediately after the ceremonial one is over ..." cited in Manmohan Ghose, 'On Social Progress in Bengal during the last 30 years', in C.Y. Chintamani, *Indian Social Reform*, p. 277.

18. Monmoyee Basu, 'Hindu Women and Marriage Law: From Sacrament to Contract', in *Women and Law*, p. 7.
19. P.N. Bose, *A History of Hindu Civilization during British Rule*, Vol. II, p. 42.
20. S. Natarajan, *A Century of Social Reform in India*, p. 43.
21. Shiva S. Dua, *Society and Culture in Northern India 1850–1900*, p. 149.
22. Flavia Agnes, 'Plurality of Hindu Law and Women's Rights Under it', in *Pre-Colonial and Colonial Legal Structures* in *Women and Law*, p. 21.
23. Kamaladevi Chattopadhyaya, op. cit., p. 53.
24. Pandita Ramabai, *The High Caste Hindu Woman*, pp. 36–38.
25. Cited in V.P.S. Raghuvanshi, op. cit., pp. 106–107.
26. S.R. Singh, *Nationalism and Social Reform in India*, p. 210.
27. B. Joardar, *Prostitution in 19th and Early 20th Centuries*, pp. 9–10.
28. Friend of India, March 30, 1865, cited in Monmoyee Basu, 'Hindu Women and Marriage Law: From Sacrament to Contract', in *Women and Law*, p. 10.
29. Edward Thompson, in Veena Das, 'Strange Response', *Illustrated Weekly of India*, February, 1988, pp. 30–32.
30. *India Today*, October 15, 1987, p. 105.
31. A.S. Altekar, op. cit., p. 128; Also, P.N. Bose, *History of Hindu Civilization during British Rule*, Vol. II, pp. 117–118; Wilson, *Essays on Religion of the Hindus*, pp. 65–66.
32. The statistics are from Edward Thompson, *Suttee*, cited in A.S. Altekar, op. cit., p. 138.
33. Veena Das, 'Indian Women: Work, Power and Status', in B.R. Nanda (ed.), op. cit., pp. 30–32. According to Veena Das, "Since we know that this was a period in which the missionaries were trying to change the policy of the Government towards Christianization of the country, one does not know how much reliance is to be placed on these records."
34. S. Natarajan, op. cit., p. 23.
35. A.S. Altekar, op. cit., p. 139; Bruce Carlisle Robertson (ed.), *The Essential Writings of Raja Rammohan Roy*, pp. 113–166.
36. Kamaladevi Chattopadhyaya, op. cit., pp. 15–20.
37. Radha Kumar, op. cit., p. 9.
38. Krishna Basu, 'Movement for Emancipation of Women in the Nineteenth Century', in *Role and Status of Women in the Nineteenth Century*, p. 36.
39. A.S. Altekar, op. cit., pp. 167–168.
40. Pandita Ramabai, op. cit., p. 32.

41. Kiran Devendra, *Status and Position of Women in India*, p. 9.
42. G.S. Iyer, 'The Hindu Joint Family', in C.Y. Chintamani (ed.), op. cit., pp. 80–85.
43. P.N. Bose, op. cit., p. 114.
44. Abbe Dubois, *Hindu Manners, Customs and Ceremonies*, pp. 337–338.
45. Shiva S. Dua, *Society and Culture in Northern India, 1850–1900*, p. 195.
46. A.M. Monoleath, *Note on the State of Education in India, 1865–66*, p. 75.
47. Documents relating to indigenous education in the Madras Presidency 1822–26; Minute of Governor Sir Thomas Munro ordering indigenous education 25.6.1822; Collector of Tinnevilly to Board of Revenue 18.10.1822, cited in Dharampal, *Beautiful Tree*, p. 84.
48. Ibid., pp. 76–77.
49. L.S.S. O'Malley, *Modern India and the West*, pp. 300–328.
50. Dharampal, op. cit., pp. 300–328.
51. Malvika Karlekar, *Voices from Within: Early Personal Narratives of Bengali Women*, pp. 49–50.
52. Pratibha Jain and Sangeeta Sharma, *Honour, Status and Polity*, pp. 123–125. In Rajput royal families, women were given military training. According to Laxmi Kumari Chundavat, who belonged to the *thikana* of Devgarh in the erstwhile state of Mewar in Rajputana, the girls of the family were taken on weekly visits to the *silahkhāna* (weaponry) to make them familiar with the weapons.
53. A.S. Altekar, op. cit., p. 25.
54. Kumkum Sangari and Sudesh Vaid (eds.), op. cit., 'Introduction', pp. 9–10.
55. Neera Desai, 'Ideas which Influenced the Status of Women', in Bisheshwar Prasad (ed.), *Ideas in History*, p. 110.
56. C.H. Hiemsath, *Indian Nationalism and Hindu Social Reform*, pp. 50–55.
57. L.V. Kaikini (ed.), *Speeches and Writings of N.G. Chandavarkar*, p. 434. (Now onwards, *Speeches and Writings*)
58. C.H. Hiemsath, op. cit., p. 53.
59. V.R. Mehta, *Foundations of Indian Political Thought*, pp. 159–160.
60. Veena Mazumdar, 'The Social Reform Movement in India, from Ranade to Nehru', in B.R. Nanda, op. cit., pp. 48–50.
61. It would be relevant to point out that 90 per cent of prostitutes of Bengal were widows and, of them, a large number came from *kulin* Brahmin and low class poor widows. B. Joardar, op. cit., pp. 9–10.
62. Yogendra Singh, *Modernization of Indian Tradition*, pp. 42–43.
63. V.K. Vashishtha, 'Rajasthan mein Sati Pratha ka Nivaran (1846–1988)', in Pratibha Jain and Sangeeta Sharma (eds.), *Bhartiya Stree*, pp. 133–54.
64. K.C. Yadav (ed.), *Autobiography of Swami Dayanand Saraswati*, 'Introduction', p. 4; P.N. Bose, op. cit., pp. 103–127.

65. Radha Kumar, op. cit., p. 8.
66. The first issue of *Spectator* in April, 1842 carried a long analytical article on widow remarriage. The article suggested the novel idea of sending a petition to the British Government, along with the signatures of the prominent individuals for legalization of widow remarriage.
67. The Secretary of the Commission J.P. Grant sent the proposal for the consideration of the *Sadar Adalats* of Calcutta, Madras and Allahabad in 1836. All the *Adalats* refused to enact a law for the legalization of widow remarriages, under the plea of violation of the sanctity of Hindu social and religious customs.
68. Vinay Ghosh, *Ishwarchandra Vidyasagar*, p. 71.
69. Bruce Carlisle Robertson (ed.), op. cit., pp. 113–166.
70. Ishwarchandra Vidyasagar, *Marriage of Hindu Widows*, p. 4.
71. Veena Mazumdar, 'Social Reform Movement: From Ranade to Nehru', in B.R. Nanda (ed.), *Indian Women: From Purdah to Modernity*, pp. 41–66.
72. Ganesh L. Chandavarkar, *A Wrestling Soul: Story of the Life of Sir Narayan Chandavarkar*, pp. 85–88.
73. *Speeches and Writings*, p. 65. It is pertinent to underscore Gandhi's progressive approach as far as reliance on *shastras* is concerned. Although he was deep-rooted in Indian tradition and relied on *shastras* as far as improvement in condition of women was concerned, he was against blind imitation of the *shastras*. For details refer, Pratibha Jain, *Gandhian Ideas, Social Movements and Creativity*, pp. 142–143.
74. Ganesh L. Chandavarkar, op. cit., p. 78.
75. Ibid., p. 93.
76. Dr Bhandarkar's Address to Social Reform Association of Madras in 1894, Ibid., p. 91.
77. *Collected Works of Vivekanand*, Vol. VII, pp. 62–63.
78. Pt Ramabai, op. cit., p. 12.
79. S.M. Dahiwale (ed.), *Understanding Indian Society: The Non-Brahmanic Perspective*, 'Introduction', p. 19.
80. *Indian Social Reformer* (Bombay) September 5, 1925, cited in G.S. Ghurye, *Caste and Race in India*, p. 161.
81. Uma Chakravarti, 'Whatever Happened to the Vedic *Dasi*? Orientalism, Nationalism and a Script for the Past', in Kumkum Sangari and Sudesh Vaid (eds.), op. cit., pp. 29–60.
82. Radha Kumar, op. cit., p. 23.
83. Ibid., p. 32; M.G. Mali, *Krantijyoti Savitribai Phule*, pp. 38–40.
84. Gopal Ganesh Agarkar, 'Common Curriculum for Boys and Girls', in Mathreyi Krishnaraj (ed.), *Remaking Society for Women: Visions, Past and Present*, Indian Association for Women's Studies, 1995, pp. 27–28.

‖Chapter 2‖

Indian Renaissance, Tradition, Dayanand and the Vedas

The vibrant movement for social and religious reform in the nineteenth century was the first all-India response to the cultural and moral challenge posed by the colonial rule. The movement was initiated by the educated middle classes in the backdrop of an ideological and cultural conflict between the British imperialists and the Indian intelligentsia. The cultural confrontation was provoked and preceded by an unabashed indictment of the Indian social and cultural practices, especially the low status of women, by the Christian missionaries and English utilitarians. The western critique evoked two types of distinctive responses from the native intelligentsia. At one level, they sought to accept the assessment as a valid and justified criticism of the degenerating state of the existing situation. Consequently, several aspects of Hindu social order and religious practices were re-examined from different perspectives. This response necessitated reform and reformulation of contemporary religious and social practices. On the other hand, they sought to assert the cultural superiority of the Indian heritage and constructed the theory of a Vedic Age to counteract the colonial critique. While they covertly accepted the validity of European criticism, the 'revivalists' wanted their own paradigm of change and continuity. Both the responses led to a critical revaluation of Indian life, both past and present, and thereby produced a discourse that sought to assign centrality to the Brahmanic scriptures. Ancient scriptures were subjected to rigorous examination by reformers like Raja Ram Mohan Roy, Ishwarchandra Vidyasagar, Mahadev Govind Ranade, Dayanand Saraswati and others.

Upholding the vitality of traditional culture was not cultural revivalism but cultural self-defence. The native intelligentsia wanted to prove that the true nature of Hindu society and religion should not be evaluated from its prevalent form. They undertook a reappraisal of Hinduism to demonstrate that its true form lay buried under a mass of irrationalities and superstitions. Such an assertion was also necessitated on account of the cultural insecurity of the Indians whose self-image had been smothered due to the strong negative perception that was being articulated by the Christian missionaries, British administrators, travellers, and others regarding Indian society and even the moral, intellectual and physical faculties of the Indians. The Indian reformers and scholars borrowed incessant support and evidence from scriptures to establish the claim of a high state of civilized existence in antiquity.

The scriptural authority was also invoked by exponents of the Indian Renaissance when they propounded eradication of social evils especially, the sensitive issues pertaining to women's situation. Roy, in his numerous tracts against *sati*, pleaded for its abolition by drawing upon the *Vedas, Smritis* and the *Bhagwat Gita*.[1] Ishwarchandra Vidyasagar's booklet, Marriage of Hindu Widows cited scriptural evidence in support of widow remarriage. The fact that reformers took recourse to *shastric* authority as a matter of expediency is adequately substantiated by the great reformer in the preface. He remarked, "I have been influenced more by compassion towards the unfortunate widows of my country than by a firm belief in their remarriage being consonant to the *shastras* ... but at the same time I may be permitted to state that I did not take up my pen before I was fully convinced that *shastras* explicitly sanction their remarriage .... For it will not be admitted by my countrymen that *mere* reasoning is applicable to such subjects. The custom must have the sanction of the *shastras*, for in matters such as these *shastras* are the paramount authority."[2] The use of scriptures was, thus, a strategic move to seek popular support for reformist measures.

To settle social and religious matters with reference to some authoritative scripture evolved as a standard practice not only amongst the reformers and their opponents, the orthodox community but it was quite pervasive amongst the colonial officials also. In fact, Lata Mani has argued, "Rammohan's shift from arguments based on reason in *Tohfat u 'l -muwahiddin* to arguments that are increasingly derived from scriptural texts had more to do with the colonial insistence on the centrality of scripture to the Indian society than on the 'feudal' or 'semi-feudal' character of the early nineteenth century Bengal."[3] Significantly, Roy himself believed that the *shastras* had no practical relevance as is borne by his letter to Lord Amherst on December 11, 1823 wherein he opposed an official move to open a Sanskrit college on the grounds that it would produce no positive or progressive impact on the students.[4] Roy felt that rather than loading the students with abstract metaphysical speculations they would benefit more by imbibing modern European knowledge. Roy was convinced that western education would widen the outlook of his countrymen.

Reinterpretation of tradition by the Indian intelligentsia was probably motivated by their desire to appropriate the discourse on Orient that had so far been dominated by the French and British scholars. Moreover, whether the latter's accounts were appreciative or critical, they spoke and wrote from a position of superiority and posited European identity as a superior one in comparison with all the non-European peoples and cultures. As Edward Said has observed, "The relationship between the Orient and the Occident is a relationship of power, of domination, of varying degrees of a complex hegemony … . The scientist, the scholar, the missionary, the trader, or the soldier was in or thought about the Orient because … he could think about it with very little resistance on the Orient's part."[5] He has compared the Orient to a woman who never spoke of herself, never represented her emotions, presence, or history. The Occident was the male who was wealthy, foreign, who spoke for her, and told his readers in what way she was "typically Oriental". The native intelligentsia probably wanted to contest this position of 'cultural domination' assumed in the early stages by the European Orientalist scholarship which had revealed India's past glory and later by the colonial officials and missionaries who, in their writings, articulated a bleak and negative perception of society and cultural heritage of the

Indians. The indigenous scholarship sought to assert its cultural superiority by seizing the initiative from the western scholarship by seeking to reinterpret their tradition and by formulating their own version of native history and cultural legacy.

Dayanand Saraswati's conceptualization of a reformed and regenerated Hinduism derived from the *Vedas* distinguished him from his contemporaries. He turned to the ancient scriptures not merely for seeking validation for isolated reform causes. Instead, he undertook the reinterpretation of the entire *Vedas* and carved out from the same an extensive blueprint of a socio-religious and political structure. It was through this reinterpreted and reformed formulation of Hinduism that he sought to respond to the moral and cultural challenge of the British rule. In his words, "I hold the four *Vedas*, the divine revealed knowledge and religious truths comprising the *Samhita* or *Mantras* as infallible and as authority by their very nature. In other words they are self-authoritative and do not stand in need of any other book to uphold the authority. I consider the four *Brahmanas* of the four *Vedas,* the six *Angas* and *Upangas*, the four *Upvedas* and the eleven hundred and seventy *Shakhas* of the *Vedas* as books composed by Brahma and other *rishis* as commentaries on *Vedas* and having authority of a dependent character." Dayanand's dogmatic insistence on the supremacy of the *Vedas*, as the source of Hinduism, marked a significant deviation in the history of the religion "which had never been strictly speaking the religion of the book. Dayanand's conviction that it was did not stem from Hindu tradition".[6]

I

Dayanand's unequivocal stand on the *Vedas* as the authentic tradition of Hinduism and as the repository of the entire knowledge of the world was formulated over a period of time. His numerous biographies and autobiographical narratives underline a consistent process of elimination of scriptural texts as the basis of Hinduism. A short chronological perusal of Dayanand's life and activities till 1870, the year when he asserted the supremacy of the four *Vedas* as the most ancient tradition from which Hinduism could be traced, would highlight the factors and influences that shaped Dayanand's consciousness during these years.

Dayanand was born in an *Audichya Brahmin* family in Tankara in 1836, a small township in Gujarat. His autobiographical accounts mention his father as a staunch Shaivite who performed the daily Parthiva Puja and forced Dayanand to do the same. Dayanand attributed his disbelief in idol worship to a small incident on the occasion of Mahashivratri, festival to venerate Lord Shiva. He saw mice running on the idol of Shiva. He could not reconcile the image of an "Omnipotent living God with this idol which allows the mice to run along its body and thus suffers to be polluted without the slightest protest". The deaths of his beloved sister and uncle impressed upon Dayanand the worthlessness of "living or caring for a worldly life". Aversion for worldly life motivated Dayanand to leave home in 1846 in search of *moksha*. His childhood accounts do not intimate his extraordinary propensity towards the *Vedas*, except that as a part of his syllabi, he had mastered the *mantras* of *Yajurveda*.[7]

Until 1860, Dayanand undertook extensive journeys in search of learned *yogis* to attain real knowledge. His quest took him to various strongholds of Brahmanical religion such as Hardwar (on the occasion of Kumbh Mela), Rishikesh, Garhwal, Shrinagar, Rudraprayag in 1854, Kedarnath, Okhimath, Joshimath, Badrinarayan in 1855 and Farukhabad and Benaras in 1856. In November 1860, Dayanand reached the hermitage of Virjanand and stayed here for three years to study Sanskrit grammar.[8]

Dayanand's sojourns during this period gave him a clear perception of the decaying conditions of Hindu religion. His disillusionment with the contemporary state of Hinduism was complete. He was particularly appalled by the Brahmanical domination over Hindu society. It was during this phase at some point of time that Dayanand abandoned the idea of freezing himself to death on the mountains of Alkapuri and instead resolved that "acquisition of knowledge and then doing good to others was a better proposition".[9]

During these years, Dayanand also initiated the process of examining the authenticity of scriptures of Hinduism. He rejected the *Tantric Shastras* as disgusting literature "full of incredible obscenities". After examining a floating corpse he found that details regarding human body given in *Shiv Sandhya*, *Hathyogapradipika* and *Kesarani Sangita* did not tally with the actual details. On the issue of relative legitimacy of scriptural texts, Dayanand's Guru Virjanand had also influenced him. He had impressed upon his disciple the division of Hindu scriptures into *Arsha*, i.e., pre-*Mahabharat* scriptures and *Unarsha* or the post-*Mahabharat* texts. Virjanand upheld the authenticity of the former and indicted the latter for the ruin of *dharma* in India. It is, however, clear that Virjanand was not responsible for Dayanand's contention that only the four *Vedas* formed the canonical source of Hinduism. Another engrossing concern of Virjanand was the regeneration of Hinduism. His concrete plan for achieving this objective was the formation of Sarvabhaum Sabha, i.e., a universal council of Hindus involving the participation of princely states, which would strive for renaissance of Hinduism.[10] Dayanand imbibed this twin concern of Virjanand, his anxiety regarding the authentic scriptural tradition of Hinduism and urgency of an organized endeavour to rejuvenate the same, quite deeply.

Dayanand left his guru in 1863 with a promise to resuscitate Hinduism and spread the knowledge of *Arsha Granthas* even at the cost of his life. His journeys until 1863 apprised him of the threat from within Hinduism, i.e., from unethical Brahmanical tyranny. His wanderings after 1863, however, made him aware of the threat from forces outside of Hinduism, i.e., from Christianity and, to a lesser degree, Islam. Before this period, there has been no mention of Dayanand's contact with Christian missionaries nor did he himself express any apprehension of challenge from their proselytizing activities. He had not yet limited the extent of Hinduism to the Vedic tradition. He was teaching grammar, *Vedanta*, *yoga*, *Bhagvat Gita* and the *Manu Smriti* during his visits to Jaipur and Ajmer in 1855 and 1856. Ghasiram, one of his earlier biographers, mentions that until 1866 in Pushkar, he converted people to Shaivism and instructed them to wear *rudraksh* and in Ajmer too, he preached Shaivism. Lekhram, another prominent and earliest biographer of Dayanand, described the reformer's attitude thus: "he criticized the idol of Shiva and he did not mention Shiva, the husband of Parvati, in fact he was against him. [But] he was still wearing *rudraksh* beads and applying ashes and teaching others to do so".[11]

In his series of lectures delivered at Poona, Dayanand had himself said, "[in Jaipur] I condemned Vaishnavism and preached Shaivism. The Maharaja of Jaipur, Ram Singh, too embraced Shaivism. This led to such widespread conversion to Shaivism that I myself distributed thousands of *rudraksh* rosaries".[12] All his biographers have substantiated his devotion to Shiva while at the same time, emphasizing his disapproval of image worship and sectarianism.

It is a scarcely known fact that Dayanand had not read the entire Vedic literature until 1866. In Agra, in 1865, he had read parts of the *Vedas*. After staying for two months in Pushkar, he came to Ajmer in June 1866. It was here that Dayanand encountered the preachers of Christianity and Islam.[13] Maulvi Murad Ali, a Muslim theologist, held discussions on various religious issues. Later, a *Shastrarth* (scriptural discourse) with Christian missionaries continued for three days. The discussion centred around three subjects – God, soul and creation. On the fourth day, the discussion on the divinity of Christ and his resurrection ended in dispute. In Ajmer, Dayanand also met Additional Deputy Commissioner, Major A.G. Davidson and informed him of the malpractices that were being carried on in the garb of religion. His reference, in all probability, was towards the baptizing activities of the Christian missionaries. Subsequently, one can observe definite shifts in his philosophy. His keen perception of the Christian challenge to the survival of Hinduism induced him to evolve a clear strategy to counteract their pervasive propaganda and intensive proselytizing activities. He strove to do this in various ways. At the outset, he sought to impart to Hinduism, a definite scriptural basis that formed a part of his efforts to transform Hinduism into an organized and unified religion. At another level, he sought to unify the Hindus by rejecting the diversity in rituals and sectarianism. Towards the end of his visit in Ajmer, he wrote *Bhagvat Khandanam*, a pamphlet in which he denounced the irrelevant ritualistic practices, as also wearing of the marks of sectarian distinction. In his words, "... abandon the application of ashes, abandon the wearing of *rudraksh,* and do not adore me, the Lord of this Universe, in the form of *Shivlinga*".[14] Dayanand is clearly indicating his disagreement with religious symbolism as signified by worship of *shivlinga* and wearing of *rudraksha* beads. From now onwards, he also made a conscious effort at narrowing down the scriptural basis of his theological, religious and social thought. Dayanand was, however, still not clear regarding the authentic tradition of Hinduism and the respective authoritativeness of its numerous scriptures.

Dayanand started questioning the authority of the *Bhagvat Gita*, *Mahabharat* and some parts of *Manu Smriti* in 1867 all of which earlier he had accepted as authoritative. During this period, he also strove hard to bring about uniformity in the rituals and ceremonies of the Hindus. He instructed people for proper performance of rituals like *Sandhya*, *Havan* and *Panchmahayajna* (five great sacrifices), observance of 16 sacraments and recitation of the *Gayatri Mantra*. The insistence on the performance of these specific ceremonies was motivated with a keen desire to do away with the baffling diversity that had so far characterized the religious life of the Hindus and thereby transform them into a homogeneous group. The inspiration for such a move must have been the homogeneity, organization and uniformity that had defined Christianity all over the world. In Kanpur, the same year, he published a declaration, in which he accepted the four *Vedas* as the only authentic source of Hindu religion. However, he had not yet distinguished between the *Vedas* and the *Brahmans*. The four *Vedas* were inclusive of their respective *Brahmans*. Even in the famous Kashi *Shastrarth* in November 1869, Dayanand had quoted the *Brahmans* and had allowed the pundits of Kashi to cite extracts from the same to prove their point of view. It was in 1870 that Dayanand firmly established supremacy of the four *Vedas* that now stood apart as the only revelation of God's wisdom communicated to the *rishis* (seers). The *Brahmans* and other books were held to be only man-made, secondary and, therefore, liable to contain errors.[15]

II

Dayanand's insistence on the *Vedas* as the sole authoritative source of Hinduism has been often criticized as a rigid and dogmatic. Pertinently, Dayanand's insistence on the infallibility of the *Vedas* led to the failure of his efforts to amalgamate the existing reform endeavours for regeneration of the Indian society. A distinctive, yet lesser known, aspect of his reform efforts was his sincere efforts to forge a functionalist alliance, based on a broad identity of ideologies and methodologies, among the reformers for revitalization of the Indian socio-religious structure. He had convened a conference of leading reformers like Syed Ahmed Khan, Munshi Kanhayalal Alakhdhari, Babu Harish Chandra Chintamani, Munshi Indramani, Keshav Chandra Sen and Babu Navin Chandra Roy on the occasion of Imperial Durbar in Delhi in 1877. He implored them to embark upon a combined endeavour to retrieve Indian society from the degenerating depths. Dayanand was able to impress upon them the urgency of a combined offensive but he utterly failed in his efforts to win them over to his convictions regarding the infallibility of the *Vedas.* His unrelenting and doctrinal stand on the issue estranged his relationship with the Brahmo Samaj and the Sat Sabha in 1878 and with the Theosophists in 1880.[16] In fact, his own close follower, Mulraj, recommended a modification in the doctrine pertaining to the divine revelation of the *Vedas*, to render the Arya Samaj a more accommodating, inclusive and liberal creed.[17]

It is indeed ironical that a reformer like Dayanand should have jeopardized his cherished dream for combining the existing reform efforts for rectification of evils that plagued the Indian society on the singular issue of revival of the Vedic culture. Perhaps, Dayanand was led by a compelling rationale in making *Vedas* the primary source of reformed Hinduism. The primary force that influenced Dayanand to adopt this unyielding and non-conciliatory stand was the vicious propaganda of the Christian missionaries against the Indian religion and society. Their vilification campaign had focused on issues like idolatry, superstitions, indecent ceremonies and also the Indian pilgrimages during which people died of disease, exhaustion, and hunger. Low status of Indian women, particularly the barbaric practices like *sati* and female infanticide, and the evils of caste system formed key aspects in their indictment of the Indian society. In addition, they also raised doubts over the authenticity of Hinduism by focusing on the lack of a divine or revealed book that could be defined as the authoritative source of the religion. Such propaganda was unleashed incessantly through books, pamphlets and public meetings. The intensity and tenacity of the vicious attack appalled the exponents of Indian Renaissance. They felt that these onslaughts against Hinduism, especially the campaign regarding the absence of an authoritative source of the faith, could produce a thoroughgoing skepticism in the minds of the followers. They felt the urgency to redefine, reinterpret and organize Hindu religion. Dayanand sought to combat this challenge by asserting the supremacy of the *Vedas* not only as the source of Hinduism but as the repository of the entire knowledge in the world. As J.T.F. Jordens has rightly observed, "All other books were considered secondary, man-made and, therefore, liable to contain errors .... He evolved that dogma over many years and the decisive influence in its emergence cannot have been any other than that of Christian missionaries and, to a lesser degree, of Muslim theologians. One should remember that most of the missionaries with whom Dayanand came into contact belonged to the Protestant churches; their religion was primarily the religion of the book and the *Bible* occupied the centre of their theology. Their propaganda concentrated on two fronts. They showed, on the one hand, the absurdity and immorality of Hindu scriptures and on the other they tried to prove the absolute and definite truth of Biblical revelation. That was exactly the approach Dayanand applied in reverse: he wanted to prove that Christianity fell with the *Bible* and that the truth of the Vedic religion was demonstrated by the absolute veracity of the *Vedas* .... The Swami went even further than the Christians in his claim that the *Vedas* contained the totality of truth, both theological and scientific."[18] It is not a coincidence that the sudden shift in his ideology regarding the supremacy of the *Vedas* occurred immediately after his meetings with the Christian missionaries.

Dayanand's keen perception of the Christian challenge and his firm faith in the efficacy of the *Vedas* to combat the menace finds categorical expression in one of his letters thus, "the Christians and the Muslims criticize Hinduism on the issues of pilgrimages, image-worship and temples. Adherence to these three rituals has rendered [the Hindus] defenseless in the face of Christian onslaughts. Therefore, even if one professes faith in pilgrimages, image-worship, temples, *Puranas*, fasts, *kanthi*, *tilak* (auspicious mark on forehead), sectarianism and incarnation, one should refute his belief in them, at least outwardly, in the presence of Christians and Muslims. Only by adherence to the *Vedas* can these practices be disowned otherwise, one would be powerless in the face of their allegations"[19]. Excessive ritualism and religious symbolism had been targeted by Christian missionaries as the dominant critique of Hinduism.

Apart from counteracting the adverse propaganda of the Christian missionaries, the *Vedas* suited Dayanand's programme of social reconstruction. Writes J. Ried Graham, "From the first hand, he knew that his people had to be led along the path of reform slowly, that all reform measures must be founded in scriptures. He was aware and made use of their tendency to follow tradition blindly. He appealed to all the Hindus, when he founded his system on the *Vedas* and exalted the position of the most ancient and venerated, if unread, scriptures of the Hindus."[20]

As far as reinterpretation of religious tradition is concerned, Dayanand had taken a dogmatic stand on the *Vedas* that were upheld as the first, foremost and the only canonical source of Hinduism. In addition, he laid stress on the uniformity of religious rituals amongst the Hindus. He insisted on the obligatory performance of certain specific rituals by all the Hindus, e.g., *Panchmahayajna* (the five great sacrifices), performance of 16 sacraments, recitation of *Gayatri Mantra* and wearing of the sacred thread. He wrote *Sanskar Vidhi*, a full-length book on the 16 sacraments, their significance, timing and the precise rituals for their performance. Even in his magnum opus, *Satyarth Prakash*, gives a section of the book giving details of the ceremonies and sacraments that should be performed by the Hindus. Similarly, he was keen on the continuity of traditional social institutions of Hinduism like *Varnavyavastha* (four-fold division of society) and *Ashram Vyavatha* (four stages of life). However, insistence on these practices and institutions was motivated with a view to inculcate a sense of unity, solidarity and oneness amongst the Hindus "putting an end to mutually antagonistic beliefs and practices which create bad blood in the country and lead to its ruin".[21] He was seeking to evolve a distinctive identity for Hindus and Hinduism. His aggressive and militant stand was necessitated in the given historical context when Hinduism had come under vicious attack from Christian missionaries. Dayanand had sought to remodel Hinduism in a manner that would render the moral challenge ineffective. He in fact endeavoured to transform Hinduism into an organized and dogmatic religion similar to Christianity. Dayanand, like other thinkers and reformers of his age, was reacting to the challenges of the time who believed that the answer was to construct a Hinduism modelled on Christianity and Islam. These were perceived as monolithic faiths sure of their rightness and aggressive in propagating their beliefs. Dayanand wanted to construct a single identity out of the bewildering variety of traditions and sects. The challenge before Dayanand was to make Hinduism aggressive so that it could be defended against the onslaughts of Christianity. This was in turn compelled by the cultural insecurity of the Hindus. The obvious requirement was a faith the Hindus could claim was superior to all others. Supremacy of the *Vedas* was, thus, crucial to the emergence of a glorious cultural past and the construction of a golden age of Hinduism. *Vedas* were projected as a unified source of Hinduism, and prime determinant of the cultural ethos and an Aryan identity. The urgency to assert the supremacy of Hinduism unfortunately led to his aggressive, parochial and intolerant posturing towards other religions.

Notes

1. Bruce Carlisle Robertson (ed.), *The Essential Writings of Raja Rammohan Roy*, pp. 113–166.
2. Ishwarchandra Vidyasagar, *Marriage of Hindu Widows,* p. 4.
3. Lata Mani, 'Contentious Traditions: The debate on *Sati* in Colonial India', in Kumkum Sangari and Sudesh Vaid (ed.), *Recasting Women: Essays in Colonial History*, p. 91.
4. Bruce Carlisle Robertson, op. cit., pp. 260–263.
5. Edward Said, *Orientalism*, pp. 6–7.
6. K.C. Yadav (ed.), *Autobiography of Swami Dayanand Saraswati*, p. 83.
7. J.T.F. Jordens, *Dayanand Saraswati: His Life and Ideas*, p. 273.
8. K.C. Yadav (ed.), op. cit., p. 24.
9. Dayanand Saraswati, *Dayanand Pravachan Sangrah* or *Poona-Bombay Pravachan*, Yudhishthir Mimansak (ed.), (henceforth *Dayanand Pravachan Sangrah*), p. 142.
10. J.T.F. Jordens, op. cit., pp. 37–38.
11. Ibid., p. 42.
12. Bhavani Lal Bhartiya, *Navjagran ke Purodha:Dayanand Saraswati*, p.42.
13. Ibid., p. 71.
14. J.T.F. Jordens, op. cit., p. 43.
15. Ibid., p. 56.
16. Ghasiram, *Maharshi Dayanand ka Jivan Charit*, Vol. II, p. 17; Y. Mimansak & Pt Bhagwat Dutt (ed.), *Rishi Dayanand ke Patra aur Vijnapan*, Vol. II, pp. 317–323.
17. Vishwaprakash, *Life and Teachings of Swami Dayanand*, p. 208.
18. J.T.F. Jordens, op. cit., p. 273.
19. Y. Mimansak and Bhagwat Dutt (ed.), *Rishi Dayanand ke Patra aur Vijnapan*, Vol. II, Letter No. 723, pp. 734–35.
20. J. Ried Graham, Arya Samaj as Reformation in Hinduism, with special reference to caste, Yale University, Ph.D Dissertation, 1943, p. 215.
21. Dayanand Saraswati, *Satyarth Prakash: Light of Truth*, English translation by Chiranjiv Bhardwaj, (henceforth *Satyarth Prakash*), p. 380.

Chapter 3

Women in the Vedic Age

The period of Indian Renaissance was characterized by a cultural encounter between the British rulers and their Indian subjects. The discourse on the relative superiority of the two cultures, the occident and the orient, privileged the scriptural tradition of India as a central theme. The debates that, thus, surfaced had many strands. Firstly, it led to a debate over the authentic tradition in India. This culminated in the hegemony of the Brahmanic scriptures like *Vedas*, *Upanishads* and *Smritis* as the repositories of the pristine tradition of India, both in the indigenous and official/colonial discourse. Secondly, status and condition of women were central component of the discourse. As Lata Mani observes, "Women became emblematic of tradition and the reworking of tradition is largely conducted through debating the rights and status of women in society. ... women and Brahmanic scripture become interlocking grounds for this rearticulation."[1] This was largely because status and condition of women had formed a central theme in the colonial indictment of Indian society, culture and people. Low status of women and their abject conditions were often cited as Indians' disability to govern themselves. Women's question became a critical tool in colonial propaganda claiming moral superiority over the subject population. This was the context for the obsessive concern for the reconstruction of the past in the nineteenth century. The exponents of Indian Renaissance and the native scholars sought to counter the western propaganda by projecting the Vedic Age as the golden period of Indian womanhood. It is, therefore, pertinent to delve into the status and condition of women in the Vedic period.

Vedic Literature and Society

The *Vedas*, claimed to be a divine revelation, form a body of literature, which is deeply cherished and venerated, even in the present times. The Vedic literary history is divided into three parts – *Samhitas* (2500 BC–1000 BC), *Brahmanas* (1000 BC–500 BC) and *Upanishads* (600 BC onwards). Historically speaking, the *Vedas*, four in number, form the earliest available textual records that throw light on the social conditions of the people in ancient India. Of the four *Vedas*, *Rig Veda*, defined as the "most ancient literary monument of India", has been dated differently by scholars from 2500 to 1500 BC. *Yajur* and *Sam Veda*, compiled by arranging some of the hymns of the *Rig Veda* are concerned primarily with the ritualistic aspects of the sacrifice. The *Atharva Veda* is the *Veda* of charms, spells and incantations. The religious and social ideals embodied in the *Atharva Veda* are at variation with that of the *Rig Veda*. Two branches of the later Vedic literature were the *Brahmanas* or ritualistic precepts and the *Upanishads* or metaphysical writings, attached to the four *Vedas*.[2]

Pertinently, the composition of the various texts which constitute the *Vedas* was spread over many centuries and ascribed to many generations of seers. Therefore, despite a broad consistency, the *Vedas* do not embody a uniform set of ideals and aspirations. In fact, the period stretching from *Rig Veda* to *Atharva Veda*, the two *Vedas* that have been most useful in the reconstruction of contemporary history, represent the formative stages of the Indian society which witnessed the formulation and crystallization of the distinctive traits, concepts and institutions of Indian religion and society. The undisputed historical significance of these texts lies in tracing these evolutionary stages of Indian civilization.

The *Vedas* are essentially religious and metaphysical texts concerned with theological and ritualistic aspects. Most of the hymns are addressed to a pantheon of Gods and Goddesses. There is no systematic or direct treatment of non-religious subjects dealing with day-to-day social, political and economic life. Yet, the scholars have drawn up a comprehensive picture of the life and conditions of the people in the Vedic Age. One of the striking features, which has consistently emerged in these sketches, is the high status held by women. The period has been upheld as the golden epoch of Indian womanhood. The portrayal of female deities, their characteristic traits and predominance in the Vedic pantheon, marriage and funeral hymns and other direct and indirect references to women project them as active participants in major spheres of societal activities. The period was marked by women's equal access to economic resources, religious rights, political participation and freedom of movement.[3]

Towards the end of the Vedic Age, especially in the *Atharva Veda*, one does observe the genesis of the theory of transmigration, which had a direct bearing on the change of attitudes towards women. The theory of transmigration gave rise to a firm belief in the survival of nourishment of manes by means of oblations offered to the dead. Over the issue of eligibility of the either sex to offer oblations, a son's claim was held up, for in a patriarchal society, the daughter had to sever her connection with her parental family after marriage.[4] Besides, the period also marked the emergence of caste rigidity and the subsequent crystallization of the concepts of purity and pollution. The way in which these concepts became central to women's body and behaviour, had serious repercussions for women's freedom of movement and also their access to productive sources. As Aryans began to concern themselves with notions of ceremonial purity, women were beginning to be considered impure and, especially so, during pregnancy, childbirth and menstruation.

Equality of Status

Vedas have abundant references which express desire for sons. In fact, *Atharva Veda* contains hymns that explicitly denigrate the birth of daughters. Scholars have treated these references as conclusive evidence of the superiority of sons over daughters in the Vedic Age. However, keeping in view the centrality of women's position in a constantly warring society and a subsistence economy coupled with non-prevalence of concepts which sought to consolidate forms of gender inequalities in the later ages, one comes across various hymns which not only express desire for sagacious and intelligent daughters but also reflect the fondness and affection of parents for girl children. In one such hymn, a simile of heaven and earth has been drawn to reflect upon the tender and affectionate bonds of parents with their daughters. Besides several hymns expressing keenness for children (*praja*), which implies both sons and daughters, goes to prove that lesser value was not attached to daughters.

The two verses, which are often quoted by scholars to convey the depreciation at a daughter's birth, are as follows:

"Preserve the babe at birth; make not the boy a female child."[5]

"Elsewhere may be effect the birth of maids, but here a boy."[6]

Dr Thomas, while explaining this waning respect and scornful treatment towards the birth of female children, writes, "Apart from her uselessness, as far as redemption from hell was concerned, social censure was becoming very strict on erring women, and child marriage not having come into vogue, the guarding of girls from improper conduct was becoming a very grave burden on parents."[7]

The achievement of intellectual feats by women demonstrates, beyond doubt, a healthy tradition of imparting training to daughters. The initiation ceremony of girls used to take place as regularly as that of boys.[8] Several hymns of the *Vedas* unequivocally underline the indispensability and significance of education for maidens.

"An unmarried young learned daughter should be married to a bridegroom who, like her, is learned. Never think of giving in marriage a daughter of very young age."[9]

The *Atharva Veda* is equally emphatic in its advocacy of female education.

"A king by observing *Brahmcharya* can protect his kingdom easily. An *Acharya* can impart education to his students, if he has himself observed his *Brahmacharya*. A young daughter, after the observance of *Brahmacharya*, should be married to a young man."[10]

Women were imparted training in spiritual as well as temporal subjects. The spiritual aspects comprised of training in religious lore, historical tradition and mythology. The scholars were divided into two classes, *Brahmavadinis* and *Sadyodvahas*.[11] The former were lifelong students of theology and philosophy. Vak, the daughter of Abhrma, to whom the authorship of hymn 125 of Book V of *Rig Veda,* embodying the unity of the universe is attributed, marks the beginning of the line of the *Brahmvadinis* who distinguished themselves in the later Vedic literature by the depth and intensity of their philosophical discourses. This hymn is one of the "earliest precursors of the non-dual doctrine of the later *Vedanta* philosophy"[12].

It goes to prove that not only mythology and tradition were taught to women, but even the most intricate principles and concepts of metaphysics formed the subjects of their study. The *Sadyodvahas* prosecuted their studies till their marriage at the age of 15 or 16. Vedic literature points to women's proficiency in fine arts too.

The completion of education was followed by marriage which was a well-recognized institution since the early Vedic days. The imperative need to increase the numerical strength of the community and the need for a settled life led to a wider acceptability of the institution. Religious beliefs of the period further enhanced the popularity of marriage. "Gods accepted no oblations offered by the unmarried ... they could be properly performed by the husband and wife officiating together. Wife was not an impediment but an absolute necessity in the religious life."[13]

On marriage, the bride was accorded the most venerable position in the household. She was at the helm of affairs. The phrase of *Rig Veda*, 'Wife, O' Maghavan is home and dwelling' underscore her position as one of unique importance. She was an object of reverence and compassion. The following hymn, exhorting her to be the empress of the household and members of the family reflects her supreme position in the household.

"... Be the bestower of happiness; be the bringer of prosperity to our bipeds and quadrupeds".

Be a queen to thy father-in-law.

Be a queen to thy mother-in-law.

Be a queen to thy husband's sisters.

Be a queen to thy husband's brothers."[14]

Likewise, in hymn XIV.1.44 of the *Atharva Veda*, her supreme position in the household is reflected.[15]

The use of the word *Dampati*, in the sense of a pair for husband and wife, exemplified their innate unity in the family and society.[16] At other places, the application of the term '*Dampati*', signifying 'Lord of the House' to both husband and wife, suggests an egalitarian family structure where wife was entitled to similar privileges and duties.

According to Prof. Indra, "The wife and husband being equal halves of one substance were regarded equal in very respect, and both took equal part in all works, religious and social."[17]

Innumerable references in the *Vedas* testify to the equal status of the wife and husband in the family and community. Scholars unanimously subscribe to women's active and real participation in the religious rituals. The wife was "on a level of equality at the hearth, which was the altar of sacrifice."[18] Wives took equal part in the performance of sacrifices and offering of oblations to fire which formed an indispensable part of the religious life in the Vedic Age. Apart from that, her principal function in the Aryan household was to keep the domestic fire, symbolic of *Agni* (Lord of the House), kindled at all hours.[19] In hymn II.39.2 of the *Rig Veda*, word *Dampativa Kratuvida* shows that household fire was tended by husband and wife.[20] Besides this, there are several references regarding joint worship and sacrifices by the couple.

Not only jointly but wives and maidens could perform worship and *yajnas* independently. In *Rig Veda* VIII. 91.1, a maiden, while returning from her bath, takes a shoot of the Soma shrub and offers it to Lord Indra in a sacrifice.[21] Similarly, Viswavara is shown as performing the sacrifice all by herself. Moreover, when the husband was on journey, the wife alone performed the various sacrifices, which the couple had to offer jointly.[22] Commenting on the religious privileges of women in the Vedic Age, P. Thomas writes, "The fact that women were considered competent enough to compose religious hymns is proof enough that they had few religious disabilities at the time."[23]

Similarly, women enjoyed an equal political and public space with men. Far from excluding women from the larger extra familial concerns of the community, their cooperation and participation in the political assembly of the clan called '*Vidhata*' was considered highly useful. *Vidhata* has been defined as the earliest collective institution or a popular assembly of the Indo-Aryans which was "performing all kinds of functions – economic, military, religious and social. It answered the needs of a pastoral and nomadic formation which hardly knew division of labour or domination of male over female ..."[24]. The *Rig Veda* and *Atharva Veda* furnish several references testifying to active participation of both men and women in the deliberations of the *Vidhata*. In a hymn, hope is expressed that the bride should be able to speak with composure in public assemblies down to her old age.[25] This hymn presupposes that not even common women were excluded from participation in public bodies. In the *Rig Veda*, the maiden is seen going to *Vidhata*.[26] In the *Rig Veda* and *Atharva Veda*, both men and women were expected to speak to *Vidhata* in their advanced age.[27] The fact that in hymn X.85.26 Surya is instructed to speak to the assembled people in the *Vidhata* goes to prove that women's participation was not a mere formality but a real one.[28]

Women reigned supreme in their role as mothers. For a community striving to increase its numerical strength, women as progenitors of race were objects of deep veneration. "The mother outlived the wife."[29] The degree of reverence which Aryans had for their progenitors is reflected in a number of hymns. The Aryans very definitely recognize the importance of the mother in the conception of female deities. Aditi, standing first amongst Goddesses, typifies motherhood. Motherhood is the essential and most characteristic trait of this divinity. She is the mother of Mitra and Varuna, Aryaman, the Rudras, the Adityas and Indra.[30] In later literature too, Aditi's character as a mother is preserved.[31] In the *Atharva Veda* and *White Yajur Veda*, she is invoked as a generous mother.[32] The following hymns bring out her motherly traits. "We call to succour in the Mother of those whose sway is just, the Queen of order. Strong ruler, far expanding, ne'er decaying, Aditi, gracious guide and good protectress."[33] Similarly, Prithvi is also spoken of as "kindly Mother Earth."[34] Similarly, in the *Atharva Veda*, Goddess Prithvi is eulogized as a benevolent Mother.[35] Saraswati is another Goddess, reflecting the innate goodness of motherhood.[36]

The endowment of motherly traits of protection, benevolence and nurturance on the female deities imbued the mother with a divine halo. This identification of the mother with female divinities in the Vedic mythology had far-reaching impact on the position of women. Even in the ages when there was a sharp decline in the status and condition of women, their position as mothers continued to be one of empowerment, veneration and even worship. The Vedic texts, thus, accorded a high status to women in their roles as mother, wife and daughter who enjoyed opportunities for public participation, education, ritual performances and artistic endeavours.

Freedom of Choices

Freedom and space available to women in a particular social structure determine to a large extent their status in the society. Judged from this standpoint, the Indo-Aryan woman was free from inhibiting customs that tend to restrict women's choices to the straitjacket of specific roles in society. The complex institutions and concepts that produced and sustained gender equalities in the later period were yet to take shape. The caste system, which enjoined purity of lineage naturally entailed restrictions on women's behaviour and mobility leading to discriminatory ethical canons for women, had not yet assumed its rigid form even towards the end of the Vedic period. Similarly, the concept of pollution which came to be associated with women due to biological processes like reproduction and menstruation was non-existent. Above all, a nomadic pastoral subsistence economy engaged in military pursuits could ill-afford to restrict women's mobility. These socio-economic, religious and political factors in turn led to the construction of a society in which women, in a large measure, enjoyed marital, ethiçal and professional autonomy.

Marital freedom emerges as one of the significant indicators of a woman's freedom to choose a way of life. Vedic literature looks upon the institution of marriage as desirable alternative for both the sexes, yet women were not bound by the marital imperative. The existence of the word *'Amajuh'* which meant a girl who grew old in her father's house without finding a husband or as they were called who sit with their father and the reference to unmarried female rishis as Apala Aitreyi[37] suggest that matrimony was not absolutely binding upon a woman. In the two hymns attributed to her, Ghosha is depicted as being unmarried and staying with her father.[38] The expression 'acceptance of even the sons of maidens' in *Atharva Veda*[39] does reflect the growing recognition of marriage as a social institution, but the society did not insist upon its obligatory character. An incantation in the *Atharva Veda* suggests that the worst fate one could think of a woman one disliked was that of a spinster forced to lead her life in her parents' or brother's house. The *Atharva Veda* also speaks of the custom of dowry to secure a groom for girls.[40]

Even with regard to selection of partners, Vedic literature does not testify to strict parental control. The hymns embodying the marriage rituals of Surya suggest the existence of *Swayamvara* marriages. The Aswins were selected as bridegrooms after they had won a chariot race.[41] Apart from these, numerous references to the existence of natural love between young people before marriage also goes to prove the discretion of the individuals in selecting their partners. The absence of endogamy also gave substantial liberty to women to choose their partners.[42] The following hymn of *Atharva Veda* (V.17.8–9) elucidates the liberal social norms:

> 'Even if ten former husbands – none a *Brahman* – had espoused a woman
> And then a *Brahman* took her hand, he is her husband, only he.
> Not *Vaishya*, not *Rajanya*, no; the *Brahman* is, indeed, her lord.'[43]

The inference that there were women who could individually have either a *Brahman* or a *Rajanya* or a *Vaishya* for a husband is indisputable. Even in the *White Yajur Veda* the seduction of a Shudra's wife by a rich Arya and an Arya'a wife by a Shudra, are not seen as gross violation of the law or social norms but merely as a loss to the husbands.[44]

Similarly, in the event of being widowed, women were not forced to lead austere and solitary lives. Neither was any stigma attached to widowhood. In the words of P. Thomas, "The early Aryans could ill-afford to let the fertility of their women go waste as the needs of building up the numerical strength of the family and the clans were paramount."[45] The scholars of the Vedic texts have expressed unanimity over the social sanction accorded to widow remarriage. Similarly, *Atharva Veda* refers to second marriage of women. It would be significant to mention that in case of widow's unwillingness to enter into a fresh alliance; such a union was not imposed on her.[46] There are also references to children born out of *niyoga* or levirate.[47]

The simplicity, utility and vitality of the institution of marriage in the Vedic Age, untouched by the customs and values that rendered it extremely inhibitive for women, had very positive implications for women's status. The prevalence and popularity of adult marriages gave women ample freedom to pursue the cherished goals of their lives. Similarly, evidences of choice marriages, widow remarriages and option to stay out of matrimony, reflect liberal attitudes towards women. As Gatwood has rightly observed, "Marital manipulation was a critical factor in changing the relatively equal Vedic woman into dependent and inferior high caste Hindu wife."[48]

The numerous references to love affairs and friendships between the sexes in the *Rig Veda* and *Atharva Veda* reflect a social environment which offered considerable liberty to both the sexes prior to marriage. In hymns I.115.2, IX.56.3 and IX.32.5 of *Rig Veda*, the word *Jara* (lover) does not denote a derogatory connotation.[49] There are several instances in *Rig Veda* wherein women violated the behavioural codes, as they were later formulated and legitimized in the *Smriti* and the epic period, yet she was not subjected to harsh retribution from society. "There was no discrimination between the male and female in anger of the Gods."[50] Vedic *rishis* had no overwhelming fear of supposed uncontrolled female sexuality, and hence, their unbigoted attitude towards female chastity and modesty. Even a wife's infidelity was pardoned in a ritual called *Varunapraghasa*. In this ceremony, which routinely took place every four months, wife of the sacrificer was asked by the priest to hold as many stalks of grass as she had lovers during this period. After the performance of this ritual, she was considered purified.[51]

Women's uninhibited participation in *Samana* stands out as the best exposition of the freedom that they enjoyed during the period. *Samana* has been described differently by scholars. Sayana has described it as a 'sacrificial ceremony'.[52] Among western scholars, Pischel thinks it to be either a "general popular festival to which women went to enjoy themselves. Young men and elderly women sought there to find a husband and courtesans to make profit of the occasion"[53]. Monier William has described it as a festival attended by the young and old.[54] B.S. Upadhyaya renders *Samana* to be a popular festive gathering of men and women, mainly grown up boys and girls, where they met and played, loved and parted. The institution served 'a great social need' of the Indo-Aryan community by bringing together at the nightly gathering, young men and women.[55] According to S.R. Shastri, the description of *Samana* conveys the meaning of a festival, rather than anything else.[56] From the interpretations of different scholars, *Samana* can be best understood as a festive gathering in which people belonging to different age groups and social strata actively participated. According to scholars, young women of marriageable age specially thronged the festival in large numbers and utilized the occasion for meeting and attracting strangers. Even grown-up spinsters and widows used this gathering for finding suitable marriage partners.[57] The festival of *Samana* which fulfilled a social need of the Indo-Aryans, speaks volumes on the extent of freedom extended to women. Free association and familiarity between the sexes, which was censured in the later ages, forms a distinctive feature of the Vedic Age.

Apart from access to liberal ethical, sexual and marital norms, women enjoyed tremendous freedom in the sphere of work. On account of unusual political and demographic factors, gendering of vocations was not prescribed. At the same, time the realm of work and profession was still free from the division of labour prescribed by the caste system. Consequently, women had wider vocational choices to choose from. The Vedic Age was characterized by the complementarity of men and women in social and economic pursuits. As worthy and equal partners of men women indulged in diverse occupations. She is eulogized as a potential mother, a learned daughter, a brave warrior, a faithful wife etc. Men in the Vedic period were so taken up with military and semi-military activities, that their reliance on women in spheres other than family and household was much greater than in the subsequent periods. Women were not dependent on men, but were very useful members of society whose cooperation was very valuable in securing prosperity in peace and victory in war. A *Rig Vedic* hymn wherein a composer calls himself a poet, his father, a physician and his mother, a grinder of corn is an outstanding example of the flexibility and freedom which an individual enjoyed in choosing a vocation.[58] Women's access to a plethora of choices in public sphere is well-conveyed in following lines.

"... a woman who splits cane ... a woman who works in thorns ... a woman who deals in charms ... a female dyer ... a female ointment maker ... a female scabbard maker ...".[59]

Weaving as a popular profession among women is suggested by numerous references.[60] Aufrecht, Muir and Griffith have explained the meaning of the word *'siri'* as the female weaver.[61] B.S. Upadhyaya, has also suggested that weaving was chosen as a career by women. Women undertook agricultural activities and manufactured bows, arrows and other war material.[62] According to A.S. Altekar, *Vedic Samhitas* have special words to denote female workers, specializing in different crafts, which disappeared in the later literature. These circumstances would show that women, even in higher circles, were manufacturing bows and arrows, baskets and clothes but gave up these professions in later times.[63] Women also took up dancing as a profession. The existence of professional women dancers is evident from the following description of the dawn.

"She like a dancer puts her embroidered garments on, as a cow yields her udders, so she bares her breast."[64]

Apart from their participation in the economic life of the society, women of the Vedic Age were highly esteemed for their creative, scholarly and spiritual pursuits. The Vedic literature testifies to women's proficiency in the fine arts. Many of the fine arts like sculpture and painting were little known in the age. Women, however, attained proficiency in dancing and music. The evidence pointing to music as an acquisition of women is as follows:

"Driving thee in Vivasvans' course, the seven sisters with their hymns, made melody round thee the sage."[65]

"Ten dames have sung to welcome thee, even as a maiden greets her lover."[66]

Few references in the *Rig Veda* testify to the provision of military training for women. Aryans, who were engaged in the fight with their enemies day and night, found it necessary to train their women in self-defence. At times, women even accompanied their husbands in the battlefield. Vispala, the wife of King Khela is such an example. She accompanied her lord to the battlefield, where she lost her leg, which was later replaced with an iron one by the Asvins.[67]

Mudgalini, Mugal's wife, is another brave warrior of the Vedic times, who is credited with having driven the chariot for her husband. She is said to have overpowered her husband's enemy who, thus, defeated took to his heels chased by her.[68] A few more examples are recorded in the *Rig Veda*. We come across several other allusions to bravery inherent in women.[69]

The intellectual feats of women are exemplified in the hymns of the *Rig Veda* that have been attributed to female *rishis*. According to the orthodox tradition recorded in *Sarvanukramanika* there were as many as 20 women among the authors of *Rig Veda*.[70] Shakuntala Rao Shastri has classified these hymns as follows: Hymns that are entirely attributed to female *rishis*; hymns that are partly attributed to female *rishis*; hymns that are attributed to female *rishis*, but are of dubious authorship.[71]

The first category includes hymns composed independently by Apala and Visvavara, who belonged to the Atri family. Apala addressed hymn 91 of the tenth book and invokes *Agni* in Book V of the *Rig Veda*, while Visvavara has composed hymn 91 of the seventh book. The second category includes hymns which have been traditionally attributed to female *rishis*, Lopamudra and Shashiyasi, addressed jointly with their spouse or some other seer. Lopamudra has composed a hymn jointly with her husband, Agastya.[72] The last category represents hymns of Ghosha, Indrani, Urvasi, Surya, Savitri, Sraddha, Kamayani, Sachi Paulomi, Sarparagini. With the exception of Ghosha, the rest are mythological or divine figures who might not have been the real authors.[73] The contemporary feminist historians of ancient India explode the myth of the superior position of women in the Vedic Age as far as scholarship is concerned. They point out that less than one per cent of the one thousand hymns of the *Rig Veda* are attributed to women which clearly show their secondary position.[74]

Women's unrestricted participation in the military, political, economic, spiritual and scholarly endeavours totally ruled out their subjection to the most flagrant restraint on women's mobility, i.e., the abominable practice of *purda*. The Aryans extended to their women full liberty of movement. "The very conception of Usha would have been an impossibility and her lovely picture, an undrawn sketch, had the *rishis* not seen their own free matrons in shining raiment. The free moving woman of the Aryan household is conspicuously present in her secondary type of Usha."[75]

During the 1990s, feminist historians sought to question this historical construction on several premises. According to Uma Chakravarti, the theory of golden age of the *Vedas* was a reaction to the attacks by colonial writers, administrators and Christian missionaries who had highlighted low status of women as an index of civilizational inferiority and consequently implied inability of Indians to govern themselves.[76] The construction of a particular kind of past and a particular kind of womanhood led to the 'invention of tradition' in which "Indian women were almost built up as superwomen ...". Moreover, this particular historical construction is derived exclusively from Brahmanical sources and is, therefore, a partial history that reflected the condition of upper class and upper caste women. In a detailed analysis of the nineteenth century nationalist responses to the strident western critique in her essay 'Whatever happened to the Vedic *Dasi*', Uma Chakravarty contends that even if one accepts that the status of upper caste women was high, it was so at the cost of exploitation of non-Aryan people, especially women. Her argument is that consideration of a particular kind of womanhood excluded various sections not only from the construction of the past but also from the concerns of the social reformers of the nineteenth century. Secondly, the Vedic texts focused on certain specific geographical areas, early texts refer to North-West of the sub-continent, later texts to the east around the mid-Gangetic valley and the *Manu Smriti* to the north of Vindhyas. From these texts, the nineteenth century historians have drawn a picture of Vedic India whereas India as an entity came into being only in the nineteenth century. Moreover, it is incorrect to argue that the process of women's subordination and evils of the nineteenth century were a response to fears for women's safety following Muslim invasions.[77] Even in the Vedic texts, the patriarchal features of society and structure of institutions like marriage and caste, that ensured women's subordination in the later ages, had started taking shape. According to them, the golden age of Indian womanhood was a selective picture of the past created in the context of the politics of the nineteenth century.

The concept of womanhood in the Vedic Age had certain disagreeable features also. In the Vedic literature, one comes across a school of thought which held women in disrepute. Derogatory and disrespectful pronouncements on women are not unknown. The perceived low status of women is shown in the hymn of the *Atharva Veda* wherein not *shudra* men but *shudra* women are preferred as expendable targets for fever to strike.[78] While referring to the disparaging remarks about women Altekar has commented, "They merely reflect the light hearted cynicism of some poets, and do not embody the considered views of the leaders of society."[79] Similarly, B.S. Upadhyaya feels, "Every society, whether ancient or modern, civilized or uncivilized has its quota of bad men and vile women, of villains and harlots .... The disparaging remarks, cited above, are but outbursts of casual passion and they refer only to individual cases."[80] Although towards the end of the Vedic Age, one can clearly identify the crystallization of ideological processes responsible for decline in the political, social, economic and ritual status of women but it did not substantially alter the egalitarian social structure. Cooperation and companionship between men and women in major spheres of societal activities formed the essence of social life of the Vedic Age. The conditions were conducive to the creation of a social milieu wherein women were not playing peripheral and secondary roles but their contribution was seminal to the growth and sustenance of Vedic civilization. Marriage was not inspired by the ideal of *pativratyam*, signifying dependent and inferior status of the wife. Women emerged as individuals in their own right with ample freedom to pursue a way of life. She was not confined to stereotyped roles within the four walls of the house. She had substantial freedom to pursue myriad social roles. While engaging in extra household activities, she took part in intellectual, political, military and artistic pursuits of life. Men and women were serving, strengthening and evolving the social structure in whatever way they could. In this flexibility of social roles lay the distinctness of the Vedic Age. Significantly, they enjoyed equal status with male counterparts in the spheres of marriage, education and religion. Remarriage of widows, absence of child marriage, considerable freedom to choose one's spouse and also the option to remain unmarried are factors that demonstrate that the institution of marriage was free from regressive customs that had led to a decline in women's status in the later ages. Women had equal access to education that included acquisition of religious and philosophical learning. The fact that they could even compose Vedic hymns clearly signifies their high status and the freedom of choices they enjoyed in the Vedic era.

Notes

1. Lata Mani, 'Contentious Traditions: The Debate on Sati in Colonial India', in Kumkum Sangari and Sudesh Vaid (eds.), *Recasting Women: Essays in Colonial History*, p. 91.
2. Shakuntala Rao Shastri, *Women in the Vedic Age*, pp. 54–55.
3. The family, that was undoubtedly the most important social unit, was patriarchal in nature as shown by references in *Rig Veda* to *pitrivitta* (wealth left by ancestors) and *pitriyana* (ways of the fathers). The patriarchal nature of social structure did have certain inherent disabilities from which women suffered yet the cumulative effect of socio-economic and political factors produced a social environment free from social conventions wherein relations between the genders, in a large measure, were marked

by cooperation, autonomy, equality and freedom of choices. Irfan Habib and Vijay Kumar Thakur, *The Vedic Age and the Coming of Iron c.1500–700 BC*, p. 13.

4. P. Thomas, *Indian Women through the Ages*, pp. 54–55.
5. *Atharva Veda*, VIII.6.25, cited from M.W. Pinkham, *Women in the Sacred Scriptures of Hinduism*, p. 26.
6. *Atharva Veda*, VI.II.3, cited from M.W. Pinkham, op. cit., p. 26.
7. P. Thomas, op. cit., p. 57. Somehow Arya Samajist scholars have put forth fresh interpretation of the controversial hymns in order to justify Dayanand's total commitment to the *Vedas*. Dr Ramnath Vedalankar, an Arya Samajist has, therefore, refused to accept this rendering of the above-mentioned hymn. According to him, this particular verse has three hymns and describes the treatment which should be given to a woman who has only daughters in order to make her produce sons. Ramnath Vedalankar, *Vedic Nari*, pp. 25–26.
8. A.S. Altekar, *The Position of Women in Hindu Civilization*, pp. 9–10.
9. *Rig Veda*, III.55.16, cited from B.S. Upadhyaya, *Women in the Rig Veda*, pp. 179–180.
10. *Atharva Veda*, XIII.3.17; XIII.3.18; XI.5.8, cited from B.S. Upadhyaya, op. cit., p. 180.
11. A.S. Altekar, op. cit., p. 10.
12. B.S. Upadhyaya, op. cit., p. 183.
13. A.S. Altekar, op. cit., p. 343.
14. *Rig Veda*, X.85.33; 42; 44; 47, cited from S.R. Shastri, op. cit., p. 17.
15. *Atharva Veda*, XIV.I.44, cited from S.R. Shastri, op. cit., p. 17.
16. *Rig Veda*, V.3.2; I.27.7; X.68.2; X.10.5; X.95.2, cited from S.R. Shastri, op. cit., p. 20.
17. Prof. Indra, *Status of Women in Ancient India*, p. 26.
18. Macdonell, *Vedic Religion*, p. 158, cited from Pinkham, op. cit., p. 18.
19. B.S. Upadhyaya, op. cit., p. 140.
20. S.R. Shastri, op. cit., p. 18.
21. Anil Kumar Tyagi, *Women Workers in Ancient India*, pp. 38–39.
22. Ibid., p. 39.
23. P. Thomas, op. cit., p. 56.
24. Anil Kumari Tyagi, op. cit., p. 37.
25. *Rig Veda*, X.85.26, A.S. Altekar, op. cit., p. 190.
26. *Rig Veda*, I.67.3, cited from Tripat Sharma, *Women in Ancient India*, p. 11.
27. *Rig Veda*, X.85.27, *Atharva Veda*, XIV.121; VIII.16, cited from, Tripat Sharma, op. cit., p. 11.
28. Ibid., p. 36.
29. Bader, *Women in Ancient India*, p. 51.

30. *Rig Veda*, VIII.25.3; X.36.3; 132.6; VIII.47.9; VIII.90.15; II.27.7, cited from B.S. Upadhyaya, op. cit., p. 4.
31. B.S. Upadhyaya, op. cit., p. 4.
32. *Atharva Veda*, VII.6.2; *White Yajur Veda*, 21.5, M.W. Pinkham, op. cit., p. 9.
33. *White Yajur Veda*, 21.5, cited from, M.W. Pinkham, op. cit., p. 9.
34. *Rig Veda*, X.18.10, cited from, M.W. Pinkham, op. cit., p. 12.
35. *Atharva Veda*, VII.1.8, M.W. Pinkham, op. cit., pp. 10–11.
36. *Rig Veda*, II.41.16, cited from, M.W. Pinkham, op. cit., p. 12.
37. S.R. Shastri, op. cit., p. 10.
38. *Rig Veda*, X.45.5; 39.3; 1.117.7; cited from, B.S. Upadhyaya, op. cit., p. 63.
39. *Atharva Veda*, V.5.8, S.R. Shastri, op. cit., p. 56.
40. Irfan Habib and Vijay Kumar Thakur, op. cit., p. 57.
41. *Rig Veda*, X.85.14; I.116.17, cited from, B.S. Upadhyaya, op. cit., p. 78.
42. *Atharva Veda*, VI.139.1–5; VI.130.1–4; VI.131.3; *Rig Veda*, I.115.2; IX.56.3; IX.32.5; IX.38.4; X.30.6; X.30.5; X.178.3; VIII.35.5, cited from, M.W. Pinkham, op. cit., pp. 38–39 and S.R. Shastri, op. cit., p. 10.
43. Irfan Habib and Vijay Kumar Thakur, op. cit., p. 56.
44. Ibid., p. 56.
45. P. Thomas, op. cit., p. 54.
46. S.R. Shastri, op. cit., p. 25.
47. *Rig Veda*, IV.42.8, cited from, B.S. Upadhyaya, op. cit., p. 108.
48. Gatwood, *Devi and the Spouse Goddess*, pp. 9–10.
49. S.R. Shastri, op. cit., p. 10.
50. Ibid., p. 37.
51. Gatwood, op. cit., p. 32.
52. S.R. Shastri, op. cit., p. 6.
53. B.S. Upadhyaya, op. cit., p. 191.
54. S.R. Shastri, op. cit., p. 191.
55. B.S. Upadhyaya, op. cit., p. 191.
56. S.R. Shastri, op. cit., p. 7.
57. Ibid., p. 7; B.S. Upadhyaya, op. cit., pp. 191–206.
58. Anil Kumar Tyagi, op. cit., p. 38.
59. White Yajurveda, 30.8.9, cited from, Pinkham, op. cit., p. 40. Some scholars contend that such participation was not indicative of equal status. On the contrary, women's work was regarded with scorn. Women who split canes and worked with thorns were considered suitable offering for goblets and demons. Woman dyer was seen as offering for sensuality, though female ointment maker was generally considered virtuous. The term '*kshetra-patni*' meaning mistress of the field may suggest respect but it may also simply imply that women too worked in the field alongside men. There are instances of slave women working with mortar and pestle and

gathering cow dung. Irfan Habib and Vijay Kumar Thakur, op. cit., pp. 56–57.

60. B.S. Upadhyaya, op. cit., p. 169
61. *Rig Veda*, X.71.9, B.S. Upadhyaya, op. cit., p. 160.
62. B.S. Upadhyaya, op. cit., p. 169.
63. A.S. Altekar, op. cit., p. 342.
64. *Rig Veda*, I.92.4, B.S. Upadhyaya, op. cit., p. 185.
65. *Rig Veda*, IX.66.8, cited from, B.S. Upadhyaya, op. cit., p. 185.
66. *Rig Veda*, IX.56.3, cited from, B.S. Upadhyaya, op. cit., p. 185.
67. *Rig Veda*, I.116.15; 112.10; 118.8; X.39.8, cited from, B.S. Upadhyaya, op. cit., p. 186.
68. *Rig Veda*, X.102.3, cited from, B.S. Upadhyaya, op. cit., p. 187.
69. *Atharva Veda*, XIV.1.47; *Yajur Veda*, V–10; VIII.16; XIII–18; *Rig Veda*, X.86.9; X.159.2; X.159.3; X.159.4; X.159.5 Ramnath Vedalankar, op. cit., pp. 22–24.
70. A.S. Altekar, op. cit., p. 12.
71. S.R. Shastri, op. cit., p. 12.
72. Ibid. p. 31.
73. B.S. Upadhyaya, op. cit., p. 181.
74. Nivedita Menon (ed.), *Gender and Politics in India*, 'Introduction', p. 4.
75. B.S. Upadhyaya, op. cit., p. 189.
76. Uma Chakravarti, 'Whatever happened to the Vedic *Dasi*? Orientalism, Nationalism and a Script for the Past', in Kumkum Sangari and Sudesh Vaid (eds.), op. cit., pp. 27–87.
77. Kumkum Roy, 'Where Women are Worshipped, There the Gods Rejoice', in Urvashi Butalia and Tanika Sarkar (eds.), *Women and the Hindu Right*, p. 10; Uma Chakravarti, 'Conceptualising Brahminical Patriarchy', *Economic and Political Weekly*, April 3, 1993, p. 579.
78. Irfan Habib and Vijay Kumar Thakur, op. cit., p. 56.
79. A.S. Altekar, op. cit., p. 339.
80. B.S. Upadhyaya, op. cit., p. 160.

‖ Chapter 4 ‖

Dayanand's Concept of Womanhood

Dayanand Saraswati's conceptualization of regenerated Hinduism and his approach to social reformation distinguished him from other exponents of the Golden Age theory, articulated during the nineteenth century. The exemplars of Indian Renaissance focused attention on women's issues and put forward their distinctive approaches and programmes for betterment in the status of women. While the reformers were convinced that improvement in women's position in the family and society was integral to a healthy society, they differed in their approaches and methods of reform. Some reformers targeted particular social evils and did not raise the larger issues of class or caste divisions. Raja Ram Mohan Roy, while deeply empathizing with the travails and deprivations of women in a patriarchal social structure, was more concerned with the eradication of *sati* and did not formulate any broader programme for reconstruction of caste system or other issues crucial for elevation of their status. Malabari has become legendary for his tireless campaign against child marriages. Similarly, Ishwarchandra Vidyasagar and Veersalingam Pantalu underwent untold suffering to popularize widow remarriages. These reformers considered legal remedy imperative for creation of awareness and eradication of social evils. Phule, Agarkar and Pandita Ramabai, while addressing the problem of women's subordination, sought more radical alternatives and envisaged transformation in the existing nature of gender and social relations. Similarly, most of the reformers undertook a large-scale interpretation of the *shastric* tradition to impart legitimacy to their reformist endeavours. The women's discourse in the nineteenth century thus incorporated multiple visions, approaches and methods of reform.

Dayanand derived his vision of reformed Hinduism exclusively from the four *Vedas*. He took a dogmatic stand on the infallibility and textual supremacy of the *Vedas* and asserted the superiority of Hinduism over all other religions. For the regeneration of the Aryan race, he carved out a grandiose blueprint of socio-religious and political structure through a painstaking reinterpretation of the *Vedas*. Integral to his vision of rejuvenated Hinduism, was his programme for regeneration of womanhood. Dayanand's construction of an alternative model of womanhood was not merely an exercise in the creation of a new self-image in which fellow Indians could take pride nor did he use fragments of the past for imparting legitimacy to isolated women's issues such as *sati*, polygamy, widow remarriage etc. Instead, he wished to recreate the idyllic conditions of the Vedic Age, characterized by equality between men and women in the spheres of education, religion and marriage. Dayanand's inclination to actualize his version of reformed Hinduism and counteract the colonial critique led him to deal with women's issues in a comprehensive manner.

Satyarth Prakash (Light of Truth), published in 1875, was Dayanand's first attempt at systematic presentation of his views on social, religious and theological issues, wherein his concept of womanhood is dealt with comprehensively. Henceforth, in his later publications, lectures and correspondence, Dayanand relentlessly strove for elaboration of his views on the woman's question and demonstrated consistency and clarity in his vision of a regenerated womanhood. Integrally linked to his larger concern for propagation of a healthy Aryan race, Dayanand's programme for raising women's status stood out for its significant deviations from the predominant discourse on women's issues. His eloquence on centrality of women's roles as mothers, a fresh approach towards the institutions of caste and marriage, concept of *niyoga* as a solution to the widow's problem and a comprehensive scheme of education were features that imparted distinctness to Dayanand's concept of womanhood.

Dayanand's visit to Calcutta in 1872 has been often treated as his earliest exposure to the women's question. However, many instances cited by other biographers reveal his prior awareness of women's issues and also his commitment to women's equality in numerous spheres. As early as 1868, in Karnawas he gave *Gayatri Mantra* to Hansa Thakurani, an old and sagacious woman. This was for the first time that a woman had been given the right to recite the *Gayatri Mantra*. It was indeed a revolutionary step. While commenting on this progressive mindset of Dayanand, his biographer Bhawanilal Bhartiya has remarked, "After centuries, in the realm of religion, Dayanand came forward and conferred on women absolute equality in all spheres, religion and worship, family and society."[1] Similarly, while teaching a rich merchant at Kanauj in 1868, Dayanand revealed his profound awareness of the evils of dowry and female illiteracy. "You have spent your money in vain. In 20–28 years, they (temples) will tumble down. It would have been better if you had done a deed that could have benefited some people of this country. You could have arranged the marriage of a daughter of a poor man; you could have arranged the marriage of these many thirty-one years old maiden daughters of Kanauj Brahmins or you could have built a school for boys and girls."[2] Dayanand advocated widow remarriage in Kanpur and Arrah before his visit to Calcutta. In Kanpur, in 1869, he had denounced child marriages.[3] It is, therefore, difficult to accept Jorden's contention that it was Calcutta that opened Dayanand's eyes to crucial problems of womanhood. The visit to Calcutta must have definitely deepened his understanding of women's issues, where issues like widow remarriage, *sati*, women's education and unequal marriages had dominated the public discourse for a long time.

His meetings and discussions with some of the leading men of Calcutta must have instilled into him an urgency regarding betterment in women's situation. He met some of the leading educationists of the time like Bhudev Mukhopadhyaya, Ishwarchandra Vidyasagar, Rajendra Lal Mitra and Ramtanu Lahiri. Deliberations with them must have reinforced his commitment to dissemination of education. Similarly, his meetings with Ishwarchandra Vidyasagar must have deepened his concern for widows. He, however, stuck to *niyoga*, his own solution for the problem of widows. In a way, Calcutta did not dilute his basic concepts and for every crucial problem of women, he continued to derive inspiration from the *Vedas*. Nevertheless, henceforth he made an effort at systematic elaboration of his views on the women's question through publications and lectures. He articulated his ideas more often and with greater clarity. He even tried to establish a profound relationship between the woes of women and the degeneration of the nation. In 1879, in the Kumbh Mela, he remarked that misery and curses of the widows were responsible for contemporary degeneration and stagnation of the country. *Biradare Hind* and *Brahma Samachar*, two prominent journals of Lahore, while testifying to Swami's intense involvement in the movement for women emancipation, wrote in 1877, "He is not only desirous for religious reform but has a keen eye on the eradication of social evils like child marriage and the caste system. He is extremely anxious for the education and emancipation of women. He says that until women are educated and liberated from the shackles of *zenana*, it is futile to hope for any perceptible progress in the country."[4] (*translation mine*).

Approach to Women's Issues

Dayanand attached great significance to women's roles as mothers in the overall regeneration of Hinduism. In the second chapter of *Satyarth Prakash* and in *Sanskar Vidhi*, he laid down meticulous rules and regulations for proper conception and post-natal care that show his deep concern for the health of the mother and child.[5] According to Uma Chakravarty, "motherhood for Dayanand was the sole rationale of a woman's existence but what was crucial to his concept of motherhood was its specific role in the procreation and rearing of a special breed of men."[6] Apart from veneration and centrality of mothers as procreators of a healthy stock of the Aryan race, Dayanand looked upon every woman and girl as a personification of creative power and, therefore, a mother. He recognized divine mother in every woman. In 1881, in Chittor while walking with some of his followers, he bowed to a four-year-old girl and remarked, "I bow to her as *matr shakti.*"[7]

The exaltation of the mother image was, however, accompanied by an equal respect for women's roles as wives. As a practical reformer, concerned with procreation of a healthy race, the institution of marriage had immense utilitarian value for Dayanand. In his words, "If the institution of marriage did not exist, all the amenities of domestic life would come to an end. None will serve another. Downright adultery and illicit relationships will increase; all men and women will be afflicted physically and mentally weakened, and will, consequently die young, no one will fear another or be controlled by public opinion. Families upon families will be blotted out of existence in consequence of disease, physical and mental degeneration .... All these evils can be best avoided by marriage."[8] He nevertheless realized that the institution of marriage was characterized by customs like unequal marriage, child marriage and prohibition of widow remarriage. Dayanand, therefore, visualized wide-ranging reforms to revitalize the institution. His perspective, on issues like child marriages, unequal marriages and position of widows, apart from being motivated by his larger concern for upliftment of the Aryan race, was aimed at redeeming the status and position of women.

Dayanand laid great stress on compatibility between husband and wife as the basis of a happy conjugal life and reproduction of healthy children. Wifehood for him meant comradeship and companionship and assistance in fulfilling life's duties and its true functions. He laid great stress on the complimentary model of conjugal relationship. Marriage was, firstly, for procreation, and secondly, for companionship and mutual assistance in life's duties and its true functions. The basic idea of relationship of wife and husband was respect, courtesy and even reverence. "Whenever husband and wife have occasion to meet or to part, whether in day or at night, they should wish '*namaste*' (respectful greeting with folded hands) to each other with affection and cordiality. The husband is the adorable God for the wife and the wife is the adorable Goddess for the husband."[9] He considered them as one unit. According to him, "the relation between husband and his wife is such that they cannot be independent of each other"[10]. He visualized a social order based on their active partnership in household, as well as in the extra-familial social sphere.

He proposed various reforms in the institution to render marriages more egalitarian and companionate. The caste rules of exogamy and endogamy rendered it obligatory for the parents to settle matches for their daughters within the same sub-caste. These rules, while strictly limiting the choice of the prospective bridegroom precipitated an intense competition for the best possible match within the same sub-caste resulting in child marriages and ill-matched marriages. He embarked upon the reform by stipulating certain basic changes in the caste structure of Hindu society. While retaining the *varnavyavastha* or the classical division of society into four major classes

– *Brahmin*, *Kshatriya*, *Vaishya* and *Sudra*, he stood for outright dissolution of the numerous castes and sub-castes. A more radical departure from traditional caste system was that assignment of classes, which was not determined on the basis of one's birth but solely depended on his *guna* or attributes; *karma* or actions; and *svabhava* or temperament.[11] The individuals were arrayed in their specific classes, after completion of studies, by the *Acharya* or by the king, after careful investigation of their qualifications and deeds. Dayanand then prescribed marriages between individuals belonging to the same class, i.e., individuals corresponding to each other in *guna*, *karma* and *svabhava*.[12]

Dayanand laid out a rational and systematic procedure for the settlement of marriages. He not only eliminated the role of family barbers and astrologers but greatly restricted the role of parents in the settlement of marriages. He was in favour of extending considerable liberty to the partners in the selection of prospective bride and bridegroom. According to him, their teachers should initiate the procedure when six to twelve months were left in the completion of their education. As the first step, the teachers should identify two students, male and female, who resembled each other in *guna*, *karma* and *svabhava* and make them familiar with each other through the exchange of diaries and photographs. He even allowed interaction between the two in the presence of elders, teachers and parents. He believed that partners should not only ascertain that they suit each other in temperament, qualifications, age and physical attributes but also with regard to their family and stature. Wedding arrangements should be preceded by enquiries about the candidates, not by means of fraudulent and meaningless horoscopes but by proper investigations.

He was in favour of extending considerable liberty to the prospective brides and bridegrooms in matters pertaining to their own marriages. He writes, "Even if parents ever think of arranging a match, it should under no circumstances ever be done without the consent of the parties, for when people choose their partners for life themselves, there is less likelihood of mutual disagreement and the children born of such a union are also of a superior order." By stressing the individual's right to select his own spouse, Dayanand claimed to revive the ancient practice of *swayamvara*. In his words, "*Swayamvara* marriage, i.e., marriage by choice, the most ancient form of marriage in India, is the best form of marriage. Before a man and a maid think of marrying, they should see that they suit each other, in point of knowledge, disposition, character, beauty, age, strength, family stature and built of the body and like."[13] Recalling the Vedic Age, he held that in ancient times, the daughters were not given away like goats and animals.[14] Dayanand even went to the extent of espousing a single status for women in the event of non-availability of a compatible partner. "The parents of a girl should never marry their daughter to a man who is inferior, wicked and unsuitable, might she remain unmarried in the house of her father till death."[15] He also advised women to marry only when they find someone who is truly qualified and suitable for them.

Dayanand emerged as one of the most vehement critics of child marriages in Indian society. According to him, the practice was untenable on the basis of *shastric* authority. Moreover, he considered the practice extremely injurious to the physical, mental and psychological development of the boys and girls. He also linked the practice to social and national degeneration. Dayanand recommended 25 and 16 years as the minimum age for marriage for men and women, respectively. He ridiculed the old notion that a father's *dharma* is destroyed if his daughter had her menses in his house, "how can the natural function of a woman be conceived as a sin of the father"[16]. He further said that children were incapable of understanding the meaning of the hymns recited to solemnize the wedding. Marriage was solemnized in the real sense of the term only when the bride and the bridegroom understood the meaning and implications of the wedding vows He ridiculed the children from early marriages as 'children of children'[17].

The ideal marriage, according to Dayanand, was between a man and woman of 48 and 24 years, respectively. The husband's age should be at least one and a half times more than the wife and maximum difference ought not to exceed double of the age of bride. Dayanand considered marriage of a girl of 16 years with a man of 25 years as 'inferior' than of a girl of 18 or 20 with a man of 35 or 40 years as 'medium'; and of a girl of 24 with a man of 48 years as 'superior' marriage.[18]

Dayanand also denounced extravagant marriages and insisted on the simplicity of marriage ceremony. He ridiculed the practice of inviting the entire caste to join in the marriage celebrations and called it "sheer madness"[19]. He ruled out the numerous ceremonies held before and after marriage, e.g., the *gauna* ceremony etc.[20] Dayanand was aware of the significance of the rituals. He, however, highly restricted the extreme ritualism of Hindu marriages to one simple ceremony, comprising of the performance of *havan* and the recitation of Vedic hymns. Similarly, he was against the custom of giving and taking of money from the brides or the bridegroom's side. He considered the *Asura* form of marriage, which involved the custom of gifts from either side, as one of the inferior kinds of marriage.[21] He vilified the practice of dowry among Kanauj Brahmins.[22]

Dayanand was perhaps the only exponent in the nineteenth century who underscored the centrality of *grihasthashram* or the institution of marriage in regeneration of Indian society. At the same time, he realized the urgency of introducing reforms in the institution. The proposed reforms in the institution of marriage were an attempt to render the institution more egalitarian and conducive to social development. By advocating basic changes in the caste system and the procedure for settling matrimonial alliances, Dayanand set aside in one stroke the numerous restrictions of caste on selection of partners. Despite his ardent and persistent championship of the institution of marriage, Dayanand did not rule out an independent and single status for women. He visualized certain conditions in which women could and should remain unmarried. It was Dayanand's intense desire to involve women in the process of women's upliftment. He wanted such women to observe life-long *brahmcharya*, for marriage would involve them in the numerous responsibilities of the family and household. Moreover, the image of a woman, who had the freedom to choose her own partner and in the event of non-availability of a compatible match remain unmarried till death rather than marry an unsuitable boy, was new to the Indian social context.

Problem of the Widows

Another area where Dayanand digressed from the reformist rhetoric of his era was in his approach to the vexatious problem of widows, who formed the most unfortunate category for the exponents of Indian Renaissance. Dayanand responded to the problem of widows in the most graphic and critical manner. He prescribed three solutions for the betterment in the condition of widows: remarriage; *niyoga* or levirate; and *brahmcharya* or celibacy. A strong advocate of strict monogamy, he prescribed remarriage only for *akshat yoni* widows, i.e., those whose marriage had not yet been consummated or child widows as they were generally called.[23] It would be relevant here to underline this emphasis on remarriage only of the *akshat yoni* widows. Even Dayanand's contemporaries were keen only for the remarriage of virgin widows.[24] This continuity is yet again exemplified in Gandhi, who prescribed remarriage only for unconsummated widows. For 'consummate' widows, Dayanand prescribed either of the two ways, *brahmcharya* or *niyoga*. Those who were not desirous of children could observe *brahmcharya* and devote their lives for the education and upliftment of women.[25] By prescribing *brahmcharya* along with adoption of sons as the best recourse for consummate widows, he chose to distance himself from the contemporary focus on remarriage as the ideal solution. While Dayanand rejected widow remarriage as it could lead to property disputes and destruction of noble families and their property through constant alienation, he refrained from adopting *brahmcharya* as the absolute remedy. His ideal solution for the vexatious problem of widows was, however, *niyoga* or levirate, i.e., allowing a widow to contract a temporary legal union with a widower for the purpose of procreation. He laid down that those who were not able to control their passions could also beget children by having recourse to *niyoga*.[26]

Niyoga was an ancient practice of the Vedic Age that allowed a union between the widow and a widower for procreation of sons. Dayanand imparted fresh dimensions to the doctrine through a reinterpretation of the ancient texts and widely increased its application in contemporary society. In its modified form, the *niyoga* doctrine was essentially voluntary in nature, the decision resting with the widow. *Niyoga* was primarily designed to fulfil the desire of a widow to procreate sons, a social requirement and a religious duty amongst the Hindus. *Niyoga* contract was to be between a widow and a widower and must be broken off after the birth of two or four sons. *Niyoga* could be contracted with any widower of one's own class or that of a higher class. If the partners continued their relationship after the stipulated period, they were liable for punishment by the state and society.[27] In the second edition of *Satyarth Prakash* in 1882, Dayanand extended the scope of these contractual relationships.[28] It was possible for wife to enter into a *niyoga* while her husband was alive if he was absent for a long time, if he was impotent or sterile, or if he was vile and violent. Similarly, even a husband could contract *niyoga* relationship for following reasons: barrenness, inability to produce a son, pregnancy, long absence, hateful behaviour and chronic disease. Dayanand felt that these contractual and temporary alliances would minimize the instances of illicit relationships, enhance the love between husband and wife which would in turn lead to the birth of good children and improvement of human race.[29] Thus, in Dayanand's ideology, *niyoga* was transformed from a practice devised for procreation of sons into a full-fledged institution for checking the degeneration of Aryan race through management of male and female sexuality.

Dayanand also distinguished between remarriage and *niyoga*. Unlike wife and husband, the partners of *niyoga* were to keep their separate households; they should come together only for intercourse; they were not obligated for the provision of financial support; every child begotten by *niyoga* was to belong by mutual agreement to one particular partner and not to both of them and acquired full legal rights within that partner's family. A married couple could produce ten children, while partners of *niyoga* could not have more than two or four children for each of the partner. In all, they could produce ten children. A man and woman could contract *niyoga* with eleven partners, one after the other.[30]

Dayanand even wanted to put a proposal to the British government to pass a regulation by which the children of widows from *niyoga* relationships be entitled to claim and obtain their rightful share of the property, both movable and immovable, of their parents and by which anyone trying to malign a widow, in anyway, be liable for punishment by the government. To this effect, he wrote a letter to Mulraj, his ardent disciple, to draft a legal document having proper laws and by-laws and he specifically wanted that the regulation be applicable to both *niyoga* and remarriage. His next letter to Mulraj expressed his disappointment that the latter had not used the term *niyoga* but referred only to remarriage. Dayanand then went on to formulate a draft himself, which was squarely designed to defend the rights of children from *niyoga*.[31] Till the very end of his life, Dayanand adhered to his concept of *niyoga* as the ideal remedy for the resolution of the widows' predicament.

Dayanand's concept of *niyoga* generated widespread controversy and criticism among his contemporaries and biographers, and even his followers. Writes Jordens, "For him sex was intimately bound up with reproduction and he found it impossible to dissociate the two. Although the many sufficient reasons for *niyoga* are very often different from the urgent need of offspring, yet whenever, he mentions *niyoga*, he adds the phrase, '*putrotpatti*', i.e., for the sake of begetting children."[32] It is difficult to comprehend as to how Dayanand planned to check adultery and promiscuity by means of *niyoga*, when he had himself highly restricted its use for procuring sons. Such a temporary union, for a limited purpose, could not have checked prostitution. Moreover, the problem of widow was not merely one of begetting children. It also involved psychological, economic, sexual and social needs. *Niyoga* was a very limited approach to the problem. It merely added to the burden of single-handed upbringing of children on widows. At a time when people frowned on remarriages of child widows, a solution like *niyoga* generated widespread opposition and ridicule from the protagonists of classical Hinduism, Christianity and Muslims who denounced the doctrine as tantamount to prostitution, adultery and a sin.[33] E.W. Sands, Home Commissioner, in his official report on the Arya Samaj in the United Provinces, characterized *niyoga* as 'license to frail flesh'.[34] His own close follower Mulraj expressed reluctance to draft a document for legalization of *niyoga*. Even the Arya Samajists were divided over their approach to the issue of *niyoga*. While the Gurukul faction led by Swami Shraddhanand strove, at least publicly, to garner support for the doctrine, the College faction distanced itself from the doctrine.[35] Ultimately, the slander campaign of Christian Missionaries and Ahmadiya Muslims forced the Arya Samajists to abandon the doctrine in 1917.[36] There was not a single instance of successful consummation of *niyoga*.

Dayanand could have easily modified *niyoga* into widow remarriage by interpretation of the hymns related to *niyoga* in the *Vedas*, but he did not do so. His letter to Lahore Arya Samaj in 1882 provides an insight into his attitude towards *niyoga* and widow remarriage. It is also reflective of his apprehension of meeting the same fate as Brahmo Samajists, if Arya Samajists declared their acceptance of widow remarriages. He wrote, "I hear that Babu Navin Chandra Roy (Brahmo Samajist leader) is in Lahore and is making efforts to arrange widow remarriages and Lahore Arya Samaj has acquiesced on this issue with

Babuji. ... They want that just as they (Brahmos) have been indicted of being Christians, the Arya Samaj should also meet the same fate. *Akshatyoni* widows, i.e., unconsummated widows, are eligible for remarriage, but for a widow, whose marriage has been consummated, there is no sin in *niyoga*. Anything contrary to this principle is contrary to *shastras,* which leads to innumerable hardships; even ostracization from caste cannot be ruled out"[37] (*translation mine*).

Dayanand tried to refrain from the radicalism of the Brahmo Samaj that had eventually resulted in their alienation from mainstream Hinduism. Dayanand once confided to one of his followers, "It is not my desire to segregate myself from the caste life of the Hindus, it is better to reform the society by remaining in it."[38] He took pains to document scriptural evidence in favour of *niyoga*. He cited historical proofs from the Mahabharata to further strengthen his doctrine. This strict adherence to principle was, however, accompanied by a realistic approach to the question of *niyoga* and widow remarriage. In his lectures at Poona in 1877, he conveyed his views on the subject with greater clarity, "It is not my wish to criticize widow remarriage in order to give support to those who oppose widow remarriage ... I am, however, bound to state that in the eyes of God, both, men and women are equal. God is just. He does not indulge in any kind of discrimination. When men have the liberty to remarry, why there cannot be remarriage for women. Today, the people have become non-Aryans. A man can keep as many women he likes ... is this not injustice? Is this not irreligious? ... What I am saying is that for the twice-born *niyoga* is desirable. In the olden days, *niyoga* was practiced extensively and, therefore, there was little need of remarriage. But in this age both remarriage and *niyoga* have been stopped and the resulting miserable sinfulness and degradation is undesirable .... All these sins are on our heads. Looking at today's social system one has to admit that widow remarriage is altogether better than that"[39] (*translation mine*). Dayanand's expediency on the issue of remarriage is indeed commendable. It would be pertinent to mention here that he never tried to restrain the Arya Samaj from commemorating and popularizing widow remarriages. Dayanand regularly received *Arya Messenger*, a journal of the Lahore Arya Samaj, which ran a 'matrimonial notice' inviting widows and also men prepared to marry them to contact the Arya Samaj of Lahore or Sitapur.

Concept of Education

Dayanand's concept of women's education formed another distinctive facet of his ideology wherein he made significant departures from the prevailing trends. His vision of a reformed Hindu society was based on diffusion of knowledge through a comprehensive system of education. He had immense faith in the overwhelming power of education in the transformation of contemporary social milieu and regeneration of the race. He asserted the right of all classes to acquire education. Dayanand condemned the Brahmins, who on the basis of some religious authority, had forbidden women to study or even hear the Vedic texts and had surpassed all limits of irrationality and irreligion to inflict punishment on women. Dayanand rejected the verses cited by Brahmins, prohibiting women to study the *Vedas*, as fabrications and upheld every individual's right to read them, "*Brahmins*, *Kshatriyas*, *Vaishyas*, *Sudras*, women, servants, aye, even the lowest of the low, so you should all do, i.e., teach and preach the *Vedas* ... and, thereby, acquire true knowledge. ... When all classes are well educated and cultured, no one can set up any false, fraudulent and irreligious practice."[40] While quoting a verse from *Shraut Sutra*, "(in the *yajna*), let his wife recite this *mantra*" he remarked, "were she not a scholar of the *Veda*, as well as of other *Shastras*, how could she in the *yajna* recite the Vedic *mantra* with proper pronunciation and accent, as well as speak Sanskrit."[41] According to him, the girls were entitled to wear the sacred thread and undergo the initiation ceremony of *yagyopavit*.

The most original feature of Dayanand's scheme of education was his insistence on its compulsory nature. He clearly laid down in *Satyarth Prakash*, "Both state and society should make it compulsory upon all to send their children (both male and female) to school after the fifth or eighth year. It should be made a penal offence to keep a child at home after that age."[42] Dayanand was thus the first renaissance reformer to visualize universalization of education and equality of educational opportunities for men and women of all classes.

Conceived primarily as a process of character formation of the individual, Dayanand's conceptualization of women's education diverged from the nineteenth century debates on women's education that were inspired by the acute problem of interpersonal adjustments within the family. Women's education was, thus, motivated to increase women's efficiency in their traditional roles of wives and mothers in order to fulfil the needs of the early generation of western educated men in India. This functionalist theory of women's education, which endeavoured to construct a new prototype of the ideal wife, was relatively unimportant in Dayanand's ideology. Development of the individual through inculcation of virtue was central to his concept of education. According to him, "education enabled a person to acquire true knowledge, practice virtue, shun vice and, consequently being freed from all sorrow and pain, enjoy true happiness". Emphasizing the crucial importance of women's education he remarked, "Just as boys acquire sound knowledge and culture by the practice of brahmcharya and then marry girls of their own choice, who are young, well-educated, loving and of like temperament, so should a girl practice *brahmcharya*, study the *Vedas* and other sciences and, thereby, perfect her knowledge, refine her character, give her hand to a man of her choice, who is young, learned and loving."[43] Dayanand, thus, broadened the scope of women's education by emphasizing education for self rather than merely treating it as a means of increasing their efficiency in their familial roles. According to Radha Kumar, "Saraswati shifted the terrain of discussion on women's education: by defining learning as a path to virtue and virtue as individually acquired. He diverged from the functionalist view of most other advocates for women's education, who argued that women needed education so as to be able to perform their duties as wives and mothers adequately."[44] While it is true that Dayanand considered household affairs as the major domain of the woman's activities. As a wife and mother, she was responsible for managing the economy, religion and health of the family. She was to carry on her study of the *Vedas* and assist her husband in the twice daily ritual of five great sacrifices or *Panchmahayajna*. In short, she had a primary role in regeneration of the race and as such was also responsible for the proper upbringing of her children and well-being of the husband. Despite placing women at the helm of household affairs, Dayanand did not make a connection between education and the roles that women were expected to perform as mothers and wives.

Dayanand formulated his distinctive programme of women's education that closely corresponded to the principles and spirit of the Gurukul system of education. Both, boys and girls were to be sent to their respective Gurukuls in the fifth or eighth year. The Gurukul should be situated in a sequestered place. The boys' Gurukul should be at least three miles away from the girls' Gurukul. The Gurukuls of the girls should be administered exclusively by women preceptors and employees and those of boys by the members of their own sex. Dayanand conceived education primarily as a process of character formation and acquisition of virtue. Therefore, proper observance of *Brahmcharya* was upheld as imperative for proper acquisition of education. The teachers had an important role to play in the moral development of the students.[45]

The curriculum of education devised by Dayanand was similar for both boys and girls. He, however, laid down the minimum and maximum period of *Brahmcharya* for both the sexes. The minimum period of education for women was till the age of 16 and maximum period was upto 24 years of age. These, however, applied only to those women who intended to marry. If women desired they could remain celibate till death and pursue the higher echclons of knowledge. For men, the minimum and maximum age of *Brahmcharya*, was 24 and 48 respectively.[46] Dayanand's elaborate system of education included the study of *Shiksha* (Phonetics) by Panini, Patanjali's *Mahabhashya*, *Nighantu* and *Nirukta* (books on Vedic vocabulary and Philology) by Yaska, *Chhandograntha* (Prosody) by Pingala, *Manu Smriti*, *Valmiki Ramayana*, selected portions of the *Mahabharata*, six schools of philosophy, ten *Upanishads*, *Vedas* along with *Brahmanas*, six *Up-Vedas* and *Jyotish Shastra*.[47] He entertained no prejudices against women's indulgence in music and dance.[48]

Dayanand also laid down the minimum level of education obligatory for both men and women. "As men should at the very least learn science of grammar, *dharma* and their profession or trade, likewise should women learn grammar, dharma (comprising righteousness, justice, honesty, proper discharge of one's duties, etc.), medical sciences, mathematics, *shilp vidya* or mechanical and fine arts at the least, for without a knowledge of these, ascertainment of truth, bearing of good children, their household affairs, preparation of food and drinks in accordance with the requirements of medical science, can never be effected. Without knowledge of arts, they cannot properly attend such matters as making proper dresses and ornaments etc. Without a knowledge of mathematics they can never keep accounts of their household properly, and without the knowledge of true religion, as taught by the *Vedas* and other *Shastras*, they cannot know what God and *dharma* are and can never, therefore, especially going astray from the path of rectitude."[49]

Although Dayanand did not conceive education as a means of remodeling gender-based social roles, he did envisage widening of the sphere of women's social roles through acquisition of education. In this context, the following statement in *Satyarth Prakash* is significant, "The *Kshatriya* women in ancient India used to be well acquainted even with military science, or how could they have gone with their male relations and fought side by side with them in battlefields, as Kekai did with her royal husband. Therefore, it behoves *Brahmin* and *Kshatriya* women to acquire all kinds of knowledge and *Vaishya* women to learn trade and mechanical arts and like and *Sudra* women, the art of cooking."[50] In his *Veda Bhashyas*, he further advocated the participation of women in active societal roles after acquiring the requisite education. He further remarks, "In the absence of the *Raja* in war, *Rani* should assume the charge of commander-in-chief, and just as the former inspires the soldiers to fight, the latter should act in a similar manner." "Just as the *Raja* is educated in the science of government or *rajniti*, similarly his wife should be trained in *rajniti*."[51]

These views of Dayanand go to suggest that he did not contemplate education merely as a ploy to reinforce traditional images and roles of womankind. In fact, with the acquisition of education, women could aspire for and have access to non-conventional roles. He wanted to exploit education as a powerful weapon in the remodelling and rearrangement of the Hindu social order. Dayanand emerged as the first reformer who advocated and evolved a comprehensive scheme of education for raising women's status not only at the level of family and society but for her own development as an individual.

Dayanand's eloquence on the general predicament of women and their position and role in society signify his deep concern for women. He accorded an equal status to women in major spheres of societal activities and laid stress on identical moral codes for men and women. He remarked, "In the eyes of God, both men and women are equal because God is just. There is not the slightest discrimination (in his regime)"[52] (*Translation mine*). Dayanand's approach to women's issues, as compared to other exponents of Indian Renaissance, was holistic and bold. He visualized far-reaching changes in the institution of marriage and redesigned the basic structure of caste system. He contended that every individual, man or woman, had substantial freedom to decide his *varna*, class and role in society on the basis of his/her accomplishments and qualifications. Such a declaration, especially as far as women were concerned, was certainly revolutionary in the Indian social milieu, wherein lives of men and women were strictly regulated and controlled by rigours of caste system. By advocating basic changes in the institutions of caste and marriage, which had a key role in the regulation and management of female sexuality in Hindu society, Dayanand struck at the fundamental elements of social conservatism, and unlike other renaissance reformers, visualized not only fragmentary but substantive changes in women's position. He introduced a totally new paradigm in the nineteenth century debates on women's education when he linked acquisition of education to the moral upliftment, happiness and growth of woman as an individual. However, Dayanand's highly unrealistic doctrine of *niyoga* as the solution to the widows' problem, which led to some of the most acrimonious arguments amongst the Arya Samajists, Christians and Muslims, suggests one of the most glaring limitations of his ideology. Moreover, his curriculum for education is inadequate to meet the requirements of the modern times. It is indeed regrettable that he tried to search for solutions to the ills of the Indian society only within the Vedic context. Yet, it would be ahistorical to judge Dayanand's approach to these issues in isolation. His ideological stance on the women's question should be studied in the larger context of his response to the nineteenth century colonial critique of the social and cultural ethos of Hinduism. It was through his well-knit response to the moral challenge of the colonial rule that Dayanand could generate urgency for raising women's status by forging vital links between his vision of the regenerated Hinduism and upliftment of women. The significance of Dayanand's contribution lay in effectively interweaving his radical ideas within the boundaries of the *Vedas*. The fact that he emphasized the continuity of the Hindu tradition led to widespread support for his ideology and initiatives in the later decades, especially in the realm of women's education and widow remarriage.

Notes

1. Bhavani Lal Bhartiya, *Navjagran ke Purodha: Dayanand Saraswati*, p. 98.
2. Ghasiram, *Maharishi Dayanand Saraswati ka Jeevan Charit I*, p. 192.
3. Lekhram, *Maharishi Dayanand ka Jeevan Charitra*, p. 642; Jordens suspects the authenticity of these statements since Dayanand had visited Kanpur several times after his visit to Calcutta. Ghasiram's statement that Dayanand preached widow remarriage in Arrah is even more doubtful since he does not provide any supportive evidence to prove his view. Moreover, Dayanand had visited Arrah shortly after his visit to Calcutta in June 1873. It is probable that Ghasiram might have confused the two visits. J.T.F. Jordens, *Dayanand Saraswati: His Life and Ideas*, p. 310.
4. Ghasiram, op. cit., Vol. II, p. 155.
5. Swami Dayanand Saraswati, *Satyarth Prakash (Light of Truth)*, (English Translation by Chiranjiva Bhardvaja), pp. 20–30 (from now onwards only *Satyarth Prakash*); Dayanand Saraswati, *Sanskar Vidhi* (now onwards, *Sanskar Vidhi*), pp. 49–97.
6. Uma Chakravarty, 'Whatever Happened to the Vedic *Dasi*? Orientalism, Nationalism and a Script for the Past', in Kumkum Sangari and Sudesh Vaid (eds.), *Recasting Women: Essays in Colonial History*, p. 56.
7. Har Bilas Sarda, *Life of Dayanand Saraswati*, p. 81.
8. *Satyarth Prakash*, p. 139.
9. Ibid., p. 110 and 382.
10. Ibid., p. 129.
11. Ibid., pp. 96–100.
12. Ibid., p. 105.
13. Ibid., p. 94.
14. Dayanand Saraswati, *Dayanand Pravachan Sangraha Arthat Poona Bombay Pravachan* (Now onwards, *Dayanand Pravachan Sangraha*, Y. Mimansak (ed.), p. 161.
15. *Sanskar Vidhi*, p. 179.
16. *Satyarth Prakash*, p. 92.
17. Ghasiram, op. cit., Vol. II, pp. 88 and 229.
18. It is incomprehensible, why Dayanand considered such an advanced age as the ideal marriageable age for men. Such an advanced marriageable age left little scope for the other two *ashrams*, i.e., *Vanaprastha* and *Sanyas*. Moreover, companionship and compatibility in marriage on which Dayanand laid great stress could not be expected between husband and wife of such disparate ages. In advocating 48 as the marriageable age of men, Dayanand was probably moved by his immense faith in the observation of *brahmcharya* upto the age of 48 years which he considered as the highest stage of *brahmcharya*. He further believed that such a person enjoyed the full life span of 400 years.

19. *Dayanand Pravachan Sangraha*, p. 162; Ghasiram, op. cit., I, p. 290.
20. *Swami Dayanand ke Patra aur Vigyapan*, Vol. II, Y. Mimansak (ed.), Appendix VIII, p. 998.
21. *Sanskar Vidhi*, pp. 177–178.
22. Jordens, op. cit., p. 118.
23. *Satyarth Prakash*, p. 129.
24. For details regarding reformist discourse on widows' rehabilitation, refer chapter fifth 'Arya Samajist perspective on issues of widowhood'.
25. In Dayanand's own lifetime, he advised Arya Samaj, Ajmer, to send Sita, a widow recently converted from Christianity, to Lahore girl's schools for the purpose of teaching girls.
26. *Satyarth Prakash*, p. 130.
27. Ibid., p. 133.
28. J.T.F. Jordens, op. cit., pp. 118–119.
29. *Satyarth Prakash*, pp. 133, 137–138 and 140–141.
30. Ibid., pp. 130–131.
31. *Rishi Dayanand ke Patra aur Vigyapan*, Vol. II, Y. Mimansak (ed.), Letter nos. 326, 321, 333, 379–380, pp. 393–396.
32. J.T.F. Jordens, op. cit., p. 119.
33. *Selections from Vernacular Newspapers published in the Punjab, 1891–1901*.
34. E.W. Sands, *Arya Samaj in the United Provinces*, p. 17.
35. Swami Shraddhanand, *Isai Pakshapat aur Arya Samaj*, in B.L. Bhartiya (ed.), *Swami Shraddhanand Granthavali*, Vol. 3, p. 190.
36. Swami Shraddhanand, 'Adim Satyarth Prakash aur Arya Samaj ke Siddhanta', in B.L. Bhartiya (ed.), op. cit., pp. 60–61.
37. *Swami Dayanand ke Patra aur Vigyapan*, Vol. II, Y. Mimansak (ed.), Letter no. 528, p. 568.
38. Ghasiram, op. cit., Vol. II, p. 237.
39. *Dayanand Pravachan Sangraha*, p. 168. While lecturing in Saharanpur, in a reply to Mahatma Munshi Chandi Prasad, he had favoured widow remarriage. He said, "Widows should get remarried. Man is not entitled to second marriage while his wife is alive, but after her death (if) he can remarry. Such a right should be accorded to the widow also." (Translation mine) *Swami Dayanand ke Patra aur Vigyapan*, Vol. II, Y. Mimansak (ed.), Appendix VIII, pp. 995–999.
40. *Satyarth Prakash*, p. 51.
41. Ibid., p. 79.
42. Ibid., p. 33.
43. Ibid., p. 79.
44. Radha Kumar, *History of Doing*, p. 22.
45. *Satyarth Prakash*, p. 32.

46. Ibid., p. 43.
47. Ibid., pp. 69–74.
48. *Dayanand Pravachan Sangraha*, p. 171. Dayanand often referred to the instances in ancient India when daughters of royal families learnt dancing. In this context, he cited the example of Uttara, daughter of the King of Virata who was trained in the art of dancing by Arjuna, the Pandava prince, while he was in exile.
49. *Satyarth Prakash*, p. 80.
50. Ibid., p. 80.
51. *Yajur Veda Bhashya*, XIII.18, p. 107.
52. *Dayanand Pravachan Sangraha*, p. 162.

Chapter 5

Issues of Widowhood

Samajist Perspective

The predicament of widows in the Indian society evoked some of the most graphic and poignant responses from Indian intelligentsia and also from British officials. Quite pertinently, most of the major reform measures concerning women were inspired by the misery of the widows. The leading reformers of the Indian Renaissance came forward with multiple solutions to relieve the misery of the widows. Abolition of *sati*, campaign against child marriage, advocacy of education and economic training were some of the major alternatives that were put forth for rehabilitation of the widows. Yet others were courageous enough to uphold remarriage of the widows as the ideal option. While it is true that the widow was marked out for special treatment, a closer look makes it clear that far from uniformity, there are nuances that define the attitudes of the reformers. Overall, the widow's question reveals that there were multiple planes on which reformers were putting forth the choices for widows. For instance, Roy, who had built up an authoritative case against *sati* by denouncing the practice in the most vehement manner on scriptural and humanitarian grounds in his numerous writings, failed to extend the argument to vindicate the option of remarriage for widows. In fact prescription of alternatives or choices for widows that dominated the indigenous discourse in the nineteenth century was beset with deep-seated social, religious and material prejudices. As Uma Chakrovarty has rightly observed, "The management of sexuality was the key to the thorny problem of widow remarriage. Throughout the nineteenth century, the most problematic category of women were widows, and reformers were attempting to resolve the problem of what to do with the widow especially since a large proportion of widows were upper caste women ...".[1]

In the nineteenth century, there was a group of reformers who advocated remarriage as an ideal remedy for the problem of widows. The Young Bengal radicals were the earliest champions of widow remarriage. Individuals like Ishwarchandra Vidyasagar in Bengal, M.R.R.T. Muttasamy Iyer, Raja Sir T. Madhava Rao, Dewan Bahadur Raghunath Rao and Viresalingam Pantalu in the south, Jyotiba Phule and Vishnu Shastri in Maharashtra, displayed unusual courage and tenacity in promoting widow remarriage even at the cost of immense financial loss and even excommunication by caste and community. In his booklet, *Marriage of Hindu Widows*, published in Bengali and English in 1855, Vidyasagar sought to prove that enforced widowhood was not prescribed by the *shastras*. In 1855, he submitted a petition to the Governor General pleading for a law to be passed recognizing widow remarriage. In the same year, J.P. Grant introduced a Bill in the Legislative Council based on Vidyasagar's petition. While debating the Bill, Grant advanced arguments based on the biological-sexual needs of the widows and the consequent moral depravity and licentious life leading them to desert their homes. The remarkable boldness demonstrated by Lord Dalhousie in carrying out the radical measure formed a significant breakthrough towards the resolution of the widows' problem. He completely disregarded the innumerable petitions submitted to the British Government against the proposed Act, The human rights argument advanced by Dalhousie was reinforced by J.P. Grant thus, "If he knew certainly that but one girl would be saved from the horrors of *Brahmcharia* by the passing of the Act, he would pass it for her sake."[2]

The Act, by and large, remained inoperative due to multiple reasons. Firstly, the Act providing for the legality of widow remarriages did nothing to secure the civil rights of the widow, who remarried. The Act declared that all rights and interest which any widow had by law in her husband's estate, either by way of maintenance or by inheritance, shall upon her second marriage lapse, as if she had then died. Moreover, on an issue like widow remarriage, the

Hindus were largely motivated by their conviction regarding the permanence of marital tie, especially in the case of women, rather than the dynamics of law and custom. The Act, therefore, encountered stiff opposition from all sections of the Hindu society. Part of the failure also lay in the approach of reformers to the issue of widow remarriage. Their vigorous attempts for widow remarriage, in the absence of simultaneous and integral movements for women's education, eradication of child marriages and unequal marriages and creation of public awareness were bound to result in the failure of the movement. The personal weaknesses of the reformers in living up to their professed ideals also resulted in the failure of the movement. As Ramabai poured scorn on reformers "who took oaths that they would marry widows but no sooner were they confronted with actual situations off they went and married pretty little maidens."[3] In addition, caste orthodoxy has been held responsible for the failure of the Act. The native newspaper, *Gujarati* has recorded the horrors of ostracization suffered by those who promoted remarriage or married widows, vividly, "The only remedy is to dispossess caste of its power of excommunicating the widow who marries again. Government sanctions remarriage and caste opposes it .... The widow and her husband, and very often her and his families, are shunned like poison .... So cruelly rigid is the system that it drew tears from that most patient Hindu martyr Karsandas Mulji .... Englishmen can have no idea of the bitterness of this social seclusion; it is worse than the bitterness of death ... ."[4]

In the last quarter of the nineteenth century, concern for condition of widows continued to engross the sympathy and attention of the reformers. However, by now the failure of the legal remedy had led to a perceptible shift in the attitude of the reformers. The failure of the Act is reflected in the fact that till 1890s only 500 widow remarriages had taken place. And even these 500 remarriages were those of child widows or virgin widows.[5] Those widows, whose marriages had been consummated, could not, and did not remarry. The reformers, deeply moved by the loneliness, suffering and dependent lives of the widows, formulated new approaches and methods to bring relief for the widows. For instance, Malabari had thought about widow remarriage as a viable option for a long time but he realized the futility of the mission and shifted his focus to eradication of infant and child marriages. He felt that problem of widowhood was largely the outcome of early marriages.

Jyotiba Phule had undertaken bold and pioneering initiatives to improve the condition of women. He had established schools for girls as early as 1848 and a widow's home *Bal-Hatya Pratibhandhak Griha* (Home for Prevention of Infanticide) in 1873. This home provided shelter to widows who were pregnant and secretly arranged for the safe deliveries of their illegitimate children and their adoption by families. In his book, *Gulamgiri*, Phule reacted sardonically when asked as to why he had refrained from seeking assistance from his community, "Those who have failed to demonstrate courage to snatch the knife from the barber who has been shaving the heads of their mothers and sisters, would be hardly useful as members of the Home". Phule probably understood that while remarriage remained an unrealistic remedy, other practical measures could be adopted to alleviate the suffering and mental agony of the widows. In fact, most of the widows who sought shelter in his Bal-Hatya Pratibhandhak Griha were upper caste women as codes repressing their sexuality were most severe. To save the widow from the humiliation of tonsured heads, Phule even mobilized the barbers into refusing to shave widows' heads.[6]

Yet another major strand of the movement that emerged from the failure of the widow remarriage movement was the emphasis on making widows' lives more meaningful through education and economic training. Even those reformers who had remained ardent supporters of remarriage for widows shifted to widow's education. This new class of reformers initiated attempts for the rehabilitation of widows as useful members of society. Sasipada Banerjee was the first reformer to fulfil this felt need of the widows when he founded the widows' home in Calcutta in 1887 to provide education to the widows. The curriculum comprised of home-science as well as academic subjects. The Home was run along orthodox lines, i.e., refraining from remarriage of widows.[7]

Pandita Ramabai, too, set a precedent in this direction when she set up Sharda Sadan in Bombay in 1897, later shifted to Poona in 1899, for educating the high caste Hindu widows. She received financial assistance from American ladies for a period of ten years for her educational movement. Like Phule, she did not consider it worthwhile to seek support from Hindu society for they would either ignore or ridicule the cause. She followed the policy of non-interference in matters of religion and no compulsion was exerted on Hindu women to abandon their ancestral faith or their caste observances. Despite this declared policy of non-interference in religious affairs, Hindus viewed the Home with suspicion, for Ramabai's conversion to Christianity was beginning to have impact on her inmates.

Ramabai had been disillusioned by the repercussions of the widow remarriage movement and, therefore, the Sadan desisted from encouraging its inmates to remarry. The Sadan was primarily engaged in enabling the widows to secure an honourable and independent living by providing them education.[8] The Sharda Sadan was rocked by intense controversy, when several girls in the Sadan embraced Christianity under the impact of Ramabai's religious leanings. Reformers like Bhandarkar and Ranade not only resigned from the Advisory Board of the Sadan but also suggested to the guardians of girls to withdraw them from the Sadan. The widows home was no longer taken advantage of by the higher castes.[9]

Ramabai's movement inspired D.K. Karve to initiate a similar experiment, i.e., widows' education. From 1893 to 1900, Karve was closely associated with the Widow Remarriage Association in the sponsorship of widow remarriages. His experiences, however, convinced him that the question being a religious one, "a high degree of moral courage was required on the part of the guardians of widows. ... It was not easy thing in those days to face excommunication from society".[10] He, therefore, thought that the best way to advance the cause was to educate widows. "Education would make them self supporting and would enable them to think for themselves." He set up Hindu Widows Home in 1900. The education for widows in the Home was employment oriented. The cause of widow remarriage continued to enamour the reformer. He, however, drew a sharp wedge between his efforts for widow remarriage and widows education and so far as the inmates of the Widows Home were concerned, he remained indifferent and never tried to promote widow remarriage. He refrained from remarriage for two reasons. Firstly, after the untoward events in the Sharda Sadan, Karve took great care to respect popular religious sentiments and despite his agnostic attitudes, saw to it that the Home did not offend Hindu orthodoxy. Moreover, he thought that it would be beneficial for the widow remarriage movement, if the Home remained detached on the issue, "And it did actually prove to be so ... in 1955 since the establishment of Home, 25 widows belonging to it had got married till that time while the total number of marriages since 1870 among Maharashtrians was only about 85."[11]

Vivekanand emerged as a strong exponent of widows' education, as the appropriate solution to the vexatious problem of widows, rather than widow remarriage. He said, "our reformers do not see where the wound is, they want to save the nation by marrying the widows; do you think that a nation is saved by the number of husbands its widows get? ... They are to be given their lost individualities; they are to be educated .... Everyone must work out his own salvation".[12] He wanted to organize widows as instructors and teachers. He also contemplated the organization of a *math* that would be managed by *Brahmcharini* widows. These *maths* would train a class of *Brahmcharinis* who would embark upon the task of regeneration and employment of women.

Interestingly, Vivekanand's attitude towards widow remarriage represents yet another school of opinion as far as choices for widows were concerned. On the question of widow remarriage, he, in fact, not only took a fairly conservative position but even an indifferent and hostile one. Vivekanand, who otherwise thought that religions would flounder if they could not wipe the widow's tears, did not endorse remarriage as an appropriate option for widows. Vivekanand, in fact, displayed absolute insensitivity towards the issue when he upheld that denial of remarriage to the child widow caused no hardship to her. Moreover, he attributed the failure of widow remarriage to scarcity of men rather than the disadvantaged position of widows as far as willingness of men to marry them was concerned.[13] His attitude towards remarriage reflects the widespread and deep-seated prejudice in contemporary upper-class society. Those reformers who were expected to take a progressive stand on the issue of widow remarriage made strange exceptions. Peary Chand Mitra, a member of Young Bengal, who even published a woman's journal, *Masik Patrika*, supported women's education and opposed early marriages but would not advocate widow remarriage. Even Bankim Chandra in his essay, *Samya*, generally considered his most radical piece of writing, does not admit of widow remarriage as readily as women's education. The essay, in fact, contends that a widow who was chaste and loved her deceased husband could hardly marry a second time. Similarly, Vivekanand saw in the love and fidelity of the widow, the Absolute or an immutable God. He actually supported Sasipada Banerjee's Widow Home, which was trying to give helpless widows some dignity and social resettlement. Even Tagore, in his lecture '*Hindu Vibaha*', delivered in 1887 felt that while second marriages were acceptable in the case of men, remarriages of women were socially more disruptive as they involved transference of name, lineage, loyalty and property to the other family.[14]

Towards the close of the nineteenth century, there was a perceptible shift in the women's question as it was articulated in the public discourse. According to Partha Chatterjee, "From then onwards, questions regarding the position of women in society do not arouse the same degree of passion and acrimony as they did only a few decades before."[15] It has been contended by some that relationship between nationalism and women's question had been problematical. Ghulam Murshid had argued that the new politics of nationalism glorified India's past and tended to defend everything traditional, all attempts to change customs and lifestyles began to be seen as aping of western manners and thereby regarded with suspicion. Vivekanand defended his retrogressive and indifferent stance on widow remarriage and child marriages in America in a conversation with Sister Nivedita.[16] He remarked that only a fool would wash dirty linen in public. In fact, according to some of his biographers, his motives in denying the sad state of Indian womanhood were "inspired by nationalism rather than Hindu chauvinism". This led to the crystallization of conservative attitudes towards social issues, particularly those that concerned women. Yet another argument that has been often extended to explain the disappearance of the early enthusiasm on women's issues is that the movement was "overtaken by the more pressing and emotive issues of political struggle". Moreover, the process of nation-making that was integral to the growth of nationalism demanded consensus and unity whereas social reform was seen as essentially divisive.[17] Partha Chatterjee has argued that the nationalist resolution of the women's question cannot be explained in such a simplistic and linear manner. According to him, this resolution was built around a separation of the domain of culture into dichotomies such as material/spiritual, home/world and feminine/masculine. While the material domain was seen as external and essentially male, wherein western models of development could be adopted, the home was the inner spiritual self, a nation's true identity, and woman was its representation. The crucial need was to preserve and defend this inner core, its spiritual essence. This premise resulted in the construction of an ideal woman, suitably educated but protected from western influence in the way she behaved, dressed and managed home. Moreover, demonstrations of self-pride led the nationalists to assert their superiority in the spiritual and, by implication, the inner domain of the woman which was seen as sacrosanct and hence an area "where the nation was acting on its own, outside the purview of the guidance and intervention of the colonial state".

The Arya Samaj, founded by Dayanand Saraswati in 1875, emerged as the most unswerving champion of widow remarriage from the close of the nineteenth century and in the twentieth century. Their advocacy of the cause assumes immense historical significance, particularly in the context of a social scenario, wherein, owing to the rise in nationalism there was a considerable decline in the interest in women issues. Their involvement in the cause can be examined in two phases – their approach towards the issue in the nineteenth century, followed by the second phase in the twentieth century, when they pursued a multi-pronged approach to achieve remarkable success in the realm of widow remarriage.

Arya Samaj and Widow Remarriage Movement in the Nineteenth Century

Dayanand had prescribed alternatives for different categories of widows – remarriage for virgin or child widows, *niyoga* for widows whose marriages had been consummated and ascetic widowhood or *Brahmcharya* for widows with children. While Dayanand had upheld *niyoga* as the ideal solution to fulfil the biological needs of the widows and also her requirement for sons, he somehow displayed remarkable flexibility when he accepted widow remarriage as a choice for widows. According to him, if men are allowed to remarry then widows should not be deprived of the opportunity to remarry. Moreover, if *niyoga* was not acceptable then widow remarriage should be permissible. Therefore, Arya Samaj had started sponsoring widow remarriage, since its inception.

Lahore Arya Samaj was the first to commemorate a widow remarriage as early as 1882.[18] As early as 1879, the advocacy of widow remarriage had become an integral part of their worship service.[19] The Samaj even started a journal *Vidhwa Hiteshi* in 1882 for championing the cause of widows.[20] The Lahore Samaj also applauded the publication of the *Social Reformer*, which carried a full page of advertisement of widows who were willing to remarry.[21] *Arya Messenger*, organ of the Lahore Samaj, also ran a matrimonial notice inviting men eager to marry widows to contact the Arya Samaj at Lahore and Sitapur.[22] Various tracts and pamphlets were also brought out by the Lahore Samaj for popularizing the concept of remarriage of widows. Some of the important ones were Munshi Jiwan Das' *Sadah-i-Haqq*, Pandit Lekhram's *Risala-i-Nawid-i-Begwan*, Ama Ram's *Masala-i-Niyoga*, and Lal Jiwan Das' *Do Hindu Bewa Aurton Ki Batchit*.[23]

The marriages conducted by the Lahore Arya Samaj were well-publicized in their journals. The major success in this direction was the remarriage of the widowed daughter of Diwan Sant Ram Chopra, who hailed from a distinguished family and was a prominent leader of the *Khatris*. On the occasion of this marriage, a widow remarriage society, the *Adhikari Bidhwa Bewa Sahayak Sabha* of Lahore, was launched under the Presidentship of Lala Hans Raj, and Diwan Sant Ram provided for the funds.[24] This marriage deeply stirred the Hindu community, especially the *Khatris*. The Sanatanists argued that the marriage was against the *Hindu dharma*. The Chopra community of Akalgarh published a treatise, pressing for the excommunication of Sant Ram Chopra. Lala Munshiram, better known as Swami Shraddhanand, published a 24-page pamphlet *Kshatra Dharm Palan Ka Gair Mamuli Mauka,* as a rejoinder to the treatise of the Chopras.[25] Interestingly, in this tract Munshiram had argued solely for the remarriage of *akshat yoni* or virgin widows. The Arya Samajists till now, like the earlier attempts for widow remarriage, were largely advocating remarriage of virgin widows.[26]

While the Lahore Samaj provided leadership, the Amritsar Samaj also performed a few remarriages. The movement had, however, not yet picked up momentum, writes Jones, "In spite of Arya tracts and publicizing of actual remarriages such instances remained relatively rare throughout the remainder of the nineteenth century."[27] The other Samajists displayed a definite disinclination towards commemorating widow remarriages. There were no instances of widow remarriages reported from the Arya Samajes of other provinces.[28] This can partly be explained by the fact that Lahore was a progressive city even in the 1880s. Its sponsorship of widow remarriage was probably because of its close association with the Brahmo Samaj in Lahore. Lahore Arya Samaj had lent its support and assistance to the Brahmo Samajist leader Babu Navin Chandra Roy, when he had come to Lahore to propagate remarriages of widows. According to J. Ried Graham, "the fact that it had been a centre of the progressive Brahmo Samaj would make for a liberal point of view".[29] The Samajists, however, did not formulate any comprehensive ideology nor did they set up an organization at the national level.

The movement was, however, beset with factors that hindered its progress. In fact, in these early years, the Arya Samajists concentrated on and devoted most of their time to education. Hence, "the removal of other social evils like child marriage and the advocacy of widow remarriage were given a back seat".[30] For the first 20 years, there was a perceptible inertia towards securing any radical reform, except educational. J. Ried. Graham has rightly remarked in this connection, "... it must be clearly recognized that Arya Samaj was still in the stage of talking about reform and aside from the college undertaking had not, yet, attempted solid reform work. It was following the lead of its founder in beginning more Samajes, in preaching and in carrying on the work of *Shuddhi* of Christians and Muslims. Yet, these activities too cannot be regarded as reforming Hindu society in the way the later Samajist enterprise did".[31]

The dissensions and divisions within the Samaj in Punjab also gave a setback to the reform endeavours of the Samajists.[32] The differences commenced on two issues; whether the education imparted in the Dayanand Anglo-Vedic College founded in 1886 should be on modern lines or on ancient Hindu lines as advocated by Dayanand. The other major disagreement was on the matter of vegetarianism and non-vegetarianism. The Gurukul party, also called the radicals (for their radical views on position and education of women and the institutions of caste and marriage), and the *Mahatmas*, condemned meat-eating as contrary to the teachings of Dayanand, while the liberals or the College party maintained that in order to be a member of Arya Samaj it was necessary only to act in accordance with the ten *Niyams* of the Lahore creed and that in other matters such as the food one ate, the Arya Samajist had the liberty of following his own convictions. The entire debate boiled down to the basic point of dispute between the two parties, i.e., the position of the founder within the Samaj. The Mahatma section claimed infallibility for the Swami and his teachings, whereas the liberals regarded him only as their leader whose teachings and opinions were not binding on them. Within a decade of Dayanand's death, the Samaj was split into two sections.[33] The schism adversely affected the social reform endeavours of the Arya Samaj.

The opposition of the Hindu orthodoxy or the so-called Sanatani Hindus had always been a retarding factor in the movement for widow remarriages. The strong reaction of the orthodox Hindus had led to the failure of widow remarriage movement in Bengal. In Punjab, the Bharat Dharam Mahamandal, the principal representative body of the Hindu orthodoxy, established in 1887, spearheaded the opposition. The Secretary of the Mandal, Pt Din Dayal led a fiery crusade against the Arya Samajists by means of *shastrarths*, tracts and lectures, quoting profusely from the *Vedas*, *Smritis* and *Puranas* for seeking legitimization for his arguments.[34] Yet another organization of the Hindu conservatives was the Sanatan Dharm Sabha led by Pandit Gopinath, which led a virulent campaign against the widow remarriage movement of the Samajists through the columns of its journal, *Sanatan Dharm Gazette*. In 1917, during its anniversary celebrations, the Sabha passed a resolution criticizing widow remarriage.[35] The Punjab Hindu Sabha, established in 1907 in Lahore, also tried to retard the movement for widow remarriage by contemplating a scheme for the welfare of the widows and orphans in 1910.[36] Due to the slander campaign of the conservative Hindus, the Arya Samaj realized the need to impart new dimensions to the widow remarriage movement.

Hitherto, the Samajists had tried to counter resistance to widow remarriage by bringing out tracts that cited scriptural authority in favour of widow remarriage. The Sanatanists were, however, quick to pick up these tactics and "turned to scriptural sources for legitimization in arguments paralleling those used by Aryas"[37]. Hereafter, the Samajists instilled urgency into the widow remarriage campaign by making it a part of the larger movement called the *Hindu Sanghathan*. They also set up a widow remarriage society called the Vidhwa Vivah Sahayak Sabha with the sole and express aim of commemorating widow remarriages.

Concept of Niyoga

The Mahatma section initiated the efforts for bringing about betterment in the condition of widows. Since they had proclaimed their belief not just in the ten *niyams* of Arya Samaj but the entire teachings of Swami Dayanand, they could not ignore his concept of *niyoga*, while dealing with the widow's question. Consequently, in accordance with Dayanand's teachings, they advocated remarriage for child widows and *niyoga* for consummate widows.[38] Swami Shraddhanand celebrated the remarriage of a child widow, in as early as the 1890s.[39] Till the 1920s, the Gurukul party upheld and propagated the doctrine of *niyoga*,[40] while the College party never took the doctrine seriously[41]

The espousal of the doctrine of *niyoga* by the Gurukul party is reflected in the Samaj journals, particularly the *Arya Musafir* and *Arya Gazette* and also the pamphlets written by prominent Samajists from time to time. The *Arya Gazette* even carried matrimonial advertisements for *niyoga*.[42] Such advertisements were received with great consternation not only by the Hindu conservatives but also the Muslims. The Arya Samajists found themselves in the midst of a fierce controversy. Gopi Nath, the editor of the *Sanatan Dharam Gazette*, led a virulent campaign against the Arya Samaj for its advocacy of *niyoga*.[43] The editor of *Hakam*, Mirza Ghulam Ahmed, denounced the doctrine as "an insult to civilization"[44]. Undaunted by the sarcasm and disparagement of its doctrine, *Arya Musafir* continued to vindicate the doctrine of *niyoga*, even devoting its entire issue titled *'Vedic Marriage and Niyoga'* of March 1901 comprising of 54 pages towards the justification of the doctrine.[45] It said, "The Mirza should know that, in the first place, it is not obligatory for such a woman to perform *niyoga*, and secondly, entering into *niyoga* in the prescribed manner has nothing dishonourable about it."[46] *Sanatan Dharma Gazette*, edited by Gopi Nath, issued a rejoinder to it in its issue of 15th March, 1901.[47] The editor denounced it as an act of adultery, which should be punishable with imprisonment. Significantly, the colonial officials too criticized the concept of *niyoga*. E.W. Sands, Home Commissioner, in his official report on the Arya Samaj in the United Provinces characterized *niyoga* as 'license to frail flesh'.[48]

Quite incredulously, in his tract entitled, *Adim Satyarth Prakash aur Arya Samaj ke Sidhant* (1917), Shraddhanand completely disowned the doctrine of *niyoga* for a society, which emulated Vedic principles. He reinterpreted the Samajist concept of *niyoga* when he upheld that the Arya Samajists did not require *niyoga* at all and the doctrine was formulated primarily for the *Pauranics* or non-Arya Samajists. He felt that since the former adhered to the Vedic precepts, their widows could enter into matrimony with the widowers. Whereas the *Pauranics* had faith in the ceremonies of *Pind Dan* and *Shradh* and for their performance, they stood in need of a son and, therefore, *niyoga* was meant for them.[49] Swami Shraddhanand did not give any cogent reasons for such an unexpected reversal of his stand on *niyoga*. The Samajists, probably considered it desirable to forsake the doctrine of *niyoga* to ward off the scathing criticism and slander campaign of Christian missionaries and Ahmadiya Muslims. Widespread disapproval of the doctrine impelled the Samajists to virtually abandon the concept of *niyoga*. Despite the sincere desire of the Mahatma section of the Arya Samajists to uphold the principle cherished by their founder, they utterly failed to bring it into practice. There is not a single instance of the successful consummation of *niyoga*.[50]

Hindu Sanghathan and the Widow Remarriage Movement in the Twentieth Century

In order to impart urgency to the widow remarriage movement, Arya Samajists linked the movement with the ideology of *Hindu Sanghathan* (Hindu solidarity or consolidation of Hindus). This ideology was disseminated through all the platforms of Arya Samaj like the Vidhwa Vivah Sahayak Sabha and the Sarvadeshik Arya Pratinidhi Sabha. Henceforth, widow remarriage movement was conceived as an essential and integral part of a broader movement for *Hindu Sanghathan*. The movement for *Hindu Sanghathan* had begun in 1906 in Punjab with the establishment of Hindu Sabhas. The movement was launched to organize Hindus as a community for their improvement generally but especially in their social and religious affairs.[51] These Hindu Sabhas were primarily concerned with the uplift of the untouchables and their integration with the Hindu society. The widow was not marked out for any special treatment.

The forceful exponent of the movement for *Hindu Sanghathan* started by Arya Samaj was Swami Shraddhanand, earlier known as Lala

Munshiram. It was a meeting with Colonel Mukherjee in Calcutta in 1912 that brought to the notice of the Swami a constant depletion in the ranks of the Hindus. Colonel had calculated from the statistical tables of the census reports that within 420 years, the Indo-Aryan race would be wiped off the face of the earth unless steps were taken to save it.[52] Swami Shraddhanand was so impressed with the facts placed by Dr Mukherjee that in the year 1923, he threw himself 'heart and soul into the movement of protection and progress' of the Hindus.

He articulated his concern on the issue with the publication of the booklet, *Hindu Sanghathan* in 1925. This extensive statement of the Swami gives an insight into the Arya Samajist concept of *Hindu Sanghathan*. The concept, while claiming to strive for the consolidation of Hindus, differed from the *Sanghathan* of the Santanist Hindus in that it was more inclusive, comprehensive and revealed a more rational appreciation of the gravity of the situation, its causes and remedies. In the first section of the book, he has undertaken an exhaustive discussion of the causes of decline of the Hindu population. Conversion to Islàm and Christianity was upheld as the primary reason for this phenomenon. To support his argument, he quoted lengthy extracts from the Census of India, 1911; to show that majority of the Muslims in Bengal and Northern India were originally Hindus. Speaking of the rise of the population from 1901 to 1911, the Swami quoted from the census report, "The number of Mohammedans has risen during the decade by 6.7 per cent as compared with only 5 per cent in the case of Hindus. There is a small but continuous accession of converts from Hinduism and other religions ... but the main reason is that their social customs are more favourable to a high birth rate than those of the Hindus. They have fewer marriage restrictions, early marriage is uncommon and widows remarry more freely."

The second cause of degeneration was the disintegration of the *varna* system, through the emergence of castes and sub-castes and the introduction of untouchability. Prevalence of child marriages and deplorable condition in which women were kept was cited as another significant reason for the diminution in the numbers of Hindus. Shraddhanand, while taking a very comprehensive view of the movement of *Hindu Sanghathan*, incorporated not only the widows' question but also the entire woman's question as a part and parcel of the movement. He considered the *Mahabharata* age as the beginning of deterioration in the position of Hindu women. He considered the reprehensible custom of child marriages as the root cause of the lowly status of women, in general and widows in particular. He said, "The result of child marriages is the following table giving exact enumeration of child widows among orthodox Hindus excluding Arya Samajists, Brahmo Samajists, Sikhs, Jains and Buddhists".

Table 5.1

Number of Child Widows

Age	*Total No. of Widows*
0–1	597
1–2	494
2–3	1,257
3–4	2,837
4–5	6,707
5–10	95,037
10–15	2,33,147
15–20	3,96,172
Total	7,37,248

Source: Census of India, 1911

"It is an appalling figure. Out of these 7¼ lakhs of child widows, there are thousands who lead a life of strict chastity, and it is perhaps due to their *tapasya* that the Hindu society still ekes out its existence. But an overwhelming majority consists of those who are compelled to leave their homes on account of their female and male relatives and to seek shelter under Mohammedan roofs or to add to the numbers of the daughters of shame. In this way, while reducing the number of Hindus they add to the numerical strength of the befitting religious societies." The fourth cause for the gradual extinction of the Hindu race was "the dislocation of the *Ashram Dharm* and the neglect of *Brahmcharya*".

In the last section of the book, Shraddhanand underscored the remedies that could vitalize and strengthen the *Hindu Sanghathan* as a movement. The first remedy was "to make the Bhartiya Hindu Shuddhi Sabha a living body," by harnessing resources in the form of sufficient finances and selfless men who can convince the Hindus to accept those brethren who had embraced other religions. The second remedy was to "revivify the ancient *Ashram Dharm* and to place it on a sound basis". This was to be done by raising substantially the age of marriage. Shraddhanand dealt a severe blow to unequal marriages, which lay at the root of widowhood, when he wrote, "no widower should be allowed to marry a virgin. If, after the death of the first wife, the widower cannot lead a life of *Brahmcharya*, let him marry at widow." The third remedy lay in allowing all unconsummated child widows, who have the desire, to remarry. It is only *Aapatdharma*.[53] The fourth remedy lay in the revival of *varna dharma* of the ancient Aryans. "The present day unnatural, immovable division into a hundred castes and thousands of sub-castes must go, if the Hindu community is to be rescued from total extinction."

Lala Hansraj, the founder member of Sarvadeshik Arya Pratinidhi Sabha, in his presidential address in the first *Sarvadeshik Arya Mahasammelan*, in 1927, restated the stand of Swami Shraddhanand on the issue of widows. He, too, viewed the problem of widows as an integral part of the *Jati Nirman* (Reconstruction of the Hindu Race), and called for an immediate solution. While quoting the Census of India, 1921, he said, "... in the last census there has been a increase of 10 lakhs in the number of Christians and 18 lakhs Muslims, while the Hindus have decreased by 7 lakhs. How can a race, which suffers a loss of 10 lakhs (of persons) every 10 years, be able to survive ...?"[54] (*Translation mine*) He thought that it was imperative to retain the widows, the orphans and the untouchables within fold of the Hindu religion to prevent it from extinction. As the most appropriate solution to the problem of widows, he suggested remarriage. He remarked, "... those widows who willingly adopt the course of *Brahmcharya* may do so, but the forcible imposition of the same leads to disaster". *(Translation mine)* He thought that it was ironical that while people willingly accepted old-age marriages, remarriages and even polygamy in the case of men, they deprived the widows of the same privileges.[55]

The Vidhwa Vivah Sahayak Sabha, the premier organization of Arya Samaj for arranging widow remarriages, too, disseminated its ideology on similar lines. The Tenth Annual Report of the Sabha had compiled the data on the number of widows in the following table.

Table 5.2
Number of Widows

Provinces	*No. of Widows*	*No. of Widows under 25*
Punjab, Delhi and North Western Frontier Provinces.	8,77,107	40,757
United Provinces	32.81.094	1.02.133
Bihar and Orissa	30,43,890	2,25,938
Bengal and Assam	28,16,374	2,05,895
Rajputana	7,52,205	44,489
Bombay Presidency	19,58,319	1,43,258
Central Presidency	10,85,990	67,689
Madras Presidency	39,43,931	2,39,310

Source: Tenth Annual Report of the Vidhwa Vivah Sahayak Sabha 1925.

The report said, "A perusal of figures will show the magnitude of responsibility for the leaders. There is no reason to cry over the loss of population, when it is being depleted of its very source. The conversion of the widows to other religions is a potent fact. No one should blame them if they cannot get peace and happiness in their parental society. Hence, each Hindu should think it his bounden duty to look to the betterment of their condition, bearing in mind that they form one tenth portion of the Hindu community of India."[56] These shocking statistics were publicized through the journals and the tracts of the Sabha and the Samaj in which the need for widow remarriage for the preservation of the Hindu race was consistently underscored.[57] The other tracts on widow remarriage, which were written in the twentieth century, also emphasized the need to preserve Hindu race by arranging widow remarriages. The prominent thread in the widow remarriage movement now was "widow remarriage not for the betterment of the widow but for that of Hindu society."[58] Special care was taken in the journals of Vidhwa Vivah Sahayak Sabha and Arya Samaj to highlight the remarriages of Hindu widows, who were reconverted from Islam to Hinduism.[59]

Cooperation of the Sanatanists

The location of the widow remarriage movement within the larger movement of *Hindu Sanghathan* was an ingenious move on the part of the Samajists. The most significant achievement of disseminating this ideology was the procurement, to a large extent, of the support of the Sanatanists or the conservative Hindus for the cause of widow remarriage. Neki Ram, the leader of the Sanatanist Hindus, made a declaration in 1927 to the effect that he would move the proposal for legitimization of *Karewa* (more or less a synonym for widow remarriage) in the Sanatan Dharm Conference to be held in Multan. He lent his full-fledged support to the widow remarriage movement in 1927 in Jullunder during the fourth regional Widow Remarriage Conference when he endorsed remarriage of both virgin and non-virgin consummated widows.[60] The Vidhwa Vivah Sahayak Sabha received this announcement with great applause. "We had never hoped that the Sanatanists would pass this resolution, but the moving of the proposal on behalf of one of the most respected and prominent Sanatani pandits goes to prove that the Sanatani scholars, too, are cooperating with us in this endeavour." The proposal read, "The widows of all *varnas,* who are unable to observe chastity, should be given, the privilege of *Karewa."* The Sanatanists extended their support to widow remarriages in various provinces. Wide publicity was given to these marriages in the Arya Samajist journals. In the princely state of Jammu, the stronghold of conservative Hindus, the leading Sanatanists passed resolutions approving widow remarriages. The first remarriage in the province was held in Bisauli district on 21 April, 1930. The marriage was commemorated with great fanfare, exactly in the same manner as that of a virgin bride, according to the Sanatani rites, and left a deep impact on the people. It was soon followed by another remarriage on 9 July, 1931 in Ratiyan.[61]

In Rajputana too, Sanatanists gave their willing consent to widow remarriages and even commemorated a few remarriages. The first widow to be remarried under their auspices in Beawar in 1934 was the daughter of an eminent Brahmin family. The *Arya Martand*, a journal of the Arya Pratinidhi Sabha, Rajasthan, called it an 'epoch-making marriage conducive to a mighty revolution in society'. In Kota and Bharatpur too, a few widow remarriages were commemorated among the Vaishyas and Rajputs, under the joint auspices of Sanatan Dharm Sabha and the Arya Samaj in 1938.[62] In the United Provinces too, the widow remarriages received approval from the Sanatanists. They were able to organize widow remarriages among some leading Sanatani families.[63] The unequivocal support of the Hindu orthodoxy to the cause of widow remarriage boosted the morale of the Samajists and provided for wider acceptance of widow remarriages.

The singular success of the Samajists in securing the support of the traditional Hindu society was the annual organization of regional Widow Remarriage Conference, in collaboration with non-Arya Samajist Hindus, from 1924 onwards in Khan Khana, in the Jullunder district.[64] In 1925, Swami Shraddhanand, who presided over the Conference, introduced a resolution which stated that no widower could marry a virgin nor should a widow marry a bachelor, and that the marriage of virgin widows should be celebrated in exactly the same manner as that of virgin brides. Moreover, children born from the union of widows and widowers should enjoy the same legal rights and privileges as those born from the first marriage. Yet another platform successfully exploited by the Samajists was the All India Widow Remarriage Conference. Swami Shraddhanand was able to steer his resolution providing for widow remarriage in the session of Conference held in Guwahati in 1926.[65] The Conference passed a resolution, which stated that the widows should have the liberty of remarrying. The All India Widow Remarriage Conference held in Ajmer reiterated the resolutions passed by the earlier conferences and decided to undertake speedy measures for remarriage of widows.[66]

The Samajists, however, failed to persuade the leaders of the Hindu Mahasabha to incorporate the widow remarriage clause as a quintessential part of *Hindu Sanghathan*. Swami Shraddhanand failed to motivate the Mahasabha leaders for adopting a broader outlook. Twice, in 1925 and 1926, he tried to introduce proposals for a resolution on the remarriage of child widows. On the first occasion, in 1925, Pt Madan Mohan Malviya dissuaded him from introducing such a radical measure, while in a later meeting he had to withdraw the resolution on child widow remarriage to avoid a split in the Mahasabha. Shraddhanand was, however, highly disillusioned by this attitude of the leaders of the Hindu Mahasabha. On both the occasions, he tendered his resignation from the vice-presidentship of the Hindu Mahasabha, which was not accepted. In fact, Shraddhanand had great faith in the role, which Mahasabha could play in bringing about the consolidation of Hindus. The entry of Mahasabha into the political arena precipitated its final break with Swami Shraddhanand.

An 'even bigger reason' for the Swami's frustration with the Mahasabha, was the failure of the latter to accept a more inclusive concept of *Hindu Sanghathan*. While referring to the issues of widow remarriage and untouchability, he remarked, "The Mahasabha does not consider it its duty to work for those social improvements, which are utterly essential in order to save the Hindu community from total ruin, and the Sabha even puts obstacles in the way of its members who try to fulfil that very duty."[67]

An appeal was also made by the Vidhwa Vivah Sahayak Sabha to the Hindu Mahasabha to seriously ponder over the distressed condition of widows. "Today, as a result of our prosecution, not one but many widows are embracing other religions .... Our Hindu leaders, despite observing all this, have been sleeping comfortably over the issue. Only by chanting the slogan of *Hindu Sanghathan*, they consider their task to be fulfilled. It is our firm belief that without doing anything concrete, it is futile to hope for *Hindu Sanghathan*. Just as we consider *Shuddhi* and upliftment of untouchables as an essential part of the *Sanghathan*, in the same way the betterment in the deplorable condition of widows should also be made an integral part of the same."[68] It lambasted the Mahasabha leaders for advancing the weak argument that widow remarriage was not sanctioned by the Hindu religion. With the entry of Hindu Mahasabha into active politics its leaders, perhaps, feared that their political clout might suffer if they raised socially sensitive issues like widow remarriage and socio-religious equality for untouchables. Despite the setback they received at the hands of the Hindu Mahasabha, it must be remarked to the credit of the Samajists that by absorption of the concept of widow remarriage within that of *Hindu Sanghathan*, they imparted to the cause of widow remarriage urgency and the dimensions of a well-knit movement.

Vidhwa Vivah Sahayak Sabha

The establishment of Vidhwa Vivah Sahayak Sabha (Society for Assisting Widow Remarriage) in 1915 imparted a fillip to the widow remarriage movement spearheaded by the Arya Samaj movement. Sir Ganga Ram, a prominent Arya Samajist, had set up the Sabha under the supervision of Sir Ganga Ram Trust Society in 1915. The chief objects of the Sabhawere to encourage and arrange widow remarriages, to popularize widow remarriages through distribution of literature and undertake activities that would facilitate the above objects.[69] According to the trust-deed of the founder, the Sabha was to continue to work till the custom of widow remarriage in the Hindu community got full currency. The Sabha did not interfere in the religions of the parties concerned and they could perform the marriage ceremony with any rites they liked.

In the first few years, the activities and branches of the Sabha were limited to the province of Punjab. Even in Punjab, the success was not immediate. It was a gradual and formidable headway because apart from the opposition of the Hindu orthodoxy, the taboo on remarriage among the twice-born castes was as common in Punjab as in the other provinces. Prakash Tondon, while lamenting the distressed conditions of widows in Punjab, has written, "Young widows, in fact, were a great problem. While people would not accept remarriage at any cost, they did not know what to do with them. The lot of widows improved somewhat with the spread of Arya Samaj, which advocated remarriage or education to befit them for a teaching job, but people were slow to react and continued to hold the same belief that God had so willed it ...".[70] In the year 1915, the Sabha could arrange only 12 remarriages. The Sabha achieved tremendous headway when it commemorated two remarriages in respectable families of Punjab in 1915.[71] The number gradually increased to 13 in 1916, 31 in 1917, 40 in 1918, 90 in 1919 and 220 in 1920. From 1920 onwards, the Sabha strove to expand the scope of its activities to other provinces. The expansion and success of the Sabha in a particular province largely depended on local response. While the Sabha did its utmost by distributing instructive and inspiring literature and sending its preachers, it was not able to achieve success if the masses of that province continued to remain apathetic to the cause. A perusal of the reports and journals highlight the regional variations, as far as success of the Sabha was concerned. Significantly, in the early years, the resources of the Sabha were diverted mainly to the provinces of Punjab and North-West Frontier Provinces (NWFP) followed by United Provinces and the Hindu pilgrim stations. Out of the seven paid workers, four worked solely in Punjab and NWFP. These provinces were visited as many as 225 and 359 times by the paid workers in the years 1923 and 1924, respectively. The reports testify that in these provinces there was a definite increase in people's support for widow remarriage. The provinces of Bengal, Madras and Rajputana, however, remained indifferent towards widow remarriage when the preachers of the Sabha visited these regions in 1923. As a result, it did not send its preachers to these provinces in 1924.[72] By 1924, the Sabha had a network of its branches all over India that kept on increasing from year to year.

The province of Punjab continued to provide leadership to the widow remarriage movement and maintained an impressive lead over other provinces well-nigh into the twentieth century. The tenth annual report, while commending the favourable response of the men from Punjab towards widow remarriage said, "It is a measure of pleasure and satisfaction that where ever a Punjabi has been found, he has tried to help the cause to the best of his ability ...".[73] Stalwarts like Dinanath Sidhantalankar were sent to Bengal from Lahore to resuscitate the dying movement.[74] A substantial number of men from Punjab even married widows from other provinces. In 1923, Punjabi men married 63 widows belonging to provinces, other than Punjab, while in 1924, this number rose to 141. Not only widowers but also bachelors belonging to Punjab were willing to marry widows.[75]

Closely following the province of Punjab, largest number of widow remarriages was celebrated in the United Provinces. The movement received an impetus in the province in the first decade of the twentieth century, when Shrotiya Shankar Dutt, an orthodox Hindu of Bijnore, married a widow and another eminent personality, Dr Mukandlal, arranged the remarriage of his widow daughter.[76] The movement spread more rapidly in the western United Provinces in the non-pilgrim stations of Agra, Lucknow, Meerut, Muzaffargarh, Kalakankar, and Jhansi where preachers of the Sabha were often sent.[77] The ruler of Kalakankar extended his active support to the widow remarriage movement. On 20 March, 1933, the ruler arranged the marriage of a *Kshatriya* widow of Baliya with his own relative.[78] Many widows got remarried under the joint auspices of the ruler and the Arya Samaj.[79] In Eastern United Provinces, there were many strongholds of orthodox Hinduism like Benaras, Gaya, Allahabad, and Hardwar. The *Choubes* and orthodox Hindus offered stiff opposition to the Arya Samaj movement. The number of widow remarriages in the United Provinces kept on increasing. *Arya Mitra*, the newspaper of the Arya Pratinidhi Sabha, United Provinces, was reporting widow remarriage almost every month.[80]

Arya Samaj, however, tried to reach out to the widows in the holy places of the Hindus that gave shelter to numerous widows. An earnest attempt was made by Arya Samaj to get them remarried. The tenth annual report of the Sabha said, "To tap the very citadels of orthodoxy, two *ashrams* for widow remarriages have been started at Mathura and Hardwar, in addition to one at Lahore and it is contemplated to extend this policy to Benaras, Tarkeshwar and other such places where poor widows without anyone to look after them are found in abundance".[81] In the year 1924, 39 remarriages were reported from Benaras, 12 from Allahabad, 1 from Hardwar and 10 from Mathura. Similar trends were noticeable in the subsequent years.[82] Despite encouraging figures from these stations, the problem of widows' rehabilitation still had enormous proportions, keeping in view the large number of widows who thronged to the pilgrimages. Arya Samaj and the Vidhwa Vivah Sahayak Sabha focused its attention on pilgrimages outside of the United Provinces – Gaya in Bihar and Navdweep in Bengal were chief among them.[83] In 1934, Pandit Dinanath Sidhantalankar himself visited Gaya to propagate widow remarriages.[84] In 1933, in the month of September, two widow remarriages were reported from Gaya.[85]

Quite ironically, the movement did not succeed in Bengal despite the fact that the earliest efforts for widow remarriage were made in the province. The Vidhwa Vivah Sahayak Sabha failed to elicit a favourable response in Bengal. It was set up in 1921 and dissolved some years later and was revived in 1931 by Dinanath Sidhantalankar.[86] There were many instances when men from Punjab married widows from Bengal, probably due to the unwillingness of men in Bengal to marry widows. They formed a sizeable number as in December 1926 Sir Gangaram had invited the Bengali widows married to Punjabi gentlemen to his home in Lahore for a tea party to enquire about their well-being in the province of Punjab.[87] The fact that Arya Samajists could revive the dormant movement in Bengal was an outcome of their tenacity and also their commitment to the cause.

Arya Samaj and the Vidhwa Vivah Sahayak Sabha, however, failed to evoke an appreciable response in Southern India.[88] Swami Shraddhanand and Jiwan Mal, a preacher of the Vidhwa Vivah

Sahayak Sabha, preached in favour of widow remarriage in Madras in 1925 and 1926 respectively. The conservative backlash by the Brahmins and non-Brahmins precluded the possibility of achieving any breakthrough in Madras and Hyderabad leading to despair among the Arya Samajists.[89]

The society in the princely states of Rajputana was also highly conservative. Widow remarriages were a taboo among the higher castes. The princely states of Loharu, Alwar, Kota, Jodhpur, and Udaipur even imposed taxes and fines on widow remarriages.[90] The Arya Samaj and the Vidhwa Vivah Sahayak Sabha pioneered the cause of widow remarriage in the princely states. The generation of awareness by Arya Samaj and the other caste reform associations led the rulers of Bikaner and Bharatpur to legalize widow remarriages in their states.[91] The efforts of the Samaj led to the commemoration of widow remarriages among the Rajputs too.

A community that received special attention from the Samajists in the region of Rajputana states were the *Marwari Vaishyas* of Marwar and their sub-castes – the *Oswals*, *Maheshwaris*, *Agarwals* and the *Khandelwals*, who were to be found in distant parts of India. The *Marwaris* were a conservative community, owing to their adherence to retrogressive social customs like infant marriages and prohibition of widow remarriages. The efforts of the Arya Samajists made a dent in the rigid attitude of the community towards widow remarriages.[92] In December 1925, 25 remarriages were commemorated among the *Agarwals* and the *Oswals* and in December 1926, 24 widow remarriages were commemorated among the *Agarwals*. The remarriage of the child widow, daughter of an eminent personality, Brij Mohan Lal Singhania, marked a significant breakthrough.[93]

The perseverance with which the Vidhwa Vivah Sahayak Sabha pursued the task of popularizing widow remarriages led to their tremendous success in promoting widow remarriages among the twice-born castes. Innumerable letters were received from widows willing to contract a matrimonial alliance. Total number of applications received from the date of establishment of this society up to the end of 1924 from widows was 1496.[94] Widows even composed poems, eulogizing the pioneering efforts of Sir Gangaram, the founder of the Vidhwa Vivah Sahayak Sabha.[95]

The widow remarriage movement was spearheaded and pioneered by men. Unlike movements for education and relaxation of *purda,* where women too, made substantial contribution, women leaders were conspicuous by their absence in the widow remarriage movement. Stree Samajs, which were formed during the last decades of the nineteenth century, as an attempt to exhort women to give up *purda* and to increase their participation in Samajist activities, never aimed at any comprehensive and radical reform in the marriage system.

Widows Homes

The Arya Samaj and the Vidhwa Vivah Sahayak Sabha upheld remarriage as the ideal solution for the vexatious problem of the widows. Deep-seated religious and social prejudices and at times, widows' unwillingness to remarry, however, rendered remarriage of widows a difficult proposition. The imminent need for the establishment of widow homes had dawned upon the reformers in the last quarter of the nineteenth century. The failure of the widow remarriage movement to gain public acceptance, by and large, motivated the reformers to take up the task of providing education, economic training and shelter to widows in homes exclusively, meant for them. The widow homes set up under the aegis of the Arya Samaj can be divided into three categories – *Vidhwa Ashrams* set up by Stree Samaj or the women's wing of the Arya Samaj; *Vidhwa Ashrams* set up by the Arya Samaj; *Vidhwa Ashrams* set up by the Vidhwa Vivah Sahayak Sabha.

The *Vidhwa Ashrams*, which were set up by the Stree Samaj are among the earliest efforts made by the Arya Samaj in this direction. Lahore Stree Samaj set up a widow's home in 1891. The home gave shelter to about forty-sixty widows and their children.[96] Ludhiana Stree Samaj also managed a widow's ashram.[97] Religious education, which included books written by Swami Dayanand, was imparted to the widow inmates of Lahore Ashram.[98] Although not much is known about their schemes for the betterment of widows, these homes were motivated by purely humanitarian concern for the helpless and persecuted widows. The homes did not strive to arrange the remarriage of their inmates. The second category included the homes maintained by the Arya Samaj. Apart from compassionate grounds, the Arya Samajists were largely moved by the fact of mass conversion of widows to Christianity and Islam. There was a sudden spurt of activities in this direction in the 1920s when the impending danger of the extinction of the Hindu race dawned upon the Samajists. The functionaries of the Samaj had not taken up this aspect of widows' betterment in the early stages apparently because of their involvement in other social reform activities, lack of funds and difficulty of locating lady superintendents for the widow homes.[99]

The All India Dayanand Salvation Mission was founded in 1924 by Lala Devichand M.A.[100] Its objectives were to rescue Hindu girls and widows from molestation; to arrange for rescue homes at important centres; to convert non-Hindus to Hinduism. The Mission had a wide network of 21 branches all over India.[101] The Mission undertook the task of rehabilitation of the widows either through remarriage or by imparting vocational training to them. The Mission also reclaimed the widows who got converted to other religions after performance of *Shuddhi*. From 1934 to 1939, the various branches of the Mission rescued 560 women.

In 1937, Arya Raksha Samiti was set up in Prayag with more or less similar objectives. The Samiti laid additional emphasis on *prachar* through lectures and *bhajans* against detrimental social practices like child marriages, unequal marriages, polygamy and dowry. In the year 1940, the Samiti reclaimed 16 widows from other religions. Twelve widows were sent back to their guardians and four were sent to Sir Gangaram Vidhwa Bhawan. Besides these two organizations for rescuing widows and untouchables, widow ashrams were set up in Agra, Kashi, Monghyr, Bhagalpur, Vasudevpur, Patna, Jhansi, Ajmer, Delhi, Bikaner and Dehradun.

The region of Ajmer was a stronghold of Christian missionaries and, therefore, threat of conversions loomed large over the Hindu society. As a result, the Arya Samajists set up 3 widow homes in the city – Rajasthan Vanita Ashram (1926); *vidhwa ashram* was attached to the already existing Shrimaddayanand Orphanage in 1924; and Shraddhanand Mahila Ashram. These widow homes undertook multiple activities for the amelioration of the widows. The primary aim of these Homes was to provide the widows a refuge within Hinduism.[102] From 1923 to 1940, Shrimaddayanand Vidhwa Ashram rescued 3,000 widows from the clutches of the infidels and gave them a new lease of life.[103] The Ashram also gave succour to 19 widows of Jodhpur state.[104]

The *vanita* and *vidhwa ashrams* also gave shelter to destitute women and those who were persecuted by their husbands and families.[105] Rajasthan Vanita Ashram, Jhansi Vidhwa Ashram, Saharanpur Vanita Ashram and Dayanand Orphanage specified this very clearly in their advertisements that harassed women, whether widows or not, were welcome in the homes. In most of the cases such persecuted women were sent back to their guardians.[106]

Commemoration of remarriages of the eligible widows constituted yet another major objective of the *vidhwa ashrams*. The rules of the Shrimaddayanand Vidhwa Ashram clearly stated one of its objectives thus: "To locate suitable matches for widows willing to remarry and arrange for their remarriages so that they can spend the rest of their lives happily. Those widows who are not willing to remarry would not be forced to enter into matrimony."[107] Matrimonial advertisements of widows willing to remarry were regularly given in the Samaj journals.[108] Constant reports of widow remarriages were received from Rajasthan Vanita Ashram, Shrimaddayanand Vidhwa Ashram and Saharanpur Hindu Vanita Ashram.[109] These *ashrams* also provided succour and shelter to pregnant widows in order to prevent them from resorting to prostitution.[110] Widow homes also provided religious education and vocational training to the widows. An effort was made to make them useful and self-reliant members of society.

Vidhwa ashrams were actively associated with consciousness-raising too. Instructive literature was distributed free of cost by these homes.[111] Inmates of Rajasthan Vanita Ashram toured Beawar, Nasirabad and Phulera and preached in favour of widow remarriage in 1926.[112] The Saharanpur Vidhwa Ashram started a journal *Hindu Sambandh Sahayak* to propagate in favour of widow remarriage and condemn practices like child marriages, polygamy and unequal marriages.[113]

The widows' homes even became targets of criticism when they fell short of their objectives. In a letter to *Arya Mitra*, Mithan Lal pointed out that *vanita ashrams* were inefficient and even if some men married the widows, the latter came back to the *ashrams*. He pleaded that instead of aiming for remarriage, the *vidhwa ashrams* should strive to make widows useful members of society. Some other articles pointed out that *vidhwa ashrams* under the auspices of Arya Samaj started deteriorating after a short period. He demanded that the *ashrams* should be run on the basis of certain specific rules.[114] The *vidhwa ashrams* increasingly felt the need to tour the villages and assist the helpless widows who were being converted to Christianity and Islam. He also emphasized the need to acquaint the Hindu widows with their own proper addresses and those of the Arya Samajist widow ashrams so that they could reach proper places and were not trapped by Muslims and Christians.[115]

The *vidhwa ashrams* set up under the auspices of the Vidhwa Vivah Sahayak Sabha, called *Ganga Ram Vidhwa Bhawans*, constituted the third category of widow homes. These were set up in Ajmer, Mathura, Lahore and Hardwar. These widows' homes were set up with the specific purpose of arranging widow remarriages.[116] The Vidhwa Bhavan at Ajmer claimed six to seven remarriages in a month and in the six months ending November 1930 it arranged as many as 40 widow remarriages.[117] Widows in Arya Samajist widow homes, who were willing to remarry, were also transferred to Ganga Ram Vidhwa Bhavan.[118]

The Samajists' endeavours for the establishment of widow homes testify to their deep concern for widows. Apart from providing for the rehabilitation and education of widows, these homes also strove to arrange their remarriages. The contribution of Arya Samaj in this sphere has been of utmost significance.

Creation of Public Awareness

The Samajists adopted publication and dissemination of literature in favour of widow remarriage as a powerful medium for educating public opinion. Till the last decade of the nineteenth century when the approach of Arya Samajists towards the issue of widow remarriage was marked with considerable restraint and moderation, they concentrated their efforts towards diffusion of progressive ideals and doctrines of the Samaj. The Lahore Samaj devoted one of its first journals, *Vidhwa Hiteshi* for articulating the grievances of the widows. Besides, their numerous journals like *Arya Magazine*, *Arya Mitra* and *Regenerator of Arya Varta* championed the cause of widows.[119] Individual Samajists published innumerable tracts and pamphlets in advocacy of widow remarriage. These tracts were written in simple, yet, effective language. Most of these tracts were in Urdu.

The advocacy of widow remarriage through diffusion of literature, received a tremendous impetus with the establishment of

Vidhwa Vivah Sahayak Sabha in 1915. One of the primary objects of the Sabha was 'to place proper literature in the hands of the public'. In pursuance of its aims, the Sabha started its Urdu journal *Vidhwa Sahayak* in October 1921 followed by an English journal *Widow's Cause*. In 1925, additional eight pages were added for the benefit of women. *Vidhwa Sahayak* justified its existence by being very useful in educating public opinion on the problems of widows in Punjab and Northern India. [120]

In 1926, the Sabha started its Hindi journal, *Vidhwa Bandhu*, particularly for widows belonging to the United Provinces, Bihar and Central Provinces even distributing free copies of the journal among poor and helpless widows and despite incurring heavy losses, the Sabha priced the annual subscription of the journal at Rs 2 only.[121] Other journals like *Arya Martand* and *Anath Rakshak* carried numerous articles and poems on widow remarriage.[122]

Publication of tracts on *niyoga* and widow remarriage by individual Samajists continued unabated in the twentieth century. The tracts, which were published in the twentieth century, were equipped with new ideological dimensions. Firstly, the imminent necessity to prevent Hinduism and Hindu race from becoming extinct was forcefully articulated. The acceptance of widow remarriage was emphasized as *Aapat-Dharm*, i.e., religion to be followed in times of crisis. Secondly, now there is a marked emphasis on equality of men and women. The Samajists were exhorted to uphold the principles of justice and fair play with regard to women, as their exponent Swami Dayanand Saraswati had done. *Vidhwa Vivah Prashnotri* by Pt J.P. Chaudhary Kavyatirth[123] was an ardent plea for widow remarriage to check the gradual diminution of the Hindu race due to non-remarriage of widows. The author claimed equal rights for both men and women as far as remarriage was concerned.[124] Kunwar Chand Karan Sarda brought out a pamphlet '*Vidhwa Vivah Karo*' in 1924.[125] The pamphlet was written primarily to arouse the Marwari community on the imminent need to resort to widow remarriages. Like the earlier tract, the author underlined the need to preserve Hindu race by relieving women and, particularly widows from their distressed conditions. Chand Kunwar Sarda, while arguing the case for widow remarriage, upheld that men and women should be treated equally. The author, at the same time, admitted that while widow remarriage couldn't be defined as an ideal marriage he described it as *Aapat-Dharma*. Vidhwodvah Vivek, written in the 1920s by Hari Shanker Dube, was a detailed argument in favour of widow remarriage based on lengthy proofs from the *Smritis* and *Shrutis*.[126]

In 1928, Ganpati Vedopdeshak wrote *Vidhwa Vivah Apaddharma Hai*.[127] The tract was primarily written for the Marwari community and dedicated to those Marwari gentlemen who had provided economic and moral support for the betterment of widows. He remarked, "Widow marriage is neither religious, nor irreligious but *Aapat-Dharma*."[128] *Nari Punarvivah Mimansa*, penned by Swami Karamnand Saraswati was a response to two books *Shastrarth* by Vamnayak and *Vidhwa Vivah Niranaya* by Pt Kaluram, which formed an indictment of widow remarriage.[129] Apart from these, tracts on the doctrine of *niyoga* are also not scarce. *Niyoga Mardan ka Vimardan* was written by Bhumitra Sharma as a rejoinder to Pandit Kaluram's *Niyoga Mardan*.[130] The numerous journals and tracts published under the aegis of the Samaj played a significant role in bringing about change in societal attitudes towards widow remarriage.

The stupendous success of Arya Samaj and its organizations in the sphere of widow remarriages is, indeed, laudable particularly in view of the failure of the earlier movements to achieve any significant breakthrough. The Samajists displayed rare passion and insight in resorting to multiple interventions to ameliorate the widows from their sad plight. The establishment of the Vidhwa Vivah Sahayak Sabha with the primary objective of promoting widow remarriages, the incorporation of the widow remarriage movement within the larger movement of *Hindu Sanghathan*, the intensive instructive propaganda and the establishment of widow homes were measures that contributed to the success of the movement. The most critical intervention was, however, the strategic move whereby the widow remarriage movement was positioned within the *Hindu Sanghathan*. It certainly gave a new lease of life to the failing widow remarriage movement. Quite pertinently, it had the effect of softening the trenchant opposition of the orthodox Hindus whose hostility had hitherto remained the major stumbling block in the widow remarriage movement. It was a paradigm shift in the widow remarriage movement in the sense that so far humanitarian concerns and sympathy for the forlorn widow had dominated the discourse on widows. The concern for widows was now translated into the larger concern for saving Hindu religion from extinction. By arousing a sense of urgency, Arya Samaj was able to elicit support and sympathy from Sanatani Hindus thus affecting the lives of a larger number of widows. While it is debatable whether raising the slogan of 'Hinduism in danger' was a tactical move on the part of Samajist leaders or their actual fear, it definitely resulted in generating a counter-movement among the Sanatani Hindus. They realized the imminent need to liberalize social norms for women and other marginalized groups to give them space, dignity and respect within the folds of Hinduism so that they were not lured by other proselyting religions. The counter-movement among the conservative Hindus formed a critical advance as now more people began to be involved in the task of social amelioration and committed to provide liberal treatment to a large percentage of widows.

Notes

1. Uma Chakravarti, 'Whatever happened to the Vedic *Dasi*? Orientalism, Nationalism and a Script for the Past', in Kumkum Sangari and Sudesh Vaid (ed.), *Recasting Women: Essays in Colonial History*, p. 59.
2. Radha Kumar, *History of Doing*, p. 19.
3. Pandita Ramabai, *The High Caste Hindu Woman*, p. 91.
4. Dayaram Gidumal, *Behramji M. Malabari: A Sketch*, pp. 196–200.
5. Radha Kumar, op. cit., p. 19.
6. M.G. Mali, *Krantijyoti Savitribai Phule*, pp. 39–40.
7. C.H. Hiemsath, *Indian Nationalism and Hindu Social Reform*, p. 272; P.N. Bose, *A History of Hindu Civilization during British Rule*, Vol. II, pp. 46–47.
8. Nicol Macnicol, *Pandita Ramabai*, pp. 56–60; Clementia Butler, *Pandita Ramabai Saraswati: Pioneer in the Movement for Education of the Child Widow of India*, p. 25.
9. *Modern Review*, January, 1899, pp. 35–42.
10. D.K. Karve, *Looking Back*, p. 57.
11. G.L. Chandavarkar, *Maharshi Karve*, p. 76.
12. *Collected Works of Vivekanand*, Vol. VIII, p. 307.
13. Amiya P. Sen, *Swami Vivekanand*, p. 71.
14. For a discussion of these retrogressive stances on widow remarriage refer, Amiya Sen, *Social and Religious Reform: Hindus of British India*, pp. 43–50.

15. Partha Chatterjee, 'Nationalist Resolution of the Women's Question', in Kumkum Sangari and Sudesh Vaid (ed.), op. cit., pp. 233–253.
16. Tapan Raychaudhari, 'Swami Vivekanand's Construction of Hinduism', in William Radice (ed.), *Swami Vivekananda and the Modernization of Hinduism*, p. 7.
17. B.R. Nanda, 'The Social Reform Movement in India: From Ranade to Nehru', in B.R. Nanda, *Indian Women: From Purdah to Modernity*, p. 54.
18. It solemnized the remarriage of a widow as early as March,1882 between two Khatris, *Arya Patrika*, March, 1882, cited from, Kenneth W. Jones, Arya Samaj in Punjab: A Study of Social Reform and Religious Revivalism, 1877–*1902*, Ph.D. Dissertation, University of California, Berkeley, 1966, p. 100.
19. J.C. Oman, who was present in the worship service on the second anniversary of the Samaj in 1899, testified to the advocacy of widow remarriage on the occasion. K.W. Jones, *Arya Dharm: Hindu Consciousness in the Nineteenth Century Punjab*, p. 45.
20. B.L Bhartiya, *Arya Samaj ke Patra aur Patrakar*, Appendix II.
21. *Regenerator of Arya Varta*, February 11, 1884, p. 5, cited from, Jones, *Arya Samaj in Punjab*, p. 101.
22. J.T.F. Jordens, *Dayanand Saraswati: His Life and Ideas*, p. 197.
23. Cited from, K.W. Jones, op. cit., pp. 100–101.
24. Not much is known about the achievements of this Sabha. The Sabha, perhaps, ceased to exist for lack of response and funds. Jones, op. cit., p. 218.
25. For details of the tract, refer, J.T.F. Jordens, *Swami Shraddhanand: His Life and Causes*, pp. 59–60.
26. The Lahore Arya Samaj, however, had no prejudices as far as non-virgin widows were concerned. In 1894, it sponsored the remarriage of an elderly couple. Both the bridegroom and the bride were of mature age and the latter had a child from her previous husband. *Tribune*, February 17, 1894, p. 4, cited from, Jones, op. cit., p. 102. In the twentieth century, this distinction was completely given up by the Samaj. Triyambak Rao Sathe in his tract, *Vidhwa Vivah Samvad*, written in 1901, had pleaded for remarriage of both categories of widows – virgin and non-virgin. Arya Pratinidhi Sabha of Punjab had agreed to the remarriage of widows upto the age of 40, Shyamji Sharma Kavyatirth, *Kya Vidhwa Vivah Adharma Hai?*, p. 57.
27. Jones, op. cit., pp. 101–103.
28. In 1882, the Ajmer Arya Samaj, after converting a Hindu widow from, Christianity, never contemplated remarriage for her and was rather keen to involve her in the process of women's education. *Swami Dayanand ko Likhe Patra aur Vijnapan*, IV, Y. Mimansak and Pt Bhagwat Dutt (eds.), Letter no. 464, pp. 481–483.

29. J. Ried Graham, Arya Samaj as a Reformation in Hinduism, with special reference to Caste, Ph.D. Dissertation, Yale University, p. 408. Dayanand had, however, cautioned the Lahore Samaj against widow remarriage. *Swami Dayanand ke Patra aur Vijnapana*, Vol. II, Y. Mimansak and Pt Bhagwat Dutt (eds.), Letter no. 528, pp. 561–562.
30. Shyamla Bhatia, *Social Change and Politics in Punjab, 1898–1910*, p. 146.
31. Graham, op. cit., p. 401.
32. Shraddhanand complained that the Arya Samaj had not made any progress since Swami Dayanand's death due to internal dissensions. *Saddharmapracharak*, June 30, 1899, *Selections from Vernacular Newspapers published in the Punjab*, received up to July 15, 1899.
33. For details regarding the conflict between the College party and the Gurukul party, refer to K.W. Jones, *Arya Samaj in Punjab*, pp. 90–93; J. Ried Graham, op. cit., pp. 403–412; J.T.F. Jordens, *Swami Shraddhanand: His Life and Causes*, pp. 29–54.
34. For details, see *Arya Patrika*, December 27, 1887, in Jones, op. cit., p. 109; Bhimsen Vidyalankar, *Arya Pratinidhi Sabha Punjab ka Sachitra Itihas*, p. 42.
35. Ibid., It would be interesting to attract attention to the liberal point of view, as regards social issues, of some of the rulers of the princely states. Maharaja Jai Singh of Jaipur was reported to have thought of legalizing widow remarriages in his state in the 1850s. The furore that followed prevented him from promulgating the order. R.S. Pareek, op. cit., p. 155. The Baroda state was well-known for its social legislation for liberalization of the social structure. *Punjabee,* November 2, 1912, *Selections from Indian Newspapers published in the Punjab*, November, 1912, Home Poll (B), November, 1912, No. 61; Maharaja Hira Singh of Nabha had also invited Mahatma Hans Raj, leader of the College party, to his state so that he might prove the validity of widow remarriage to the orthodox Hindus. The Maharaja, then, took appropriate measures to permit widow remarriage in the state. Sri Ram Sharma, *Mahatma Hansraj: Maker of the Modern Punjab*, p. 144. Similarly, the ruler of Bharatpur, most likely under the influence of Arya Samaj, declared widow remarriages legal in his state in 1926, *Vidhwa Bandhu*, January, 1926, p. 22.
36. *Tribune*, September 15, 1909 and September 27, 1910.
37. Jones, op. cit., p. 109.
38. *Arya Musafir*, May, 1900, *Selections from Vernacular Newspapers published in the Punjab*, received upto May 12, 1900.
39. M.R. Jambhunathan (ed.), *Swami Shraddhanand: An Autobiography*, p. 114.
40. In public, Shraddhanand lent his whole-hearted support to the doctrine of *niyoga*. Apparently, there seemed to be a consistency in his views. In private, however, Shraddhanand entertained doubts regarding Dayanand's interpretation of the verses relating to *niyoga* in the *Vedas*. He

thought that the verses in question refer to remarriage and not *niyoga*. This vacillation and inconsistency in Shraddhanand's stand on *niyoga* comes across very clearly in his letters to Ram Krishna, Pradhan, Arya Samaj, Jullunder and his son Indra. *Indra Vidyavachaspati Collection*, Letters to Ramkrishna dated 16.5.1894; 5.7.1908; 6.7.1908; 9.5.1910; to Indra on 25.2.72, *Vikram* era.

41. In 1916, J.C. Oman questioned Lala Lajpat Rai, the leader of the College party, "The teaching of Swami Dayanand, in regard to *niyoga* is, I understand, taken by all his followers, as an essential part of the master's doctrine, Am I right?", Lala Lajpat Rai remarked, "No, *niyoga* is not an essential doctrine of the Samaj". Swami Shraddhanand, leader of the *Mahatma* section expressed his dismay over this assertion of Lala Lajpat Rai. Swami Shraddhanand Isai Pakshpat aur Arya Samaj, in B.L. Bhartiya (ed.), *Swami Shraddhanand Granthavali*, Vol. III, p. 190. In his book, *The Arya Samaj*, Lajpat Rai confirmed that over this particular doctrine, there is difference of opinion amongst the Samajists.
42. "A friend of the publisher of the notice being a staunch Arya Samajist of 40 years of age and having no children from his own wife, who is ill, is desirous of entering into *niyoga*, according to the injunctions of Swami Dayanandji with a widow or with a woman who has got no children by her own husband. If in the family of an Arya Samajist there is any such woman, she should apply to an Arya Samajist, care of Kalu Ram, Musafir, Store Keeper, Military Works Service, Mean Meer". *Arya Gazette*, April 12, 1900, *Selections from Vernacular Newspapers published from the Punjab*, received upto April, 1900, p. 218. A similar kind of advertisement for *niyoga* appeared in the *Arya Mitra* (published from Moradabad in United Provinces) from Jaini Lal Gupta of Bulandshahr District, *Arya Mitra*, March 16, 1901, *Selections from Vernacular Newspapers published from the Punjab*, received upto March, 1901, Para. 17.
43. *Sanatan Dharma Gazette*, April 30, 1900, *Selections from Vernacular Newspapers published from the Punjab*, received upto May 12, 1900, p. 231.
44. *Selections from Vernacular Newspapers published from the Punjab*, received upto October, 1900, Paras. 6 and 570; *Hakam (Kadian)*, April 17, 1900, received upto April, 1900, p. 218. Anwar-ul-Islam, April, 1901, SVNPP, received upto June, 1901, p. 361.
45. *Selections from Vernacular Newspapers published from the Punjab*, received upto September, 1900, Paras. 16 and 17.
46. *Arya Musafir Magazine*, September, 1900, *Selections from Vernacular Newspapers published from the Punjab*, received upto October, 1900, pp. 570–571.
47. Ibid., received upto March, 1901, Para. 18, p. 201.
48. E.W. Sands, *Arya Samaj in the United Provinces*, p. 17.

49. Adim Satyarth Prakash aur Arya Samaj ke Sidhant, in B.L. Bhartiya (ed.), op. cit., Vol. III, pp. 60–61. Shraddhanand's unequivocal statement regarding his change of stand on *niyoga* was followed by a series of articles by him and others on the subject of *niyoga* in his journal *Saddharmapracharak*; Swami Shraddhanand, Niyoga ke Liye Hetu, *Saddharmapracharak*, January 5, 1918; Niyoga aur Swami Shraddhanand, Ibid., February 23, 1918; *Swami Shraddhanand aur Niyoga*, Ibid., March 9, 1918; Niyoga aur Swami Shraddhanand, Ibid., March 18, 1918.
50. In the United Provinces, some widow remarriages took place in the nineteenth century, which were called *niyoga* by a few newspapers of the Arya Samaj. In fact, they were widow remarriages and the term *niyoga* was employed only to prove Arya Samaj's commitment to the doctrine. Indra Vidyavachaspati, *Arya Samaj ka Itihas*, Vol. I, p. 290.
51. *Tribune*, September 15, 1909.
52. For details regarding Shraddhanand's attempts to mobilize Hindus through the ideology and movement of *Hindu Sanghathan*, refer, Swami Shraddhanand, *Hindu Sanghathan*.
53. The *Smritis* lay down the rules to be followed in times of extreme distress or calamity and such rules constitute, what is called *Aapatdharma*.
54. Raghuvir Singh Shastri (ed.), *Sarvadeshik Arya Mahasammelann ke Adhyakshiya Bhashan*, pp. 20–21.
55. Ibid., For Lala Hansraj's views, also see, Sri Ram Sharma, *Mahatama Hansraj: Maker of the Modern Punjab*, pp. 76–79.
56. *Tenth Annual Report of the Vidhva Vivah Sahayak Sabha.*
57. Hindu Vidhwaein aur Hindu Dharma, *Vidhwa Bandhu*, January, 1926, pp. 1–2; Navdeep Mein Vidhwaon Ki Durdarsha, Ibid., January 27, p. 12; Ek Vidhwa Ki Karun Katha, Ibid., November 27, p. 10. This story is a true incident narrated by Shri Veni Madhav Prasad Singh, in which a widow who got converted to Islam expressed her resentment against the Hindu society thus "I consider it better for myself and my fellow sisters to forsake that Hindu religion, which has condemned me to this state of degradation. If, in my lifetime, I happen to meet a Hindu widow, I would advise her to follow the same path". The author concludes 'wake up, Hindus, listen to the fearful wailings of widows, which signify the ruination of Hindu community'; Bengal Ki Vidhwaein, Ibid., December, 1927, p. 407; Hindu Istriyon Ki Loot, Ibid., p. 9; Bhuliye Mat, Bharat Ki Do Karor Vidhwaon Ko, Ibid., p. 11; Bengal Mein Vidhwaon Ki Samkhya, Anath Rakshak, February, 1926, p. 11; Hinduon Ka Hwas, Ibid., p. 12; Hindu Vidhwaein Musalman Banti Hain, *Prabhat*, May 11, 1926. The *Prabhat* while publishing a news item from *Indian Daily Mail* of 20 April said, " ... every proud Hindu should read the following ... with a heavy heart and bend his head in shame": "Recently in the Jamnagar State, many widows got converted to Islam and married Muslims. This incident has sent shock

waves in the Hindu community, who demanded a law from the officials of the State to prevent further conversions to Islam". The paper further said, "... this is one example of how Hindus continue to remain slaves of customs and traditions in order to commit atrocities on the widows. Instead of learning something from the commotion that has been generated by the recent conversions of the widows, they desire to perpetuate persecution by means of a law". (*Translation mine*) Vidhwashram, *Arya Mitra*, December 14, 1933; Vidhwaen Dharadhar Bedharm Ho Rahin Hain, this was an advertisement put by the Jhansi Vidhwa Ashram, which was regularly published in the journals of the Arya Samaj in Hindu and Gujrati, *Arya Mitra*, May, 1925; *Vidhwa Bandhu*, November, 1927, p. 6; Vidhwa Vivah Ki Avashyakta, *Arya Mitra*, October 18, 1934; Vidhwaon par Samaj ka Atyachar aur us ka Phal, *Arya Martand*, April 5, 1928; Chetavani, *Anath Rakshak*, July, 1925; Hindu Vidhwaon ki Kathortam Heen Dasha, Ibid., September, 1924; Vidhwaon par Atyachar, Ibid., September, 1927; Vidhwaon ke Prati Hindu Janta ka Kartavya, Ibid., July, 1925; Aushadhi, Ibid., February, 1926; Do Karod Hindu Vidhwaon ki Sudh Le (An appeal published by Rajasthan Vanita Ashram) *Arya Martand*, July 4, 1928.

58. Well-known preachers of the Arya Samaj, Swami Survanand and Purvanand in their discourses on widow remarriage in Amritsar exhorted people to strengthen the hands of society and ameliorate their own condition by taking to widow remarriage, *Tribune*, February 24, 1918.
59. These advertisements were generally published under the heading 'Shuddhi aur Punarvivah'. For details, see, *Arya Martand*, April 24, 1928; June 14, 1929; *Arya Mitra*, March 9, 1933; *Vidhwa Bandhu*, January, 1926, p. 11.
60. *Vidhwa Bandhu*, January, 1927, p. 4.
61. *Vidhwa Bandhu*, August, 1930, p. 21.
62. For details of these marriages see, *Arya Martand*, July 10, 1934; *Arya Martand*, June 6, 1938.
63. The most commendable one was celebrated in Meerut District. Pandit Mukhtar Singh, a leading Sanatanist Brahmin and the chief of 84 villages in Meerut, got married to the widowed daughter of Pt Data Ram. *Arya Martand*, June 6, 1928. In Mathura, too, the *Vidhwa Vivah Sahayak Sabha's* attempts bore fruit when they succeeded in arranging the remarriage of the child widow belonging to a highly distinguished family of the *Agarwals*, with the cooperation of the Chief of the *Biradari*. *Anath Rakshak*, December, 1925, p. 14 and *Vidhwa Bandhu*, January, 1926, p. 10.
64. From 1927 onwards, the Conference was named 'Doaba Widow Remarriage Conference' and it was resolved that, hitherto, it may be held in places, other than Jullunder, for a wider diffusion of widow remarriages. *Vidhwa Bandhu*, November, 1927, p. 30.

65. Jordens, *Swami Shraddhanand: His Life and Causes*, p. 161.
66. *Arya Mitra*, December 21, 1933.
67. Jordens, op. cit., p. 156.
68. *Vidhwa Bandhu*, November, 1927, p. 33.
69. *Tenth Annual Report of the Vidhwa Vivah Sahayak Sabha*, p. 1.
70. Prakash Tondon, *Punjabi Century*, p. 109.
71. For details see, *Tribune*, October 27, 1915; November 6, 1915.
72. For details regarding the numbers of widow remarriages, refer, *Tenth Annual Report of the Vidhwa Vivah Sahayak Sabha*, p. 2. In 1923, Bengal was visited nine times, Rajputana and Madras, once, Ibid.
73. *Tenth Annual Report of Vidhwa Vivah Sahayak Sabha*, pp. 2–3.
74. *Vidhwa Bandhu*, August, 1930.
75. *Tenth Annual Report of Vidhwa Vivah Sahayak Sabha*. In January, 1926, out of 32 men desirous of marrying widows 16 were bachelors; 12 of them belonged to Punjab. *Vidhwa Bandhu*, January, 1926, pp. 38–42. Similarly in January, 1927, out of 54 men desirous of marrying widows, 30 were bachelors, 27 belonged to Punjab. Ibid., January, 1927, pp. 38–42.
76. S.R. Singh, *Nationalism and Social Reform in India*, p. 210 and Indra Vidyavachaspati, op. cit., p. 290.
77. In July, 1928, Devendra Chandra Dhoot preached widow remarriage in Jhansi, *Arya Martand*, July 25, 1928; in October, 1934, Ved Prakash Vedalankar preached widow remarriage in Gonda and set up *Vidhwa Vivah Sahayak Sabha* there, *Arya Mitra*, November 22, 1934.
78. *Arya Mitra*, April 6, 1933.
79. For details, see *Arya Mitra*, February 23, 1933; November 23, 1933.
80. For details see, *Arya Mitra*, February 23, 1933; March 9, 1933; March 30, 1933; April 6, 1933; April 27, 1933; June 8, 1933; June 15, 1933; June 29, 1933; July 6, 1933; July 13, 1933; July 20, 1933; October 10, 1933; November 23, 1933; September 6, 1934; October 10, 1934; November 22, 1934, December 6, 1934.
81. *Tenth Annual Report of the Vidhwa Vivah Sahayak Sabha*, p. 3.
82. For details see, *Vidhwa Bandhu*, January, 1926, pp. 10–11 and 36–37; January, 1927, pp. 27–34.
83. Ibid., January, 1930, pp. 11–12.
84. *Arya Mitra*, November 22, 1934.
85. *Arya Mitra*, September 17, 1933; September 6, 1933.
86. *Vidhwa Bandhu*, August, 1930, p. 22.
87. *Vidhwa Bandhu*, January, 1927, p. 19.
88. *Tenth Annual Report of the Vidhwa Vivah Sahayak Sabha*, p. 3.
89. *Madras Prant Mein Vidwa Vivah*, an article by Dinanath Sidhantalankar, *Vidhwa Bandhu*, August, 1930.

90. Santosh Yadav, *Unnisvin aur Biswin Shatabdi Mein Strion Ki Stithi*, pp. 153–154.
91. Ibid., p. 155; *Vidhwa Bandhu*, January, 1926.
92. See, Marwarion Mein Vidhwa Vivah Andolan, *Vidhwa Bandhu*, January, 1926, p. 13; Akhil Bhartiya Maheshwari Sabha, Pandharpur aur Vidhwa Vivah, Ibid., November, 1927, pp. 21–23.
93. *Vidhwa Bandhu*, January, 1926, pp. 22–37; January, 1927, pp. 22–37.
94. *Tenth Annual Report of Vidhwa Vivah Sahayak Sabha*, p. 11.
95. "Dhanyavad hai us prabhu ka jisne paida kiya Sir Ganga Ram ko … , Shrimati Kamla Devi, *Vidhwa Bandhu*, January, 1927, p. 19.
96. *Tribune*, September 27, 1910.
97. *Tribune*, October 24, 1891, cited from, Jones, *Arya Samaj in Punjab*, p. 107.
98. Rajendra Jigyasu (ed.), *Mahatma Hansram Granthavali*, Vol. 4, p. 128.
99. Pandit Visnu Lal Shastri, op. cit., p. 98.
100. The *Arya Directory* (1941) gives 1924 as the year of its establishment while Dr Ganga Prasad Upadhyaya has laid down 1933 as the year of its establishment. G.P. Upadhyaya, *Origin, Scope and Mission of Arya Samaj*, p. 21.
101. *Arya Directory* (1941), pp. 189–89.
102. The advertisements released by these *ashrams* highlighted the urgency of retaining the widows within the precincts of Hindu religion. *Vidhwa Dharadhar Bedharm Ho Rahin Hain*, Advertisement put up by Vidhwa Ashram, Jhansi, *Arya Mitra*, May, 1925; *Do Karod Hindu Vidhwaon Ki Sudh Le*, Advertisement put up by Rajasthan Vanita Ashram, *Arya Martand*, July 4, 1928; *Bhuliye Mat, Bharat Ki Do Karod Vidhwaon Ko*, Advertisement put up by Saharanput Hindu Vanita Ashram, *Vidhwa Bandhu*, December, 1927, pp. 11–12.
103. *47th Annual Report of Shrimaddayanand Orphanage*.
104. *Our Services to Jodhpur State*, a pamphlet brought out by Shrimaddayanand Orphanage, Ajmer.
105. *Arya Martand*, July 4, 1928; *Arya Mitra*, May, 1925; *Vidhwa Bandhu*, December, 1927, pp. 11–12.
106. In 1931, three out of nine such women were sent back to their guardians, whereas in 1932, four out of five women were sent back to their guardians. *36th and 38th Annual Reports of Shrimaddayanand Orphanage*. In 1926, Rajasthan Vanita Ashram restored 12 out of 35 women rescued and sent to their respective guardians. *First Annual Report of Rajasthan Vanita Ashram*, Ajmer.
107. *Shrimaddayanand Vidhwa Ashram Ke Niyam*, (Source: Shrimati Paropkarini Sabha, Ajmer).
108. The matrimonial advertisements of widows of Rajasthan Vanita Ashram were generally released in *Arya Martand*, a journal of the *Arya Pratinidhi Sabha*, Rajasthan, *Arya Martand*, July 15, 1928; February 9, 1928; June 15,

1938; April 1, 1938; April 15, 1938; July 15, 1928. Shrimaddayanand Orphanage released the details of its widows keen to get married in its journal, *Anath Rakshak*. Saharanpur Hindu Vanita Ashram published such advertisements in its journal, *Hindu Sambhand Sahayak*.

109. In 1926–27, Rajasthan Vanita Ashram commemorated seven remarriages. *First Annual Report of Rajasthan Vanita Ashram*. It arranged 13 remarriages from November 1, 1925 to October 31, 1926, two in 1933 and six in 1929, *31st 38th and 34th Annual Report of Shrimaddayanand Orphanage*. Also, *Vidhwa Bandhu*, December, 1927, p. 11; *Vidhwa Bandhu*, December, 1927, p. 11.

110. In 1926–27, nine widows delivered children in Rajasthan Vanita Ashram. *First Annual Report of Rajasthan Vanita Ashram*. Also, *Vidhwa Bandhu*, December, 1927, p. 11; *Shrimaddayanand Vidhwa Ashram Ke Niyam*; *Arya Mitra*, May, 1925.

111. In 1925, Jhansi *Vidhwa Ashram* published a tract Dilli Ka Khunkhar Maula. Copies of the tract and other publications of the Ashram were distributed free of cost, *Arya Mitra*, May, 1925.

112. *First Annual Report of Rajasthan Vanita Ashram*.

113. *Vidhwa Bandhu*, December, 1927, pp. 11–12.

114. *Arya Mitra*, November 22, 1934.

115. *Anath Rakshak*, September, 1926.

116. *Tenth Annual Report of the Vidhwa Vivah Sahayak Sabha*, p. 3.

117. *Arya Martand*, October 9, 1931, cited from, R.K. Saxena, *Education and Social Amelioration of Women in Rajasthan*, p. 183.

118. See, *Annual Reports of Shrimaddayanand Orphanage* and *Anath Rakshak*, December, 1925.

119. See, *Arya Magazine*, April, 1883 and July, 1883.

120. *Tenth Annual Report of the Vidhwa Vivah Sahayak Sabha*, p. 12.

121. *Vidhwa Bandhu*, January, 1926, pp. 3–4.

122. 'Kya Vastava Mein Vidhwa Vidhan Ki Samasya Samajik Vishwa Ke Hwas Ka Mool Karan Hai', by Pt Ram Bhajan Mishra, *Arya Martand*, December 17, 1937; Divya Sandesh, by Vaidya Bhushan Pt Haridutt, Ibid., February 9, 1928; *Anath Rakshak*, the monthly journal of Dayanand Orphanage also highlighted the plight of widows in its columns. Vidhwaon Aur Anathon Ki Vritti Ka Prashan, *Anath Rakshak*, April, 1911; Hindu Vidhwa Ki Dard Bhari Kahani, Ibid., December, 1925; *Vidhwa Vivah*, Ibid., December, 1935.

123. J.P. Choudhary Kavyatirth, *Vidhwa Vivah Prashnotri*, Tract Parcharak Mandal, Kashi, 1927 (Source: Dayanand Shodh Peeth, Chandigarh).

124. Ibid., p. 5.

125. Ku. Chand Karan Sarda, *Vidhwa Vivah Karo*, Vedic Yantralaya, Ajmer, 1924.

126. Harishankar Dube, *Vidhwodvah Vivek*, Mahesh Pustakalaya, Ajmer.

127. Ganpati Vedopdeshak, *Vidhwa Vivah Aapatdharma Hai*, 1928; Other important tracts were Shyamji Sharma Kavyatirth, *Kya Vidhwa Vivah Adharm Hai*; Akhilanand Sharma, *Vaidhavya Vidhvansan Champu*; Ganga Prasad Upadhyaya, *Vidhwa Insaf* aur *Vidhwa Vivah Mimansa*; Triyambak Rao Sathe, *Vidhwa Vivah Samvad* and Narayan Dutt Sharma Kashyap, *Vidhwaon par Atyachar.*
128. Harinandan Ayurvedacharya in a pamphlet written by him underscored the need to set up more widow homes to provide shelter and dignity to the widows. Harinandan Ayurvedacharya, *Vidhwa Vivah Vichar*, Arya Samaj, Bikaner, 1920.
129. Swami Karmanand Saraswati, *Nari Punarvivah Mimansa*, Arya Samaj, Hyderabad Deccan, 1932. Other tracts that underscored the urgency of widow remarriage in order to save the Hindu society were *Hindu Strion ki Loot ke Karan, Hinduon Jago, Hindu Jati ki Raksha ke Upaya, Vidhwaen aur Desh ka Nash, Dukhdayi Durvysan, Shri Swami Shraddhanandji ka Balidan* and *Hindu Sanghathan ka Mool Mantra*
130. Bhumitra Sharma, *Niyoga Mardan ka Vimardan*, published by Raghuvir Saran Dublis, 1920; Lakshman Aryopdeshak, *Niyoga Praman, Arya Musafir Mission Granthmala I*, 1900; Other tracts on *niyoga* were Lakshman Aryopdeshak's, *Niyoga Praman* and *Tahajivul Mirza ya Niyoga* in 1901 in response to Tahajivul Mirza's, *Arya Dharma*; *Niyoga Niranaya*, written in the 1920s, constituted yet another lengthy document on *niyoga.*

‖Chapter 6‖

Liberating Women

Marriage, Caste and *Purda*

Dayanand had undertaken a holistic appraisal of the reforms critical for the resurgence of Hindu society. He had laid down an all-inclusive scheme of reforms in major spheres of societal activities – marriage, education, religion, caste and status of women. While Dayanand's major concern was the regeneration of the Hindu race, he laid great emphasis on the centrality of women as individuals, wives and mothers in bringing about this transformation. However, to equip and enable women to fulfil this historic role, many evil practices, especially those related to marriage and caste, had to be eradicated. The institutions of marriage and caste, which emerged as the basic organizing structure of the Indian society, had determined to a large extent the social life and behavioural norms for both, men and women. However, over the period of time, rules and regulations that governed these two institutions became crucial instruments for controlling and managing female sexuality. Women's behaviour became critical to the preservation of ritual purity of the caste. If women indulged in behaviour, especially in the arena of marriage and sexual relationships, that violated the rules, norms and values of a particular caste then not only the purity of women but ritual purity and honour of the entire group was endangered. Different notions regarding male and female sexuality meant that while caste rules controlled and regulated lives of both men and women but the latter were punished severely and, at times much more brutally for their transgression. Multifarious control mechanisms were devised to control and contain female sexuality resulting in child marriage, marriage within sub-caste, prohibition of widow remarriage, permanence of marriage tie and curtailment of freedom of women. Women were constrained from exercising choices especially in the realm of marriage, sexual relationships, dress, mobility, education etc. Many social reformers like Vivekananda, Jyotiba Phule, N.G. Chandavarkar and Pt Ramabai looked upon caste as the greatest hurdle to the betterment of the condition of women. The crystallization of caste system and its concomitant notions of ritual purity in the post-Vedic period thus had serious implications with regard to the position of women. Quite significantly, these restrictions were more widespread amongst the upper castes while amongst the lower ranked castes control over women's sexuality was not so stringent. Therefore, any caste that aspired to rise in caste hierarchy viewed curtailment of women's freedom and strict control over their sexuality as necessary attributes to be practiced by them in order to raise their ritual status. A brief perusal of the caste system and its implications for women makes it clear that substantive changes in the status of women demanded reform in the norms that governed marriage relations. However, any relaxation in these norms would have been possible only with liberalization in the hegemonic and rigorous control of the caste over the lives of women. Dayanand had, therefore, prescribed fundamental changes in the institution of marriage and caste that remained pertinent to the low status of women in the Hindu society. After his death, the Arya Samajists endeavoured to realize the exponent's vision as far as reforms in these institutions were concerned.

Campaign against Unequal Marriages

As a practical reformer, concerned with procreation of a healthy race, the institution of marriage had immense utilitarian value for Dayanand. He nevertheless realized that the institution of marriage was plagued by customs like unequal marriages and child marriages. Dayanand therefore visualized wide-ranging reforms to revitalize the institution. His perspective on issues like child marriages, unequal marriages and position of widows, apart from being motivated by his larger concern for upliftment of the Aryan race, were aimed at redeeming the status and position of women.

Dayanand laid great stress on compatibility between husband and wife as the basis of a happy conjugal life and reproduction of healthy children. Wifehood, for him, meant comradeship, companionship and assistance in fulfilling life's duties and its true functions. He laid great stress on the complimentary model of conjugal relationship. His immense faith in the team of husband and wife as the basis of social progress demanded compatibility of *guna*, *karma* and *svabhava*. Consequently, Dayanand emerged as a steadfast champion of equal marriages. While conforming to popular Hinduism by proposing marriage between individuals belonging to the same caste, he radically diverged from the Hindu orthodoxy, when he pleaded for the determination of caste on the basis of merit rather than on birth.

Dayanand's concept of equal marriages demanded a virtual rejection of caste rules and was tantamount to inter-caste marriage. The Samajists realized that substantive reforms in the institution of marriages should be preceded by a relaxation in the norms, rules and regulations that governed the caste system. However, they desisted from resorting to social radicalism in the nineteenth century and therefore approached the subject with tremendous caution. Throughout the nineteenth century, the Arya Samaj was too complacent on the issue of inter-caste marriages. In the 1890s, when Mahatma Munshiram, later Swami Shraddhanand, tried to bring up this particular reform by proposing that marriages of Arya Samajists should be arranged not in accordance with the rules of the caste, but on the basis of compatibility of *guna*, *karma* and *svabhava* of the partners, he was ignored by the conservative elements within the Samaj as an extreme radical. The Samajists expressed little inclination to disregard completely their caste ties with traditional Hinduism. In this connection, Jordens has rightly observed, "For the first twenty years, the Punjab Arya Samaj had remained extremely moderate, in the sense that its members were very reluctant to put any of the social principles of the Samaj into hard practice. Their social and ritual way of life was utterly dominated by what one could call caste orthodoxy."[1]

Quite significantly, even in the nineteenth century some leading Arya Samajist leaders had taken initiative in this direction. The leaders of the Punjab Arya Samaj had dispensed with their caste names as early as 1886. The five leaders elected by the College Party in 1898, Lala

Hans Raj, Lala Lal Chand, Lala Ishwar Das, Lala Mul Raj, Lala Lajpat Rai for holding talks for the merger of the two groups did not use their caste names. Similar was the case with the five leaders elected by the Gurukul section – Lala Munshiram, Lala Ram Krishan, Lala Rala Ram, Rai Peda Ram and Lala Dev Raj. Another remarkable instance that exemplifies the progressive stance of the Samajists in Punjab was the conferment of the title of '*Pandit*' on Gurudatt, a Vaishya by birth, to commemorate his intellectual feats, academic excellence and knowledge of *Vedas*.[2] In the rest of India, however, Arya Samaj did not even resort to these symbolic gestures to repudiate caste.

The *Shuddhi* movement is another example that suggests some kind of caste reform. Apart from reclaiming Hindus who had converted to other religions, it was used for raising the status of the untouchables.[3] Dispensation of caste names and reclamation of low castes, however, did not lead to an erosion of caste hegemony. Moreover, the Arya Samajists were unswerving in their loyalty to caste customs, particularly in the domain of marriage alliances the Samajists adhered to the conventional rules.

The failure of the Samaj in undertaking any bold steps on the issue of reformation of caste system began to be perceived by radical and younger groups as indifference towards the exponent's vision. The articles in the journals of the Samaj sought to explain this failure. For instance, it was contended that tedious progress in this direction was on account of the fact that a small number of Arya Samajists were placed in a hostile atmosphere where they had to confront conservative Hindus who were opposed to any kind of reform.[4] Moreover, some articles contended that while Arya Samajist men were progressive in outlook, their women in the homes still adhered to a traditional way of life, thereby inhibiting the cause of reform. It was also argued that threats of excommunication by the community or *biradari* loomed large over the Samajists if they advocated radical reform, particularly those related to marriage and caste.

. The persistent apathy of the Samaj towards securing a reform, which was highly cherished by their exponent, led to the emergence of radical wings within the Samaj, which demanded compliance with Dayanand's ideology.

These radical groups belonged to the Mahatma section of the Punjab Arya Samaj. Arya Shiromani Sabha, set up by Dr Chiranjilal sought to bring into actual practice the ideals and directives promulgated by Swami Dayanand. Abrogation of all caste regulations regarding commensality and marriage formed one of their cardinal principles. They aspired to evolve families where husband and wife were "real companions"[5] The Sabha, however, failed to realize its ideals, for its leaders left for England.

Arya Bhratri Sabha, with similar aims but a more radical approach was set up in 1895. The members decided to forsake caste restrictions among themselves. The caste was to be decided on the basis of *guna*, *karma* and *svabhava* and in the settlement of marriages they would disregard orthodox rules and would adhere to the four classes as suggested by Swami Dayanand. Unfortunately, even the Arya Bhratri Sabha never went beyond the stage of formulation of ideals. Referring to the Arya Bhratri Sabha and its proposals for reformation of caste system, J. Ried Graham has remarked, "Although the Arya Bhratri proposals were in line with Dayanand's marriage reforms, in fact, one may say that this was the first earnest attempt to take Dayanand's caste reform proposals seriously, nevertheless the majority of the Arya Samajists realized that it meant a full break with the castes, to which they belonged. Instead of being a moderate reform policy, it was as far-reaching in its effects as the Brahmo Samaj's open repudiation of caste. Arya Samaj, as a whole, was not ready to break with old caste divisions". Even more radical than these two organizations was the Arya Dharma Sabha founded in 1897. It was in favour of drastic changes in the position of women and the caste system. This organization also failed to make any headway as far as relaxation in caste rules was concerned.[6]

The failure of the Samaj to make a dent in the unbending rules of the caste, despite its ideological repudiation, led to disparaging observations. Farquhar, in his book, *Modern Religious Movements* (1916) criticized the Arya Samajists for indulging in "far more talk (on the issue of caste reform) than action."[7] Even the *Census of India* 1901 (North Western Province & Oudh Report) made the following observation, "they hold to the four-fold division into *Brahmin*, *Kshatriyas*, *Vaishyas* and *Sudras*, but the general trend of opinion seems to be towards the doctrine promulgated in the Institutes of Manu and the *Mahabharata* that caste should not be regarded, merely as determined by birth, for a man's occupation, knowledge of the *Vedas*, and way of life must also be considered. To accept such a view in entirety could involve cutting adrift from the Hindus of today, and the Aryas are not at present prepared to do this, but the reform of the caste system is steadily kept in view, and some advance has been made. While no case has been reported to me in which a marriage has been effected between the totally unconnected castes, I have heard of two marriages which would undoubtedly conflict with the ordinary views of orthodox Hinduism. In one, a *Dai Ghar Khattri* married his daughter to an *Arora* and in the other a *Sanadhya Brahmin* girl was married to a *Bajpai Brahmin*".[8]

The Samajists, in fact, found themselves in dilemma that a leading Arya Samajist Ganga Prasad Upadhyaya expressed thus: "Some people complain that in this respect the Arya Samaj has been too slow. It should be admitted that there remains much to be done. But if you take into consideration the fact that the Arya Samaj has not isolated itself from the Hindu society and one aim of the Arya Samaj has been to carry the Hindus with it, you will find that the Arya Samaj has not been idle".[9]

The tardy progress of the Arya Samaj, however, did not deter Swami Shraddhanand, the spokesman and leader of the Mahatma section of the Samaj, to carry on an unrelenting campaign for advancing the cause of equal marriages. In his first journal, *Saddharmapracharak,* he made an impassioned appeal to the Arya Samajists to put the tenets of Swami Dayanand into practice. He urged them to disregard caste regulations and open a register to facilitate marriages on the basis of *guna*, *karma* and *svabhava*. *Varnavyavastha*, the first pamphlet, which Munshiram published in his *Saddharmapracharak,* reproached the Arya Samaj for "despite a great deal of lip service, nothing concrete has been done to show that it really believes in principles". He appealed to the Samajists to seriously ponder over two areas of caste reform – marriage alliances and commensal regulations. While laying great stress on individual action, he said, "We do not agree with those who hold the opinion that everything will right itself with the passage of time. Time does not heal anything unless society itself moves. And society, which is but a collection of individuals does not move unless its members are prepared to do so".[10]

Shraddhanand proved his commitment to the cause when, he arranged the wedding of a Brahmin widow girl Sumitra with a non-Brahmin doctor Gurudatt in 1909.[11] His radicalism was subjected to scathing criticism from both the groups within the Samaj. While the moderates held that such radicalism would prove detrimental for the nascent Samaj, the radical groups took him to task for not commemorating his own daughter's marriage in a similar fashion. Shraddhanand silenced the diatribes of the radical wing when a year later he married his own daughter Hemant Kumari to Sukhdeo, an Arora.[12] *Arya Patrika*, which had become the organ of the radical groups from 1896 onwards, highly appreciated the marriage, "This is the first marriage in the province in which a leader of thought and opinion ... has done away with unreasonable distinctions of caste. Who is there, among the educated classes in India that does not feel the tyranny of caste and the fearful havoc that it is playing in our society? We have seen fathers burst into tears at the sight of the wretched plight in which their daughters had been placed by an unrelenting irony of fate .... [They] had to limit the selection of matches to their own castes. No suitable matches could be found and they were compelled, much against their will, to give away their [educated] daughters to unlettered and ignorant shopkeepers. The evil consequences of such unions manifested themselves in constant quarrels between the husband and the wife and the oppression of the latter by the former. For the people thus circumstanced – for men who have already have a bitter experience of caste restrictions and for those who wish to avoid them – here is an example to follow".[13]

In 1911, Swami Shraddhanand gave a clarion call the *Hindu Sanghathan*. The resuscitation of the '*Varna Dharma*' formed an intrinsic part of the movement for *Hindu Sanghathan*. He advocated a slow and gradual elimination of the traditional caste system along with its numerous castes and sub-castes. He said, "In the first place, all distinctions of sub-castes must cease, and no non-caste sects amongst the Hindus be recognized ... there should be no difficulty in all the sub-castes and even non-castes consisting of the so-called untouchables being absorbed in the four principal castes." The second stage involved the beginning of free marriage relations, "to begin with within the castes and *anuloma* marriages ought not to be introduced. And gradually in the third stage, *pratiloma* marriages ought to be introduced. And lastly, *guna*, *karma*, i.e., character and conduct should become the determining factors in fixing the *varna* of an individual".[14]

Swami Shraddhanand also strove to revive the ancient custom of *Swayamvara*. The commemoration of the ritual upheld by Dayanand as a form of choice marriage and also an attempt to fix marriages on the basis of compatible temperament and qualifications rather than on the basis of caste rules. Inspired by his writings in the *Saddharmapracharak*, Dhanpatrai of Kantak had requested him to arrange the *Swayamvara* of his daughter Bhagwandevi. His efforts, however, proved abortive due to the stiff opposition of the caste. He felt highly dejected when Bhagawandevi was married off to a widower, with one child.[15] In March 1923, a *Swayamvara* was organized by the Jodhpur Arya Samaj. The proceedings of the *Swayamvara,* however, took a lamentable turn when none from the large assemblage of men was willing to come upon the stage for his selection as bridegroom. A spectator of the entire drama woefully remarked, "In this situation, is it appropriate to boast that the debate over the question of caste has been fully resolved and marriages are performed on the basis of *guna* and *karma*. It is manifest that activism is still found wanting in the *Arya Jagat*".[16] The first successful *Swayamvara* was held in Lucknow, in December 1916. The bride, granddaughter of Pyarelalji, interviewed the prospective bridegrooms individually and selected Pt Vasudev of Kashi.[17] Yet another *Swayamvara* was accomplished in Kanpur in February 1926.[18] The concept of *Swayamvara* marriages was, however, a utopian proposition in a society where rules of caste and the subordinate status of women rendered it impractical.

The unrelenting crusade of the Gurukul section against the strictures of caste had a liberalizing impact on the Arya Samaj as a whole. Hitherto, the Gurukul party had spearheaded the reforms in the institutions of caste and marriage. Despite their compliance with the cause of equal marriages, the involvement of the leaders of the College party in its furtherance was insignificant. The second decade of the twentieth century saw the movement for inter-caste marriages and equal marriages gathering momentum among both the factions of the Arya Samajists. Lala Lajpat Rai, leader of the DAV faction highlighted the need for equal marriages in his new book, *The Arya Samaj*. Ruling aside caste as a major determinant in marriage alliances, he considered love and attachment between the husband and wife as the basic requirement for a happy marriage and this could come only with some social companionship before marriage. He not only suggested that girls should see their prospective husbands before marriage but that the "parties to marriage must know each other before they are united in wedlock".[19] He held that in ancient times, courtship was not altogether unknown in the Hindu society. In 1922, Bhai Parmanand and other leaders of the DAV faction founded the Jat Pat Todak Mandal with the express aim of promoting inter-caste marriages and interdining.[20]

A *Varna Vyavasthapak Mandal* was set up for determination of *varnas* of the Arya Samajists. The Sarvadeshik Arya Pratinidhi Sabha directed its attention towards caste reform in the 1920s. In December 1927, a resolution was passed, requesting the provincial Pratinidhi Sabhas and the *Updeshaks* and workers under their auspices, to motivate people to dispense with their caste names in the forthcoming census surveys and enlist themselves as *Arya*. [21] In March, 1934, the Sabha resolved that the officials serving on the governing committees of the provincial and *Sarvadeshik Arya Pratinidhi Sabhas* should only be those who had repudiated the traditional caste hierarchy and its strictures. It was also decided that attempts would be made to include the following by-laws; "any individual conforming to caste by birth would be ineligible for serving on the working committees of the Pratinidhi Sabhas, both at the provincial and national levels".

Despite the untiring efforts of the Samajists for the promotion of equal marriages, marriages on the basis of *guna* and *karma* were still very scarce, even among the Arya Samajists.[22] Inter-caste marriages were not held lawful by the Hindu law and the Samajists viewed this as a big hurdle. They, therefore, initiated an intensive campaign for the enactment of a law that would provide for the legality of such marriages. In the Arya Maha Sammelan in Mathura, it was resolved that henceforth, consistent efforts would be made in this direction.[23] Choudhary Mukhtar Singh and Ghanshyam Singh Gupta moved the bill for the same in the years 1930 and 1935, respectively. In 1937, Arya Marriage Validation Act XIX was passed by the Central Legislature, which provided for the legitimacy of inter-caste marriages among the Arya Samajists.[24] Even after the passing of the Act, the Samajists pursued the cause with great vigour. In 1937, Arya Pratinidhi Sabha, Rajasthan appealed to the Prime Minister of the Jodhpur state to legalize inter-caste marriages and widow remarriages held under the auspices of the Arya Samaj. In response to their plea, the Jodhpur State Council recognized the Arya Marriage Validation Act, 1937. In the year 1942, the Arya Samaj in Jaipur persuaded the ruler of the erstwhile Jaipur state to enforce the Act in his state.[25]

The Samajist crusade against ill-matched marriages had a liberalizing impact on the educated classes of the Hindu society. While it is difficult to concede that they succeeded in breaking the walls of tradition and custom, it can be convincingly argued that they were instrumental in making a dent in the hegemonic structure and strictures of the caste that had so rigourously controlled the lives of men and particularly women. The relaxation in the rules related to marriage had a favourable impact on the status of women who suffered immeasurably on account of caste rules. While the Samaj was criticized for its partial success in this sphere, it is seldom realized that it required tremendous courage, perseverance and zeal to challenge and erode entrenched structures and practices. These changes were indeed revolutionary, particularly if they are appreciated keeping in view the social structures and social context of the times when they were espoused and executed.

Campaign against Early Marriages

The problem of early marriage, like that of equal marriages, was inextricably linked with the strictures of the caste. The rule regarding marriage within one's own sub-caste led to the paucity of suitable matches, resulting in early marriages. Slowly and gradually, child marriages became a part of the normative behaviour and discipline required from members of the caste. The Samajists had grave apprehensions of engendering a virtual break with caste if they insisted on grown-up marriages. Dr Burns, in the census report of the North Western Provinces and Oudh, observed, "The Samaj holds strong views on the subject of marriage and it is laid down that girls should not be married before the age of thirteen, and that a more suitable time is fourteen to sixteen, while bridegroom's should be at least eighteen The question of age of marriage, is, however, merely a portion of the wider question of caste restrictions as a whole, and, in regard to these, it may be said generally that the preaching of the members of the Samaj is in advance of their practice".[26]

Like other issues related to marriage and caste, in this domain too, it was the Mahatma section of the Samaj, which initiated a fiery crusade against child marriages. The first lecture of Swami Shraddhanand, the tireless crusader of the nascent Samaj, in the Jalandhar Arya Samaj in 1885, was on the 'Evils of Child Marriage and the Veneration of *Brahmacharya*.'[27] Towards the end of the century, the Samajists came out with innumerable tracts and pamphlets on the evil of child marriage. Some of these were Munshi Chatar Biharilal's *Risala-i-Dharma Mitra* in 1893, Bawa Chajju Singh's '*Brahmcharya* versus Child Marriage Tract No.1' in 1893, 'A Well Wisher of the Hindus, Claims of the Arya Samaj on the Hindus', in 1900.[28] Swami Shraddhanand wrote a number of articles in his *Saddharmpracharak*.[29]

The child marriages, however, continued to be rampant, not only amongst the Hindus in general, but even amongst the Arya Samajists. The census of the North Western Provinces and Oudh gave the following number of married girls, for every 10,000 females:

Table 6.1

Number of Married Girls per 10,000 Females

Age	*Hindus*	*Mohammedans*	*Jains*	*Aryas*
0–10	157	116	56	82
10–15	602	457	419	442

Source: Census of India 1901, Vol. XVI, p.156.[30]

The child marriages received a setback with the spread of education among the boys and girls. The DAV schools adopted a practical approach towards the removal of the practice when a rule was laid down that no married boys would be admitted to the primary section.[31] Later on, it was resolved by the Management Committee of the DAV College that boarding house facilities would not be extended to those who were married.[32] This was followed by denial of admission to married students to the middle section of the DAV School.[33] Due to the spread of education, the marriageable age of girls increased on its own. The girls admitted to Kanya Mahavidyalaya were not allowed to leave the school in most of the cases, till they finished the course of 12 years.[34] Partly, due to the spread of education among the Samajist girls, the marriageable age of Arya Samajist women was higher than the general Hindu women. E.A.W. Blunt, a census officer in 1911, made the interesting observation that whilst the number of married or widowed Hindu girls under 10 years is 61 per 1000, in northern India, the similar number among the Arya Samajists is only 21 and of those a majority were probably married before conversion.[35] Like the widow remarriage movement, the efforts to raise the age of marriage, too met with stern opposition from the orthodox Hindus. Pandit Din Dayal[36], who spearheaded the slander campaign against the Arya Samaj, delivered innumerable lectures advocating marriage of girls below ten years of age.

In the meantime, Swami Shraddhanand launched his fiery crusade for *Hindu Sanghathan* and included grown-up marriages as yet another dimension of the movement.[37] For the preservation of the Hindu race, he appealed for the revival of the ancient *Ashram Dharma* according to which the minimum marriageable age for males should be 25 and 18 for females. The Samajists published tracts to justify their stand on grown-up marriages. Pandit Chuttanlal Swami wrote a tract '*Vivah Vayo-Vichar*' in 1927. The leader of the College party, Lala Lajpat Rai, too, wholeheartedly joined the crusade against the evil practice.[38]

Har Bilas Sarda, a prominent Arya Samajist and a member of the Central Assembly moved a Bill in the Assembly known as the Child Marriage Restraint Bill. The Bill was introduced in the Assembly on 15th September 1927. In his speech the Legislative Assembly in Simla, he remarked that the primary object of the Bill was to put a stop to child widowhood. The secondary aim of the Bill was 'to remove the principal impediment to the physical and mental growth of the youth of both sexes and the chief cause of their premature decay and death'. Har Bilas Sarda considered the Bill as a modest attempt 'to recognize that female children, even amongst Hindus, have certain inalienable rights and that the state with any pretensions to civilization will deem its duty to protect them, without heeding the vagaries that masquerade in the guise of social customs'. Sarda strengthened his argument by citing the authority of *Manu Smriti* and *Dhanwantri*. "My Bill", he remarked, "does not go against the spirit or the letter of any religious behest; for no *Shastras*, ancient or modern, enjoin that a girl must be married before she attains puberty".

Sarda faced stiff opposition from the Government. The Home Member declared that he would oppose the Bill.[39] Har Bilas Sarda tried to mobilize public opinion in his favour. He appealed to the wives of the members of British Government in India to support the Bill. He also wrote to the woman members of the House of Commons in Britain to appeal to the British Government in India to be neutral rather than actively oppose the bill.[40] The bill was passed on 23rd September, 1929. The Child Marriage Restraint Act is also known as the Sarda Act, due to the contribution put in by Dewan Bahadur Har Bilas Sarda. The Act established minimum ages for marriage; 18 for boys and 14 for girls. The Act suffered from numerous limitations. The declaration of Home Member that the 'Child Marriage Act though passed would not come into force till April the following year', was strongly condemned by Har Bilas Sarda on the grounds that it would lead to thousands of child marriages. The Government, however, refused to change its stand.[41]

Moreover, the provisions number four and five of the Sarda Act hindered its implementation. Firstly, there was no first class magistrate in the villages to prevent such marriages. Secondly, it was difficult for a man of ordinary means to arrange Rs 100 to file a suit in such cases. At times, the parents eager to marry off their children at an early age, simply ignored the Act, and considered the fine of Rs 100 as an additional expense on the occasion of marriage.[42]

Arya Pratinidhi Sabha of the United Provinces directed its sub-Sabhas to discourage people from performing child marriages failing which a legal notice would be served to the following: the bride and the bridegroom; both the *purohits* and barbers, close relatives and friends of both the parties present on the occasion; the district officer and the *daroga* of the police station.[43] The Samajists left no stone unturned to enlighten and educate public opinion on the subject. Kunwar Chand Karan Sarda made an ardent appeal to the people to bring such cases to the notice of the law courts. When any such case reached the courts *Arya Mitra*, journal of Arya Samaj in United provinces, publicized the case and the decision of the court.

To commemorate early marriages, people started going to the native states and the French colonies since the Act was not applicable there. The Arya Samaj therefore, shifted the focus to princely states to motivate the rulers to enact laws against child marriages. Arya Samaj in Jaipur appealed to the ruler of the state to introduce the Child Marriage Restraint Act. The law became operative in Jaipur from 1945 onwards. The decision of the ruler of Jodhpur state to enforce a law for eradication of child and unequal marriages was welcomed by the Arya Samaj of Sardarpur and Punjwa. This announcement had led to a fierce opposition from the orthodox Hindus who sent many letters and petitions to Maharaja Ummed Singh to repeal the same.[44]

The Arya Samajists were, however, disillusioned by the failure of the Act to check the enormous difference between the age of the bride and the bridegroom, which was not very uncommon in those days. The Arya Mahila Conference, held in Lahore, pondered over the issue and held that while the Act would put an end to early marriages, it failed to provide against marriages between a 14-years old girl and a 70-years old man.[45] The editor of *Vidhwa Bandhu*, Shanti Swaroop Vidyalankar, remarked that while some Indian states had accepted resolutions, which disallow marriage between man and women of disparate ages and the British government should enact a similar law.[46] The Sambhar Arya Samaj demanded legislation for prescribing the maximum difference between the age of the bride and the bridegroom.[47]

Marriage Customs

Prolonged ceremonies and excessive ritualism formed an integral part of the Hindu social and religious system in the nineteenth century. Hindu marriages had been reduced to a myriad of innumerable and cumbersome ritualism and customs, taking a heavy toll of an individual's savings. This vicious system was perpetuated and strengthened by the priests who were required to conduct the ceremonies. Large sums, in cash or kind, were given to priests in the form of *dakshina* on each and every ceremony associated with marriage. A major portion of this expenditure was borne by the bride's family. Apart from the expenditure entailed on the performance of ceremonies, there was the reprehensible custom of dowry, which involved the customary payment of a fixed sum of money or gifts to the bridegroom's family. Coupled with the senseless obligation of dowry and costliness of rituals was the highly unproductive expenditure incurred on fire-works, dances by prostitutes, and other forms of extravaganza. All these factors relegated the daughter to a subordinate position in the family. Ganga Prasad Upadhyaya had remarked in this connection, "To have a daughter in the family is to constantly burn in the fire of hell. Where to get money from? No money, no marriage. Several families have met a tragic end."[48]

The Samajists mounted a vigorous campaign against the Hindu orthodoxy for the simplification of marriage rituals and this formed one of their earliest efforts to reform the institution of marriage. Dayanand's *Sanskar Vidhi* had already provided his followers with a series of simple Vedic ceremonies. However, the 'process was both long and difficult' as the Samajists had to fight a grim battle with the Hindu orthodoxy for the acceptance of reformed and simple Vedic rituals. [49]

When the Arya Samaj came forward with its own set of simplified rituals, it posed a threat to the economic position of the *Brahmins*. The Arya Samajist rituals excluded altogether the services of the traditional *Brahmin* priest. Any Samajist himself could conduct them or he could utilize the services of any leading official or educated member of the Samaj. As a consequence of this new development, the Sanatanist *pandits* consolidated themselves and made a concerted attack on the Arya Samajist rituals. Besides, the reformation of marriage rituals was a formidable task, for unlike the question of death ceremonies, which could be altered by one man if he was sufficiently strong-minded, marriage required the agreement of the two contracting families, who in turn needed to face the wrath of their respective lineages. More often than not the decision lay with the groom's family, while the bride's family acquiesced. From 1886 onwards the Samaj insisted on and increasingly conformed to the marriage rituals of the *Sanskar Vidhi*. These ceremonies were short, meaningful and inexpensive as compared to the elaborate and extravagant ceremonies of popular Hinduism.

In the early years, these marriages created uproar in society. Among the first few marriages, commemorated according to Vedic rites, was the marriage of daughter of Mahatma Kirparam. People assembled in large numbers to witness the ceremony and the *Brahmins* offered tremendous opposition to the Vedic rites.[50] Similarly, the marriage of the daughter of Lala Amir Chand in 1888 performed with simple rituals was considered a radical step. The marriage elicited great applause and admiration from the Samajists. The Samajist press gave wide publicity to such marriages. Samaj journals also carried matrimonial advertisements of those desirous of getting married in "strict accordance with the Vedic rites". Despite all these measures, the Samajists themselves could not give up the ritualism of mainstream Hinduism.

The end of the nineteenth century saw the emergence of radical groups within the Arya Samaj – Arya Shiromani Sabha, Arya Bhratri Sabha and Arya Dharma Sabha. They insisted on simple and purely Vedic nature of all rituals. They encouraged the introduction of the Vedic ceremonies laid down in Dayanand's *Sanskar Vidhi*. Munshiram, the leader of the Gurukul party and himself a radical, appealed to the people to cut wedding expenses through the columns of his journal, *Saddharmpracharak*. The Samajists came out with various tracts insisting on the use of Vedic rites. Some of the important ones were *Guldasta-i-Islah*, written by Devi Lal Verma in 1890, Lala Jiwan Da's *Islah-i-Mu'asharat-i-ahl-i-Haved* and *Sawal-o-Jawab Mutazammin hal-i-Arya Samaj* published in the years 1885 and 1891 respectively.

Slowly and gradually, the reformed rituals found acceptance among the Arya Samajists and particularly the new professional classes who had come under the influence of the Samaj. The "revival of Vedic ritual in modern form without temple and priest made a direct appeal to Punjabi intelligentsia".[51] The Samaj, of course, virtually failed to elicit a favourable response towards its rituals and ceremonies from the non-Arya Samajist Hindus who still adhered to the traditional norms of popular Hinduism.

The Samajists, in their attempts to simplify the marriage ceremonies, tried to do away with some of offensive aspects of traditional marriages. They condemned the singing of indecent songs on the occasion of marriage. They wrote their own purified versions. Mai Bhagwati, the first woman preacher and *updeshak* of the Arya Samaj, replaced the traditional women's songs used at the time of Hindu marriages. Her songs were compiled by Pandit Bhaj Datta in a volume *Gayan Sanskar*, published in Amritsar in 1890. Similarly, Mahatma Munshiram, later Swami Shraddhanand, published a compilation, *Arya Sangitmala,* consisting of Urdu hymns along with a selection of Vedic *mantras*. The Arya Samaj had their own singers called *Bhajniks* who were quite popular even among the non-Arya Samajists.

Other indispensable items of the Hindu marriage ceremony were the fireworks and dances by prostitutes. You could not think of a marriage ceremony without them. Beg, borrow or steal, but remember no bride's father would receive you if your wedding party has no prostitute to dance and no fireworks, writes Ganga Prasad Upadhyaya, a prominent scholar of the Arya Samaj. "The Arya Samajists were the first to raise their voice. They argued with elders, used all kinds of persuasions and even boycotted such parties when their other efforts failed. Several wedding parties had to return in protest; others were pulled out to stop marriage alliances. But perseverance and constancy had their reward".[52]

The Arya Samaj condemned the custom of dowry in unequivocal terms. The Kumar Sabhas, the youth wing of the Samaj, made a commendable contribution in this field. In 1940, the Arya Kumar Sabhas observed an anti-dowry campaign week. Over the years, the Samajist marriages came to be known for their simplicity. "The Kumar Sabha was instrumental in persuading the Kashmiri *Pandits* to spend moderate amount of expenditure on the marriage ceremonies.[53] Impressed by their desire for simple marriages, Deputy Commissioner of Gurgaon wrote, One great result of this (spread of Arya Samaj) has been the diminution in expenditure on marriage and other occasions, which is a wave in the right direction".[54]

Purda

The Mahatma faction that had taken a lead as far as women's issues were concerned and spearheaded the efforts for the relaxation of restrictions imposed by observance of *purda*. The broad-based system of female education, initiated by the Mahatma section, did much to discredit *purda*: "Educated girls began to regard this practice as irksome".[55] The Samajist educational institutions for women organized regular educational tours leading to relaxation of restrictions on freedom of girls. Lala Devraj exhorted the students of his school, Kanya Mahavidyalaya to discard the practice of *purda* and 'emerge like tigresses'.[56] The Gurukul party led a sustained campaign against the practice of *purda*. This was exemplified even in the personal lives of the leaders since the last decades of the nineteenth century.[57]

The Samajist leaders denounced the practice of *purda*. In an article entitled 'Awakening of Women', H.B. Sarda enumerated the disadvantages of the custom of *purda* and made a strong plea for its removal. While calling the practice, 'a positive hindrance' he remarked, "*Purda* must be abolished ... *Purda* and innumerable disabilities imposed on her are insurmountable obstacles in the way of her fulfilling her desire and prevent her from performing what she regards as her duty .... Whatever their origin, these handicaps must now be removed and removed without delay .... Make her free and she will break man's chains".[58] Swami Shraddhanand highly appreciated the cordial relations between men and women in Maharashtra due to non-observance of *purda* by women.[59] The Samajist journals, too, carried on an intensive propaganda against the retrogressive practice of *purda*.[60]

Arya Samaj's crusade for emancipation of women from the abominable practice of *purda* led to awakening among the Samajist women. Some of the Samajist women demonstrated great courage in challenging the abominable practice. Once, when leading Arya Samajist educationist Satyavati was travelling with a group of girls from her school, Kanya Mahavidyalaya, Jullunder she immediately removed the curtain put before the ladies coach in the train. The event created a furore, since *purda* was rampant in Bihar. When the Station Master tried to dissuade her from doing so, she retorted, "The practice of *purda* is harmful. We cannot sit in *purda*. This curtain has to be removed." To avoid further consternation, arrangements for her and the group were made in the first class compartment. When Satyavati was touring the United Provinces, participating in the movements of the Indian National Congress, she was appalled by the pervasive practice of *purda* in the region. To protest against her unveiled face, men themselves used to sit with veils on their faces.[61] The most effective manner in which the Samajists resisted the practice was by encouraging women's participation in the activities of the Samaj. The Mahatma section proved to be very progressive in this direction, too. Their women members were allowed to attend the daily worship service, without any *purda*, along with men; while those of the College section held their separate service for themselves with a woman preacher.[62] Slowly and gradually, however, these restrictions were done away with. Lady members of the Samaj "not only came out of the house to attend the Samaj functions and meetings, they also sat out in the open and participated in Samaj functions". Samajist women like Satyavati and Sarladevi Chaudhrani not only discarded *purda* but had also delivered fiery public speeches on political issues.[63]

Participation of women became an integral feature of the Samaj's functions. This was something striking and unusual in the Indian social context in the nineteenth century. The *Tribune* carried the following description of the anniversary celebrations of the Gurukul section of the Samaj in Lahore in 1901. "The most notable feature of the city Samaj anniversary was that ladies openly took part in them and among the speakers there were several ladies.[64] Similarly, during the centenary celebrations of Swami Dayanand Saraswati's birth in Mathura in 1925, the observers were "very impressed by the great number of women participating, they were not anglicised but utterly free from *purda*, going about freely attending the functions, they chose to attend without attracting undue notice anywhere ..."[65]. Women participated in the processions in large numbers "saying that the treasures of Vedic wisdom were opened to us by Dayanand. Thousands of widows and orphans who were there were living monuments of the greatest work done by the Samaj in the last fifty years".[66]

The women also sang *bhajans* in the congregations. In Jhang district, women themselves were so enthusiastic about the activities of the Samaj that it was decided to let them attend weekly meetings along with men.[67] In almost all the Arya Samajs of Punjab, women's participation in the weekly conferences of Arya Samaj and annual functions of the Gurukuls and schools had become a regular feature.[68] Women of Haryana, too, discarded *purda* in large numbers and participated in the activities of the Samaj. The Hissar Arya Samaj had enough women members that a woman's branch had to be set up.[69] In the United Provinces and Rajputana, the relaxation of *purda* was slow but steady.[70] A letter to the editor of *Saddharmapracharak* complained that while great progress has been made in Punjab, towards removal of *purda*, United Provinces still lagged behind. The complainant further remarked that while in the annual functions of Bareli Samaj women participants were without *purda*, it was, however, distressing that officials of Arya Samaj, Biharipur had to issue nine notices, on the occasion of its annual function that "full arrangements for *purda* would be made". Leading Samajists religiously took their wives to the functions of the Samaj.[71]

The necessity for women preachers to preach the message of the Arya Samaj among women, particularly those living in seclusion, dealt a heavy blow to the practice of *purda* among the Samajist women. As compared to Brahmo Samaj, where a heated debate arose, when a leading Brahmo's wife was appointed *Dharma-pracharika*, on whether women should be 'honoured' in this way, which raged for years, women preachers were more readily accepted within the Arya Samaj, probably as some have suggested because 'of their loose-knit structure, in which many preachers were self-appointed'. However involvement of women was a conscious policy of the Arya Samaj. The employment of female *updeshaks* or missionaries was one of the chief objects of Arya Pratinidhi Sabha.[72] Mai Bhagwati, one of the women preachers of Arya Samaj used to address large public gatherings even in the last quarter of the nineteenth century. [73]

Stree Samaj

The immense potential of the Samajist women as preachers and *updeshaks* came into prominence with the emergence of Stree Samaj or women's wing of the Samaj in the last decade of the nineteenth century. Scholars have extended various explanations for the emergence of the Stree Samaj. J.N. Farquhar has treated Stree Samaj as just another attempt of the Arya Samaj to copy Christian missionaries' methods of preaching and conversion. According to him, the other ways in which Arya Samaj imitated the missionaries were their tract society, Arya Kumar Sabha, orphanages and their work among depressed classes.[74] Quite different is the view of J. Ried, Graham who has argued that there were constant complaints in the journals of the Samaj that the "Arya Samaj consisted of men who can talk in terms of social reform but that women in the homes till hold the orthodox ideas and insisted on the orthodox ceremonies. Therefore, the Arya Samaj's efforts at reform were not able to go forward. It was evidently to help meet this situation that the Stree Samaj was founded in 1912."[75] However, Stree Samaj had come into existence long before 1912. By 1912, there were as many as 60 Stree Samajs.

Moreover, the founding of the Stree Samaj did not signify the backwardness of Arya Samaj women, but exemplified their progressive outlook. Their emergence was in keeping with the progressive ideology of the founder and Arya Samaj and not merely an expedient move to meet any crisis. Stree Samaj movement was pioneered and led by women and was reflective of their keenness to increasingly associate themselves with the preaching and spreading of the Samaj's message. The Stree Samaj came into existence largely for those women, whose restricted lives deprived them of listening to the lectures held in the men's Arya Samaj and also could not derive any benefit from the books on women's upliftment, published by the Arya Samaj from time to time.

The earliest Stree Samaj was founded in Ludhiana and Lahore followed by Ajmer, Dehradun, Meerut, Badayun, Lucknow, Kanpur and various other places.[76] The primary function of the Stree Samaj was the popularization of the religious tenets and activities of the Samaj. The Ajmer Stree Samaj founded in 1904 played a significant role in this direction in the province of Rajputana.[77] Their meetings were held every fortnight on Friday, which commenced with the performance of *Havan* followed by singing of *bhajans*, prayers to God, recitation of Vedic hymns, a sermon from *Satyarth Prakash* or any other scripture. Newspapers were also read out. The most commendable feature of these weekly services was the participation of non-Arya Samajist women. Ajmer Stree Samaj had its separate *Bhajan Mandali.* Regular lectures were organized to enlighten women on issues like women's education, evils of *purda*, widow remarriage and removal of social customs like child marriage etc. The prominent women of Ajmer Stree Samaj were Gulab Devi, Shyam Devi, Sidhkunwar Bai, Sukhda Devi, Kaushalya Devi, Ganga Devi, Nani Bai, Satyavati Devi, Krishna Devi, Jawahar Devi etc. Tours to the province of Rajputana were organized by the Samaj to preach Samajist ideology. It was laid down in the report of the Ajmer Stree Samaj, "... all the sisters are kindly requested that whenever there is occasion for them to go out of town and wherever they may go, they must within their means, preach at least little bit of religion."

Gulab Devi, Pradhana, 'Stree Samaj' and Manorama Devi of the Ajmer 'Stree Samaj' were the chief motivators and activists of the *Purdah Niwarak Mandli* in Ajmer.[78] Parvati Devi (wife of Shri Harbilas, Sarda) and Sukhda Devi (wife of Shri Chand Karan Sharda) participated in the session of All India Women's Conference. The members of the Stree Samaj also performed ceremonies in the homes of the Arya Samajists, in accordance with the *Sanskar Vidhi* of Dayanand Saraswati.

The leaders of the Stree Samaj not only popularized women's education, but made substantial contribution to the cause. Gulab Devi, devoted her entire life to the cause of women's education and set up Kanya Pathshala in Ajmer. She set up *Rajasthan Stri Shiksha Nidhi* to promote and facilitate women's education in the whole province.[79] Godavari Devi of Stree Samaj, Beawar donated her property to Kanya Pathshala in Beawar.[80] The Stree Samaj of Ludhiana ran a female Vedic Pathshala under its auspices as early as 1891.[81] Stree Samaj of Ludhiana and Lahore even ran widows' homes for providing food and shelter to widows and orphans.

The significant role played by Stree Samaj towards generation of awareness among women has not been sufficiently appreciated. It was quite remarkable that as early as the last decade of the nineteenth century and early decades of the twentieth century, women came forward to undertake reform activities for the social betterment of women. In fact many exponents of Indian Renaissance had suggested that the most effective means of bringing about change in women's position would be through their own initiative and involvement. One serious drawback, wrote Rai Bahadur P. Anand Charalu, "... is that in minor as in graver matters, the effort has been solely on the part of the males ... so long [we have been working] as with the lever without the fulcrum; a good percentage of a strong contingent of self reliant, self respecting and let me add, self assertive womanhood is what I look upon, as the fulcrum".[82] Vivekanand, Pandita Ramabai and Karve who felt that "self help is the best help and women should not depend on others" articulated similar views. The wide network of Stree Samaj went a long way towards relaxation of *purda* and spread of education. The fact that they continued to give importance to rituals and customs of Hinduism while attempting to combat social evils made them much more acceptable.

A reappraisal of the reforms undertaken by Arya Samaj in the institutions of caste and marriage reinforces the complex nature of problems that characterized the attempts to raise women's status. Any endeavour to improve women's position was inextricably linked with institutions of marriage and caste. While Dayanand had realized the imperative need to reform these institutions for resurgence of the Hindu society, the Samajists realized much to their consternation, that it was an uphill task to erode the customs and practices that had become so entrenched over the centuries. In fact, this particular sphere of reform had been considered so sacred and sensitive that few reformers had the audacity to even question the inequality and irrationality that had been so deep-rooted in these institutions. The Samajists, too, had approached the reform with a great deal of caution and even hesitation. However, after initial dithering they initiated efforts to bring about progressive changes in the norms that governed the institutions of marriage. It bears testimony to the earnest efforts of the Samaj to liberate women from the control of regressive customs, practices and institutions. They tried to liberalize the institution of marriage not only through their campaign for equal marriage and crusade against child marriages but by denouncing the practice of dowry and pleading for simplification of marriage ceremonies they tried to do away with practices that demeaned women's status. Their campaign for equal marriages necessitated reforms in the caste rules which had become deeply entrenched. Even in the 1920s, it was not easy to contravene the rigorous control of the caste system over the lives of the people. Arya Samaj, however, displayed tenacity of purpose and indomitable courage when they took multiple measures to combat the stranglehold of the caste system. While it is true that even in the twenty-first century the stranglehold of caste continues to dictate social behaviour, Arya Samaj should be given due credit for challenging the ubiquitous hegemony of the caste and more so for placing this particular reform on the public agenda.

Notes

1. J.T.F. Jordens, *Swami Shraddhanand: His Life and Causes*, p. 47.
2. Shyamla Bhatia, *Social Change and Politics in Punjab, 1898–1910*, pp. 144–145.
3. *Census 1911*, *Punjab Report*, p. 149, cited in, Shyamla Bhatia, op. cit., p. 137.
4. *Arya Patrika*, May 15, 1897; October 19, 1895; July 28, cited from, J. Ried Graham, Arya Samaj as a Reformation in Hinduism, with special reference to caste, Ph.D. Dissertation, Yale University, p. 415.
5. J.T.F. Jordens, op. cit., p. 48.
6. Jordens has treated Arya Dharma Sabha as a separate organization of the radicals, while Indra Vidyavachaspati refers to it as yet another name for Arya Shiromani Sabha, Indra Vidyavachaspati, *Arya Samaj Ka Itihas*, p. 288.
7. Swami Shraddhanand was highly incensed at this allegation of Farquhar. In retaliation, he wrote a pamphlet, *Isai Pakshapat Aur Arya Samaj*. While clarifying Samaj's position, he wrote, "This article reveals that *Padri Sahab* has not bothered to find out about the numerous inter-caste marriages

commemorated in Punjab and has confined his enquiry to police reports and the lectures of the College Party. If he had met the leaders of the Mahatma party, he would have come to know that nineteen out of twenty Arya Samaj men do not get married before the age of twenty-five and the daughters in Arya Samajist homes remain unmarried till they find a match who is compatible in *guna, karma* and *svabhava*", Bhavani Lal Bhartiya (ed.), *Swami Shraddhanand Granthavali*, Vol. III, p. 191.

8. *Census of India*, 1901, NWP and *Oudh Report*, p. 86.
9. Upadhayaya, Ganga Prasad, *Origin, Scope and Mission of Arya Samaj*, p. 106.
10. Jordens, op. cit., p. 49.
11. Regarding Sumitra and Gurudatt's marriage, Swami Shraddhanand had remarked, "When history of Arya Samaj will be written, names of Sumitra and Gurudatt will be written in golden letters". Swami Shraddhanand's letter to Sumitra, *Indra Vidya Vachaspati Collection*, Correspondence between Shraddhanand and Sumitra, Group I (b).
12. Jordens, op. cit., p. 49. Earlier Swami Shraddhanand had celebrated the marriage of his elder daughter in conformity with the regulations of the caste with all traditional extravaganza.
13. *Arya Patrika*, November 16, 1901, *Selections from Vernacular Newspapers Published in the Punjab*, received up to December, 1901.
14. Swami Shraddhanand, *Hindu Sanghathan*, pp. 185–186.
15. Swami Shraddhanand, *Kalyan Marg ka Pathik*, cited from, Bhavanilal Bhartiya (ed.), *Swami Shraddhanand Granthavali*, Vol. I, p. 187.
16. *Anath Rakshak*, April, 1933.
17. *Saddharmapracharak*, December 30, 1916.
18. *Prabhat*, February 23, 1926.
19. *Modern Review*, January, 1920; Kiran Devendra, *Status and Position of Women in India*, p. 26.
20. J. Ried Graham, op. cit., pp. 537–578.
21. A similar resolution was passed in 1938, Raghubir Singh Shastri, *Sarvadeshik Sabha ke Nirnay 1908–1960*, pp. 2–9.
22. Some inter-caste marriages among the Samajists were reported occasionally in the Samaj journals. For details, see, *Saddharmapracharak*, August 24, 1916; December 11, 1915; *Arya Mitra*, June 15, 1933; June 29, 1933; February 23, 1933; October 18, 1934; for more instances, see, Bhimsen Vidyalankar, op. cit., p. 34 and R.S. Pareek, *Contribution of Arya Samaj in the Making of Modern India*, p. 133; During the *Antarjatiya Vivah Sammelan* in Hyderabad, organized by the Arya Samaj in 1944, four inter-caste marriages were arranged, *Fourteenth Annual Report of Arya Samaj*, Hyderabad.
23. Harishchandra Vidyalankar, *Arya Samaj ka Itihas*, p. 40.

24. For details, see, A pamphlet by Ghanshyam Singh Gupta, *Arya Vivah Act,* Sankshipt Itihas aur Vistrit Vyakhya.
25. *Arya Samaj, Jaipur ke Sau Varsh: Smarika aur Itihas*, p. 118.
26. *Census of India*, 1901, NWP and *Oudh Report*, p. 86.
27. This lecture of Swami Shraddhanand was well-attended by leading citizens and lawyers of Jalandhar, like Babu Madan Gopal and Babu Salamat Rai. The hall was filled to capacity. The lecture had a resonant impact on the audience. As soon as the lecture came to an end and Munshiram was being congratulated by the audience, the Sirt (a Brahmin who cooks food) of the Devraj family delivered the news that the marriage of Devraj's son has been fixed up with the daughter of Lala Bhavani Dass Munsiff. At this Babu Madan Gopal burst into hysterical bouts of laughter and in the midst of it, said, "Sir, your lecture, indeed, had a great impact on me." The reason was that the betrothed couple was hardly one and a half years old. The present incident coveys, at great lengths, how early Samajists became objects of humiliation and ridicule due to the conservative way of life of their own family members. The leaders of the Mahatma section, however, were possessed with courage of conviction and tenacity of purpose. Lala Devraj refused to comply with the repeated pleas of the bride's family for marriage, at the cost of, ultimately, breaking the marriage alliance. He married off his son at the age of 25 to a well-educated and grown-up bride. *Kalyan Marg Ka Pathik* (An Autobiography of Swami Shraddhanand), in Bhawani Lal Bhartiya (ed.), *Swami Shraddhanand Granthavali*, Vol. I, pp. 105–106.
28. Cited from, Jones, op. cit., pp. 100–101; Kiran Devendra, op. cit., p. 28.
29. Jordens, op. cit., p. 49.
30. Vishnu Lal Shastri, *Handbook of Arya Samaj*, p. 5.
31. Shyamla Bhatia, op. cit., p. 145.
32. Shri Ram Sharma, *Mahatma Hans Raj*, p. 76.
33. *Saddharmapracharak*, November 27, 1915.
34. Satyaketu Vidyalankar (ed.), *Arya Samaj Ka Itihas*, Vol. III, pp. 251–253.
35. Blunt, *The Caste System of Northern India*, p. 331, quoted in C.H. Hiemsath, p. 298.
36. Vishnulal Shastri, op. cit., p. 103.
37. See, Chapter IV, for an appraisal of the concept of Hindu Sanghathan of Swami Shraddhanand.
38. Lajpat Rai, *Unhappy India*, pp. vii-viii.
39. *Speeches and Writings: Har Bilas Sarda*, pp. 33–39. The Government's reasons for opposing the Act were later officially revealed as concern that another Age of Consent Bill would lead to unrest, Government of India, Report of the Age of Consent Committee, p. 11; C.H. Hiemsath, op. cit., p. 11.

40. *Har Bilas Sarda: Recollections and Reminiscences*, p. 68, cited in, R.S. Pareek, op. cit., p. 147.
41. The provisions of the Act were as follows:

    (1) The marriage of the boy or girl married at a minor age is prohibited and liable to punishment. (2) The guardians of such a boy or girl married in minor age would be deemed responsible for it and subject to be penalized. (3) Within one year of marriage the case can be filed. (4) No magistrate other than the first class one can hear such cases. (5) The sponsorer of such a case shall have to deposit Rs 100 as security so that in case of default the other party may demand the loss, R.S. Pareek, op. cit., p. 149. For a detailed commentary on the Act, see, Kunwar Chand Karan Sarda, *Sharda Act Arthat Bal Vivah Nishedh Kanoon*.
42. C.H. Hiemsath, op. cit., p. 348.
43. *Annual Report of the Pratinidhi Sabha*, United Provinces from October 1, 1931 to September 30, 1932, cited from, R.S. Pareek, op. cit., p. 149.
44. *Mahakma Khas, Marriage Legislation File No.C/5/1*, Vol. V, 1940, p. 1; R.S. Pareek, op. cit., p. 149.
45. *Vidhwa Bandhu*, January, 1930, p. 30.
46. Ibid., p. 30. Although the exponents of Arya Samaj vigorously campaigned for eradication of the practice of child marriages, one come across matrimonial notices for girls under the age of 16 years, even in the 1930s, in the Samajist journals. For details see, *Arya Mitra*, February 23, 1933; December 28, 1933; *Arya Martand*, April 1, 1938; February 5, 1935; January 29, 1935.
47. Santosh Yadav, op. cit., p. 138.
48. G.P. Upadhyaya, *Origin, Scope and Mission of Arya Samaj*, p. 100.
49. For details regarding simplification of marriage ceremonies refer, Jones, op. cit., pp. 96–98.
50. *Arya Pratinidhi Sabha, Punjab ka Itihas*, p. 31.
51. Prakash Tondon, op. cit., p. 34.
52. G.P. Upadhyaya, op. cit., p. 99. For Samajist viewpoint on dowry see, G.P. Upadhyaya (ed.), *Dahej*, Tract No. 9, *Arya Tract Mala II*.
53. Ghulam Hasan Khan, *Freedom Movement in Kashmir*, p. 51, cited from, Shiv Kumar Gupta, *British Attitude and Policy towards Arya Samaj, 1875–1920*, pp. 90–91.
54. *Census of India*, 1901, Vol. XVIII, p. 116, cited in, Shiv Kumar Gupta, op. cit., p. 91.
55. Shyamla Bhatia, op. cit., p. 146.
56. Lala Devraj took two of his girl students to Kangra, where they delivered lectures on female education. On August 30, 1912, Shrimati Savitri alongwith Kumari Lajjawati and Kumari Suvira, students of Kanya Mahavidyalaya, Jullunder, went to Simla. During their tour, they gave

lectures on the value of women's education and also collected funds for their school. Shrimati Gulab Devi along with two girl students of her school, Arya Kanya Pathshala in Ajmer, toured Sojat, Bharatpur and Hathras in 1908. Satyaketu Vidyalankar (ed.), *Arya Samaj Ka Itihas*, Vol. III, p. 252.

57. Acharya Ram Dev was expelled from his home when he induced his wife into giving up *purda*, Ram Chandra Javed, *Panjab Ka Arya Samaj*, p. 51, Pandit Lekhram, too, exhorted his wife to increasingly associate herself with the activities and functions of the Samaj. Swami Shraddhanand, *Arya Pathik Lekhram*, cited from, B.L. Bhartiya (ed.), *Swami Shraddhanand Granthavali*, Vol. IV, pp. 86–87.
58. *Bombay Samachar*, November 12, 1928, cited from, *Speeches and Writings: Har Bilas Sarda*, p. 28.
59. Swami Shraddhanand, *Kalyan Marg Ka Pathik*, p. 143.
60. Savitri Devi Vidushi, 'Parde Ki Kupratha', *Prabhat*, August, 1937; Shyamkanta Devi, 'Parda Paap Hai', *Vidhwa Bandhu*, August, 1930, pp. 8–12; Hindu Mahilaon ko Sandesh, *Arya Mitra*, August 2, 1930; Purna Kalakumari, 'Bharat Mein Nari Samaj' Mein Parde ka Sthan, *Arya Mitra*, July 2, 1932; Vidyavati Seth, 'The Pardah System', *Vedic Magazine and Gurukul Samachar*, Shravan, 1968.
61. Satyaketu Vidyalankar, op. cit., p. 264.
62. H.W. Newinson, *The New Spirit in India*, p. 294.
63. Shyamla Bhatia, op. cit., p. 146.
64. *Tribune*, December 31, 1901.
65. *Leader*, April 2, 1924, cited from, Jordens, op. cit., p. 158.
66. *Indian Social Reform*, Vol. 34, Feb. 23, 1924, cited from, J. Ried Graham, op. cit., p. 445.
67. *G.I. Home Poll (B)*, April, 1908, pp. 42–49, cited in, Shyamla Bhatia, op. cit., p. 146.
68. For details, see, *Saddharmapracharak*, November 25, 1916; Indra Vidyavachaspati, op. cit., Vol. II, p. 24.
69. Shyamla Bhatia, op. cit., p. 146. In Haryana, Mai Bhagwati, the first woman preacher of Arya Samaj exercised a powerful influence on the women there.
70. K.W. Jones, op. cit., pp. 107–108.
71. On the advice of Swami Shraddhanand, Pandit Lekhram started taking his wife to the annual functions of the Arya Samaj, Swami Shraddhanand, 'Arya Pathik Lekhram', in B.L. Bhartiya (ed.), *Swami Shraddhanand Granthavali*, Vol. IV, pp. 86–87. Gulab Devi also, accompanied her husband, Mathura Prasad, a prominent Arya Samajist of Ajmer, to the functions of the Samaj. *Smarika*: *Shraddheya Chachiji ke 111th Janamotsav Par*, pp. 3–4.

72. *Panchala Pandita*, November, 1900. Nothing was, however, done for the fulfillment of this important objective till 1900. Lala Devraj, the leader of the conservative section, criticized the *Pratinidhi Sabha* for 'absolute inactivity' in this direction under the lame excuse of 'paucity of funds', *Panchala Pandita*, November, 1900.
73. The *Tribune* had carried a following report on one of her meetings, 'Of late it has been difficult to get well-cooked dishes at any house in Haryana, and few people stop at Haryana for fear of indigestion.' Radha Kumar, op. cit., p. 32.
74. J.N. Farquhar, *Modern Religious Movements in India*, pp. 124–125, cited from, Bhavani Lal Bhartiya (ed.), op. cit., Vol. III, p. 173.
75. J. Ried Graham, op. cit., p. 145.
76. Vishnu Lal Shastri, *Handbook of Arya Samaj*, p. 88.
77. For details regarding the activities of Ajmer Stree Samaj, refer, *Arya Stree Samaj, Ajmer Ka Vivran: 1960 AD to 1913 AD*, p. 2.
78. Santosh Yadav, op. cit., p. 138.
79. *Smarika: Shraddheya Chachiji ke 111th Janamotsav Par*, p. 6.
80. Santosh Yadav, op. cit., p. 137.
81. *Tribune*, October 24, 1891 and September 27, 1910, cited in, K.W. Jones, op. cit., p. 107.
82. Rai Bahadur P. Anand Charlu, 'On Social Reform: A Statement', in C.Y. Chintamani (ed.), *Indian Social Reform*, p. 29.

Chapter 7

Pioneers of Women's Education

The social reformers in the nineteenth century displayed remarkable agreement over the issue of women's access to education for raising their status and also linked it to social health. Nevertheless, debates over women's education were defined by deep disagreement over how the issue needed to be addressed. The prevailing views regarding women's distinct nature and roles, as separate from men, were vital in determining nineteenth century discourse on the nature and extent of education to which women should have access. Despite the fact that education was now being conceived as a major instrument for bringing about change in societal attitudes and practices, "the purpose of educating women according to these reformers, was not to make them independent, but to train them to perform their functions as makers of home, hence the emphasis on home science and simpler liberal arts rather than the manly subjects like mathematics, science or professional courses like law, engineering etc."[1] Except for widows, who were now being given some kind of economic training, the primary aim of women's education was to produce better wives and mothers and also to enhance their specific feminine attributes.

Keshub Chandra Sen, leader of Brahmo Samaj, known for his radical stance on issues of caste and marriage, emerged as one of the leading exponents of women's education in Bengal in the 1870s. Quite surprisingly, however, his vision of women's education was characterized by conservative attitude towards women's roles in society. He maintained that women's highest duty was to care for her husband and family and therefore, science, logic and mathematics were totally irrelevant for them. He was convinced that progressive views on women's education would only 'unsex them' and were basically 'highly revolutionary and fraught with grave danger to society'.[2] D.K. Karve, despite his progressive posturing on the highly contentious issue of remarriage of widows, had firm faith in gendered roles for men and women. The aim of Mahila Vidyalaya, established by him in 1900, was to train women to be good wives, mothers and neighbours. He said, "We lay emphasis on home life as the chief sphere of a woman's activities. Here her proper place is found as wife and mother .... Women, as a class, have different functions to fulfil in the social economy from those of men .... That they are as integral a part of the social organism as men, is beyond question, but that the office, they have to fill is different ... If men and women, therefore, are to be fitted by education to bear their own respective shares in the preservation, development and evolution towards perfection of the whole community, they must be brought up on two different lines."[3] Karve designed different educational courses for men and women keeping in view the differentiation in their 'conscious individuality'. The curriculum of the Mahila Vidyalaya consisted of a practical knowledge of English, simple Arithmetic with elements of Book-Keeping, Domestic Economy, Physiology, a practical knowledge of the Art of cooking and child nursing, Anatomy and Hygiene. Similarly, Vivekanand, too focused on home and family as the centre of women's activities. He said, "We must see to their growing up as ideal matrons of home in time .... It is only in the homes of educated and pious mothers that great men are born." His curriculum for women's education was calculated to meet this primary goal. Sewing, culinary art, rules of domestic work, upbringing of children, religious scriptures, literature, Sanskrit formed the core of his scheme of education for girls.[4] Chandavarkar, too, advocated female education for limited purpose of training them to be 'good housewives' and 'good companions of life'. He remarked, "I am entirely with those who hold that such education as we impart to women must not unfit them for the duties and obligations which they have to fulfil as the presiding deities of our homes".[5]

Nevertheless, there were a few voices that advocated a liberal and broader concept of education for women. These reformers had great faith in the liberatory potential of knowledge rather than merely viewing education as an aid to improve women's efficiency in their traditional roles. Ramabai, for instance, desired education to "dispel the illusion of many superstitious beliefs, the wrong ideas that now keep women in subjection".[6] She even sought to view women's education as a means to prepare women for roles outside the family. The careers which she visualized for women were medicine, teaching and nursing. In her evidence before the Indian Education Commission, she urged that special training should be given to women teachers and they should receive higher salaries than men. The aim of her Mukti Sadan in Kadagaon was to make the inmates economically independent.

Dwarkanath Ganguly, leader of Sadharan Brahmo Samaj, stood out for his unusually advanced and rational attitudes towards women's status and education in society. While advocating equal status for women, he held that both men and women had equal opportunities in life. He saw no justification for a separate syllabi and a limited period of education for girls. In 1874, he set up Bangiya Mahila Vidyalya to conduct novel experiments in female education. He evolved his educational system on the belief that women were entitled to learn every branch of knowledge. He even succeeded in admitting two of his female students Kadambini and Sarala in the Calcutta University, at a time when no British University had opened its doors to women. His wife Kadambani went on to become a doctor. Undeterred by the slander campaign of the Hindu orthodoxy, he even sent her abroad for higher studies in medicine.[7]

Gopal Ganesh Agarkar held the most revolutionary views on the nature and objective of women's education. He made a fervent plea for co-education and common curriculum at a time when such ideas were upheld as absolutely untenable. He attributed women's exclusion from higher education to men's fear of losing their hegemony over women. "The fact of the matter is that those who acquire power are ever reluctant to relinquish it ... ". He further stated, "Each person should have the freedom to pursue tasks in accordance with one's capacity. This will benefit both males and females and the world at large. There ought to be competition between men and women in every field of science or art. If women are incompetent in science and art they should be declared so only after their abilities are actually tested."[8] His reasoned arguments on equality of educational opportunities for men and women, however, failed to evoke a favourable response.

Women's education, thus, emerged as a fiercely debated subject as it necessarily involved the inevitability of new familial, social and physical arrangements. The question of purpose, quality and extent of women's education thus became an important area of discussion. Paucity of women teachers, proper transportation, appropriate dress for schools, early marriage, requirement of reading material for their respective curriculum etc were some of the factors that had to be resolved to render women's education a viable proposition.

Arya Samaj and Early Efforts for Diffusion of Education

Till the early half of the nineteenth century, the state of female education was marked by extreme backwardness and utter neglect. The British Government did not take up the subject until 1849, when Lord Dalhousie informed the Bengal Council that, henceforth, its functions were to embrace female education.[9] The first girls' school recognized by the British Government was founded shortly afterwards. The Charles Wood Despatch of 1854 directed that female education should receive the frank and cordial support of the British Government as by this means a far greater proportional impulse is imparted to the educational and moral tone of the people than education of men. However, the Government's reluctance to allot adequate funds to girls' education, its unwillingness to promote it at the expense of boy's education and the fear of arousing popular prejudices hindered the cause of women's education.

The Christian missionaries made the first real beginning in the furtherance of the cause. Apart from the innumerable schools that the missionaries opened in several parts of India, they innovated *zenana* teaching and succeeded in getting access to *purdanashin* women in the seclusion of their homes. Slowly and gradually, the system of *zenana* education spread in various parts of India, particularly in the *purda* -dominated North India.[10] *Zenana* teaching came to be viewed with sheer trepidation and suspicion by both, Hindus and Muslims. Commenting on the sharp reaction of the Punjabis to *zenana* teaching, K.W. Jones has written, "Punjabis strongly resented *zenana* missionaries for tampering with their womenfolk and violating the sanctity of their homes. On occasions, they accused the missionaries of kidnapping and girl stealing ... The *zenana* mission produced not merely the cry of 'religion in danger' but a more damning one of subversion in the home".[11] The education imparted by the Christian missionaries could never claim popularity among the masses.

Swami Dayanand Saraswati, the founder of Arya Samaj, envisaged education of both, men and women, as the key to the resurgence of Hinduism. He envisaged a concrete plan of education for men and women. After the death of the founder, the Samajists initiated their movement for diffusion of education among men and women in 1883, when they set up Dayanand Anglo-Vedic (DAV) School for boys in Lahore. In the subsequent decades, the Arya Samaj made a phenomenal contribution to the growth of education. Their distinctive contribution lies in creating urgency for the cause among wide sections of Indian society.

The idea of founding a DAV school and college was announced in a massive meeting of the Arya Samajists, held within a week of Dayanand's death, in order to fulfil the founder's dream and perpetuate his memory. The announcement was greeted with uproarious applause and seven to eight thousand rupees were collected on the spot. Even women and children came forward with their contribution for the cause. "The collection in itself was a sign of change".[12]

The Dayanand Anglo-Vedic Trust and Management Society was set up in 1886 with the objective of starting an Anglo-Vedic institution, which shall include a school, a college and a boarding house as memorials in honour of Swami Dayanand Saraswati. The purpose of the school would be to encourage, improve and enforce the study of Hindi literature, classical Sanskrit and of the *Vedas*. The school also intended to promote the study of English literature and sciences, both theoretical and applied. It also aimed at providing technical education. However, the basic emphasis of the movement was on 'cultural reclamation'. The DAV College Movement was an "experiment in purely indigenous enterprise" as the College management was entirely in the hands of elected representatives of such Arya Samajists who contributed to its funds. The syllabus of the school included the study of modern subjects to enable the students to advance intellectually and also to secure jobs. The College taught Sanskrit, Hindi, English,

Persian, Philosophy, both eastern and modern, History, Political Economy, Logic, Elementary Physics, Chemistry and Higher Mathematics. While at the same time a consistent effort was made to strengthen the cultural roots of the students. The College started Ayurvedic classes, instituted a research fellowship for a critical study of ancient scriptures, set up a Theological Department and a Vedic Studies Department.[13] In 1899, Sanskrit had replaced Persian, and by 1914, the language received a further impetus when the students of high school were compelled to know it for college entrance examinations.[14] Quite significantly, no government aid was sought for the College. The DAV College promoters were, therefore, confronted with acute paucity of funds. To overcome this predicament, they devised unusual methods. *Atta* fund, *Raddi* fund, small monthly cash collections and annual donations collected at the time of anniversary celebrations were some of the means which ensured the flow of funds for the institution. Referring to the system of *Atta* collection in the aid of DAV College, *Indian Mirror* remarked, "The Hindus of Punjab are setting a noble example to the rest of their fellow countrymen in India."[15] Besides, the Samajists set a noble example by replacing the tradition of giving gifts to *Brahmins* on auspicious occasions by giving donations to the College fund. The donations poured in, primarily from the middle classes. The aristocracy remained apathetic to the movement.

The founders of the movement had decided to provide free education but the paucity of funds and Government regulations prevented them from doing so. However, the fee charged by the College was 50 per cent less than that of the Government schools and colleges. The DAV School and College emerged as the most popular in the province. By the end of first month in June 1886, 350 students had enrolled in the school. The Government recognized the school in 1889. In 1914, the strength of the school was 1,737. Whereas, the College had 347 students in 1901–02 and which further increased to 457 in 1907.[16] The DAV College Movement proved that English education could be imparted to the students, without endangering their cultural moorings. The DAV College Movement became the harbinger of an extensive educational movement not only within the Samaj but also among the Sanatan Dharmis, Sikhs and the Muslims.

The DAV colleges emerged as centres of social reform and social service also. The students were encouraged to engage in charitable and welfare activities like orphan relief, collection of funds, adult education, women's education, distribution of instructive literature etc. The major drawback of the DAV College Movement was its utter neglect of and indifference to women's education, an issue that would later prove to be a source of conflict between the DAV faction and the Gurukul faction, the latter emerging as champion of female education.

Early Attempts at Women's Education

The leaders of the Mahatma section, Lala Munshiram, more popularly known as Swami Shraddhanand, and Lala Devraj, spearheaded the early efforts for women's education. The rapid progress and immense popularity of the DAV College Movement drew their attention towards the cause of women's education. In some of his most forceful and acclaimed series of articles on women's education titled *Adhura Insaf* (Incomplete Justice) in his journal, the *Saddharamapracharak*, Swami Shraddhanad pleaded for women's education on the basis of equal rights for women and men. Reiterating Dayanand's stand on women's education, Shraddhanand remarked, "Women have precisely the same rights over spiritual knowledge, like men have; just as parents impart education to children in childhood according to the dictates of the *Vedas*, and send them to the Gurukuls, immediately after the *Yagyopavit*, in the same manner, girls should be treated".[17] Shraddhanand condemned the promoters of DAV College for their apathy towards women's education and depriving them of their '*basic rights*' (emphasis mine). He brushed aside the popular belief that wife's fulfillment lay in the service of her husband and upheld that as human beings women had identical claims over the acquisition of spiritual knowledge. The Mahatma section, the champion of women's causes, cherished education, primarily, as a means for spiritual and moral advancement of human beings. The leaders of this section seldom highlighted the materialistic and worldly aspect of education for men and women. Great emphasis was laid on the moral and religious content of education. This outlook of the Mahatmas was also reflected in their syllabus for women.

In addition to improvement in women's lives, the primary impulse towards women's education in the nineteenth century was provided by the necessity to produce better mothers and companionate wives. The Samajists also linked acquisition of education to the centrality of women's role in the procreation and evolution of the human race. Dayanand's major concern was the regeneration of the Hindu race. Consequently, he had laid great emphasis on the improvement of conditions in which women gave birth to children. He had devoted an entire chapter in *Satyarth Prakash* on 'Conception and Motherhood' laying down in great detail the rules, regulations and precautions to be observed by the prospective mother so that she gave birth to healthy children and thereby revitalize Hindu race. Degeneration of the race was often attributed to the birth of sickly and weak children leading to colonization of India by the British. Swami Shraddhanand had articulated his concern for the consolidation of a strong and vigorous Hindu race in his campaign for *Hindu Sanghathan*. It was felt that mothers played an important role in forming children's consciousness and also in his intellectual, moral and physical development. Women's education was pertinent not only to women's own intellectual and self-development but equally critical for the sake of their children and husbands and most significantly for a rejuvenated Hindu race. Shraddhanand, while making a plea for women's education, wrote, "It is a well-known fact that the early education of a child takes place under the guidance of his mother." Samajist discourse on women's education thus also restated the conventional arguments extended by the reformers in the nineteenth and twentieth centuries. At another place, he argued, "Without women's education no nation, race, and society can progress. Women are the basis of human society. Therefore, it is imperative to reform them first."[18] Lala Harkishan Lal, a prominent Arya Samajist, remarked, " ... Women should be educated to the highest level, they were capable of ... because it is the women who stand most in the way of social reform".[19] In addition to the social benefits of educating women, the Samajists considered acquisition of knowledge critical for women's self-fulfillment as individuals. Swami Shraddhanand and Lala Devraj felt that women, as individuals, would be able to secure more contentment, security and happiness from their lives, if they were intellectually advanced.[20]

The Samajist campaign for women's education was thus inspired by multiple objectives. The earliest school for girls was set up as a part of Ferozepur Orphanage on the advice of Swami Dayanand.[21]

Another girls' school was set up at Meerut during Dayanand's lifetime. After the death of Dayanand, Lahore Arya Samaj set up a *putri pathshala*, followed by Shraddhanand's initiative in Talwan but both the schools had to be closed due to lack of funds and unworthiness of the school teacher. The Amritsar Samaj opened three girls' school in 1885.[22] In 1886, Jullunder Samaj opened a '*Jenana* school' on the monthly expenditure of Rupee one. The report of the school in 1886 recorded six students. The dearth of a good female teacher, paucity of funds and lack of students led to the closure of the school. The subsequent two attempts failed to evoke a favourable response. Till this time, the Samajists' involvement in the furtherance of female education was sporadic. Urgency to the cause was provided by the threat posed by proselyting activities in the girls' schools run by the Christian missionaries.[23] Plans were drawn up and a committee was set up in July 1890 to expedite the establishment of a girls' school. In August 1891, the Kanya Pathshala was formally inaugurated. The school witnessed steady progress. Till the end of 1892, the number of students rose to 55. By February 1895, the Pathshala had nearly a hundred pupils.[24] In March, the same year a boarding house, the *Kanya Ashram*, was attached to the school and by the end of the year the Ashram housed students even from Poona and North-Western Provinces. This act, according to K.W. Jones, "in itself marked a daring departure as the school now took on the additional responsibility of guarding the morality of its students".[25]

The success of the Kanya Pathshala encouraged its founders to envision a scheme for higher education for females. In 1892, Lala Devraj announced the Jullunder Samaj's plan to set up a Kanya Mahavidyalaya, a girls' high school.

Progress of Women's Education: Ideological Debates and Barriers

Lala Devraj's announcement regarding the establishment of a school for higher education for women at a projected cost of Rs 2,50,000 was viewed with utter dismay by the DAV College faction and brought out into open the fissures within the Samaj, regarding female education. A bitter polemic ensued between the DAV faction and the protagonists of female education, the Mahatma section, on the subject of higher education for women. While the former were not against women's education, in their view primary education was sufficient for women. Lal Chand and Lajpat Rai, prominent leaders of the College faction justified the standpoint of their faction in a series of articles in the *Tribune* and the *Dayanand Anglo Vedic Samachar*. It was also felt that higher education for women would not only be detrimental to the expansion of men's education but would also deplete the resources for primary education for women.[26] Lala Lajpat Rai further believed that while men's education was backed by strong inducements, the education of girls was unaccompanied by such motives. These arguments were illustrative of the debate against women's education.

The stringent opposition of DAV faction to the scheme for higher education for women was probably not so much over the supposed benefits of women's education as their need for meagre funds. The DAV faction viewed Kanya Mahavidyalaya as a contender for the scanty funds available for education. The clash became virulent, when the customary appeal for DAV College funds, at the annual function of the Amritsar Samaj, was followed by a similar appeal for Kanya Mahavidyalaya, Jullunder. The DAV faction insisted on primary education for girls and demanded that while the local funds might be utilized for this purpose, the provincial funds should be reserved for the DAV College. The cause of female education formed one of the primary causes of rift between the two groups of the Arya Samaj. In addition to the deep disagreements that characterized, and quite evidently, impeded the progress of women's education, the usual deterrents that hampered the cause were also there. The leaders of the Mahatma section nevertheless strove relentlessly against odds to create conditions favourable for the growth of women's education.

In the last two decades of the nineteenth century, the Samajists came out with several tracts to vindicate women's education as socially useful and for individual development of women. Swami Shraddhanand's advocacy of female education in his series of articles *Adhura Insaf* was followed by Lala Devraj's article, *'Ek Anpad Stree Ki Yatra'*. Lectures were also organized by the local Samajes in which the need and significance of women's education was emphasized.

Scarcity of female teachers was yet another major obstacle in the progress of women's education. Various suggestions poured in even from non-Samajists and also the Government to meet this requirement. The *Tribune*, in an article, 'Female Education in Punjab' in March, 1904 put forward the view that the school attached to the Ferozepur Orphanage of the Arya Samaj, if properly developed and aided, could provide teachers for the girls' school.[27] In 1906, there were 30 orphan girls of the Ferozepur Orphanage, serving as teachers in girls' schools. The proficiency of these teachers can be judged from the fact that the Education Department was giving higher salaries to these teachers. The Samajists, however, were pessimistic about the experiment, for the girls, sooner or later, had to enter married life. Women of respectable families could not go to the *moffusil* towns away from their husbands. To cope with the dearth of teachers, the Samajists educated their own wives and daughters so that they could teach in the girls' schools. Moreover, it was also felt that inhabitants did not object to the employment of male teachers provided they be elderly man of good character.

Lala Devraj proposed a plan to rear up girl *Brahmcharinis* who shall dedicate their entire lives to the task of women's education. In October, 1900 many students of Kanya Mahavidyalaya had taken the vow of remaining *Brahmcharinis* to serve the cause of female education.[28] Lala Devraj, also, pleaded for training Hindu widows for the purpose. He said, "Widows have no encumbrances like married women. They can regard the labour as a great *brat* (vow), their time would be employed in a healthy manner and their character strengthened".[29] Lala Badri Das and Shrimati Savitri Devi set up a residential institution for educating widows on the lines of Karve's Widows Home at Poona. The experiment of employing widows as teachers, however, could not resolve the problem of paucity of teachers.

The scarcity of funds was another major impediment in the realization of the objective of female education. The Mahatma section devised the same methods for collection of funds, which had been resorted to by the College faction. They instituted a *Raddi* fund and took up begging in the streets to raise funds for the Pathshala. Collections were also made on the anniversary functions of the various Samajes. Generous donations from the supporters of female education also facilitated the growth of women's education. Apart from funds, another major problem that the Samajists faced was the non-availability of text books in Hindi.

Hardships did not dishearten the Arya Samajists who persevered in their efforts to realize their vision of women's education. By the end of the nineteenth century almost every Samaj affiliated to the Mahatma section had a Kanya Pathshala attached to it.[30] It would be worthwhile to examine in detail two institutions for women's education – Kanya Mahavidyalaya, Jullunder and Mathura Prasad Gulab Devi Arya Kanya Pathshala, Ajmer. The detailed study would provide an understanding into the distinctive concept of women's education as evolved by the leaders of the Arya Samaj. It would also give insights into the bitter struggle of the Samajists for facilitating new familial, institutional and academic arrangements for facilitating women's education.

Kanya Mahavidyalaya, Jullunder

Kanya Pathshala, Jullunder established by the pioneering efforts of Lala Dev Raj and Lala Munshiram in 1890 was the first leading institution for girls set up by Arya Samajists. It was subsequently raised, to the status of a Mahavidyalaya in 1896. Despite innumerable hurdles, including the stern opposition from a section of the Arya Samajists, the Mahavidyalaya made steady progress over the years. The number of students kept on increasing – from 134 students in 1897 the school had enrolled 389 students by 1914.[31] A widow's home was also attached to the school in 1914.

The curriculum of the Mahavidyalaya laid great emphasis on religious content. It included *Ved Path* (*mantras* from *Aryabhivinay* and the *Vedas*), singing of hymns, *chhannds* and *dohas* and performance of *Sandhya* and *Havan*. Great stress was laid on proficiency in Sanskrit. Apart from religious education and Sanskrit, Arithmetic, Geography, basic Science, History, Hindi and English were also taught. In addition to academic subjects "such arts ... as are necessary for the female sex were also included in the curriculum. Girls were taught sewing, knitting, embroidery and cookery. The Jullunder Stree Samaj assisted in teaching these skills. Students were also trained in the art of music, which formed an essential part of the syllabus. The teaching of music, which had come to be associated with dancing girls and prostitutes, was viewed with extreme displeasure and dismay by the conservatives. From November 1900 onwards, provision for *Vaidhyak Shiksha* (medical science) was also made. The girls of the Mahavidyalaya were also trained in the skills of public speaking and elocution. There was a *Vagvardhini Sabha* (debating society), which encouraged students to develop oratory skills. The students of Kanya Mahavidyalaya put their proficiency in public speaking to good use during tours when they delivered lectures on female education and collected funds during the process. Students were also sent to other places to learn various arts and handicrafts.

The medium of instruction was Hindi, an unprecedented step at a time when Urdu and English were the predominant languages. According to K.W. Jones, "The emphasis on Hindi, both in the teaching and in the publications of the Kanya Mahavidyalaya is consistent with general tendency for Hindi to be used by women and to be considered a woman's language. English and Urdu were court languages used by men. Men only used Hindi while writing to their wives". The use of Hindi necessitated the writing of new books. Lala Devraj wrote at least three-dozen books for girls in Hindi. Moral education was most carefully imparted in the Mahavidyalaya. A remarkable feature of the Kanya Mahavidyalaya was the significance attached to physical education. The education report for the years 1897–1902 observed that the only institution where physical education for girls had received careful attention was the Kanya Mahavidyalaya, Jullunder. Lala Devraj devised a special set of physical exercises for girls.

Lala Devraj evolved interesting and simple methods of imparting knowledge to women, through stories and anecdotes. He deliberately refrained from making acquisition of knowledge burdensome for girls. He and Lala Munshiram even pondered over the advisability of doing away with examination system for women.[32] Prizes were also distributed on the occasion of annual functions of the Mahavidyalaya.

Funds for the Kanya Mahavidyalaya were not as forthcoming as for boys' education. The school did not attract large donations. Deputations comprising of students and teachers were sent to different places at regular intervals for collection of funds. Despite paucity of funds, the authorities of Kanya Mahavidyalaya resisted from accepting Government aid. Lala Devraj highly cherished the autonomous nature of the institution as regards its curriculum, examinations and management. After his death in 1935, however, due to serious constraints, the authorities of the Mahavidyalaya started adhering to the curriculum and examination system of the Government universities.

Kanya Mahavidyalaya, Jullunder, epitomized the supreme dedication, sacrifice and enthusiasm of Lala Devraj for the cause of female education. His relationship with the students was marked by companionship, reverence and affectionate regard. He was fondly addressed as *Chachaji* by the students. The founders of the Mahavidyalaya had to encounter social prejudices, financial constraints and paucity of institutional devices to realize their cherished dream. The struggle against the odds was indeed extremely punishing and required a great deal of courage, determination and sacrifice at a time when a section of the Samajists themselves were not fully convinced about the utility of higher education for women. In fact as Durgadas reminisces, "Against this social background [of prejudices and taboos regarding women's education] one can readily understand the sensation caused by the opening of girls' institute the Kanya Mahavidyalaya, at Jullunder. As the girls in uniform, yellow saris after the fashion in Vedic times, trundles along in tongas (horse carts) past our high school, the boys ran to the roadside to gape at the spectacle. On the occasion of the anniversary, a chorus of girls draped in saris appeared on the platform to sing a religious song. How indeed could the orthodox put up with the indignity of girls from respectable families being exposed to public gaze? Stones and shoes came hurtling on to the stage".[33]

Kanya Mahavidyalaya also exemplifies the distinctive model of women's education as evolved by Arya Samaj. The curriculum was broad based and inclusive. While the founders did realize the need to train girls in the art of home-making, their motivation for women's education was not restricted to the narrow purpose of making them good wives and mothers. Equal emphasis on the religious, moral, physical, aesthetic and intellectual development of the students was the objective of Kanya Mahavidyalaya. The holistic nature of education was reflected in the curriculum that they framed for the students. Moreover, Lala Devraj, unlike his contemporaries, did not have a narrow vision of women's education. He wanted Kanya Mahavidyalaya to evolve exclusively as a women's university. Kanya Mahavidyalaya had far-reaching consequences in terms of fostering a spirit of individuality among its students. The graduates of the Mahavidyalaya played a commendable role in the removal of social practices like dowry and *purda*. Some of them even took part in the freedom struggle. Above all, the Kanya Mahavidyalaya set the ball of female education rolling. A large number of Kanya Pathshalas, closely modelled on the pattern of Kanya Pathshala, Jullunder, were set up by Arya Samajists in the United Provinces, Punjab, Rajputana, Bihar and West Bengal.

Mathura Prasad Gulab Devi Arya Kanya Pathshala, Ajmer

Mathura Prasad Gulab Devi Arya Kanya Pathshala was another notable institution set up at Ajmer. It formed one of the earliest endeavours of the Samaj for diffusion of education amongst girls. The school had its beginnings in 1898 when Gulab Devi and her husband Mathura Prasad, leading Arya Samajist of Ajmer, started teaching a group of girls and women from the neighbourhood. The school was formally set up in 1908.[34] As is evident from Table 7.1, the numerical strength of the school kept on increasing:

Table 7.1

Number of Students in Arya Kanya Pathshala, Ajmer

Year	*No. of Students*
1914	61
1923	117
1924	105
1925	127
1926	113
1927	129
1928	142
1929	168
1932	210
1941	322

Source: The 28th and 31st Annual Reports of Gulab Devi Arya Kanya Pathshala, Ajmer; p.109, Arya Directory, 1941.

The avowed purpose of the Pathshala was to train women to be efficient housewives with strong religious and ethical values.[35] The curriculum of the school was formulated to serve this specific purpose. The students of the Pathshalawere proficient in the performance of *Sandhya* and *Havan*. In addition to this, selections from the *Vedas*, *Chanakyaniti*, *Ramayan* and writings of Swami Dayanand were also taught to the students. Girls were also taught child rearing and home management. Cookery, embroidery, sewing, knitting and other useful skills were also imparted to the girls in the higher classes. Sanskrit was also included in the syllabus. The books of the Government schools were prescribed only for the middle classes. The examinations till the fifth standard were held by the school in affiliation with Arya Putri Pathshala and Dayanand Anglo-Vedic School, Ajmer independently of government schools and curriculum. The students of the middle section appeared for the middle examinations of the Government schools. Some girls also appeared for the Kanya Vinodini examinations of Mahila Vidyapeeth, Prayag.

Education was imparted free of cost. Poor students were supplied with books and other requisite material. As a matter of principle, the school did not accept any aid from the Government. The institution, therefore, suffered due to paucity of funds. The annual reports of the Pathshala continuously emphasized the need for a permanent fund. Various projects like a boarding house, drinking water facilities for students, specialized teachers for different subjects, purchase of sewing machines were shelved due to want of adequate resources. Despite the fact that Gulab Devi donated her entire property to the Pathshala, it depended for its continued existence on the donations of supporters of female education. Emulating the example of Kanya Mahavidyalaya, Jullunder, Pathshala also sent deputations of students to different places for collection of funds.[36] Till 1912, the school was under the personal management of Gulab Devi, wife of Mathura Prasad. The institution was then handed over to Arya Pratinidhi Sabha, Malwa and Rajasthan. Some years later, Arya Samaj, Kesarganj, Ajmer, took over the management of the school. In 1940, on the advice of Gulab Devi, it was placed under a trust.[37]

The Pathshala owed a great deal to the unremitting dedication of Gulab Devi. She donated her entire life, resources and energies to the cause of women's education. Early in life, she accepted the utility and value of female education. She crusaded for the cause when institutional and formal education was totally unacceptable in the feudal and conservative milieu of the region. She, along with her associates had to suffer hardships and abject humiliation when they sought to collect funds and students for their school. Being childless herself, she advised all such women to engage themselves in the task of women's education. To propagate the cause, she wrote and published innumerable pamphlets and books. She established *Rajasthan Stri Shiksha Nidhi* to facilitate the spread of education in the province. She campaigned incessantly for the cause outside the region also.

Gulab Devi was the Pradhana of Stree Samaj, Ajmer and Up-Pradhana of Shrimati Paropkarini Sabha, Malwa and Rajasthan. In 1938, she presided over the *Arya Mahila Sammelan*. From all these platforms, she articulated the need for resurgence of Hindu womanhood. She had passed the St. John's ambulance examination and was actively associated with famine relief and flood relief. She had also desired to establish an Ayurvedic college for women. Her dynamism induced the students of Pathshala into taking a prominent part in the activities of Stree Samaj.

Till her death in 1963, she remained the most decisive influence on the students of the Pathshala. She daily organized *Sandhya*, *Havan* and religious sermons. Her personal supervision over students went a long way in inculcating religious and ethical values in the girls. It was her personal rapport with the students that even after they left the Pathshala and got married, they willingly came forward to assist her in the activities of the Pathshala. Due to financial constraints and social taboos against women's education, the Pathshala could not develop into an institution for higher education for women but she did envisage its expansion into a college. It was her cherished dream that women, after acquiring higher education, should become useful to the society and nation.

Kanya Gurukuls

The immense popularity and stupendous success of the DAV College and School as an educational movement failed to satisfy a section of the Arya Samajists. The radical groups within the Samaj desired actualization of the educational ideals of Swami Dayanand Saraswati. With this objective in mind, Arya Bhratri Sabha pioneered the movement for Gurukul system of education. The persistent opposition and apathy from within the ranks of Arya Samaj, however, retarded the progress of the movement. The first tangible support for Gurukuls came forth after Lala Munshiram wrote a series of articles on the significance and utility of Gurukul system of education in *Saddharmapracharak* in 1897.

The primary aim of establishing Gurukuls was to build up an educational system that could enrich and enhance moral virtues and preserve the institution of *Brahmcharya*. Dayanand had cherished education as a process of character formation. The Mahatma section of the Samaj felt that DAV College faction had been utterly neglecting this fundamental aspect of education. In this context, Swami Shraddhanand remarked, "Gurukul is an educational institution founded with the avowed aim of reviving the ancient institution of *Brahmcharya* ... . In an age where the values are economic, the standard of respectability is wealth and tutelary goddess of worship is worldly success, it is difficult to understand that the moral stamina cannot be strengthened, independence of character cannot be fostered, absolute rectitude, and supreme righteousness cannot be made dominant spring of action, and righteous incentives to conduct cannot be made operative in an atmosphere of luxury and bodily comfort".[38] The Gurukul system of education was also intended to check child marriages, avoid evils of cities and materialism.

Gurukul system of education was also meant to give a fillip to the study of the Vedic literature and its varied branches, to revive the study of ancient Indian philosophy and literature, build up Hindi literature by incorporating into it all that was best in occidental thought. "The predominant idea", according to Lala Lajpat Rai, "was to give a good trial to the system of education propounded by Dayanand in his works. High proficiency in Vedic Sanskrit and character building on Vedic lines were the objectives of the scheme".[39]

The idea of Gurukul was also prompted by the idea of evolving and strengthening the Vedic institutions of *varna* and *ashrama*. In the words of Swami Shraddhanand, "Without the establishment of the *ashrams*, the establishment of the *varnas* is not possible, because the *varna* is based on the *ashrama*. Without a Gurukul how can the *ashramas* be instituted?" K.W. Jones has described the desire for Gurukul as a corollary to the Samajists' rising interest in caste reform. Gurukul was defined as a centre to train children for caste leadership. [40]

With these objectives in mind, Mahatma Munshi Ram started making efforts to set up an educational seminary embodying Dayanand's ideals of education. In 1902, they started a Gurukul for boys in Kangri, three miles below Hardwar. The model of this Gurukul was the ancient universities of India like Taxila. On entrance, the boys took a vow of chastity, poverty and obedience. They were to remain in the Gurukul for a period of sixteen years. During this period, the pupils were not allowed to visit their parents, "except under exceptional and urgent circumstances. The boys were subjected to strict discipline, though at the same time parental, personal and even tender in its mode of application".

The syllabus of the Gurukul envisaged twelve years in the lower section and six years in the college section. The curriculum of the lower section included Sanskrit and Vedic studies. In this section, the students were taught Vedic studies and also instructed in the religious thought of Swami Dayanand. In the college, the students chose a course for specialization. Out of the two options, one provided for study of the four *Vedas*. The students opting for this branch had to choose a professional course in Economics, Agriculture or Ayurvedic medicine. This compulsory combination was devised to enable students to earn their livelihood in the *Grihasthashram*. In the alternative scheme, the students were expected to specialize in English with Mathematics, Science or Western Philosophy. Apart from this, great attention was paid to the observance of *Brahmcharya*, performance of *Sandhya* and *Havan* and character formation of the students.

The remarkable feature of the syllabus was the due regard that was accorded to English. The *Niyamavali* of the Gurukul, while justifying the inclusion of English remarked, "Apart from the fact that the study of English as an essential part in any educational scheme, is a political necessity for India, the truth cannot be gainsaid that useful information can be had on every conceivable subject embodied in the almost inexhaustible literature of that language ... a fair knowledge of that language would materially help him (the student) in his course in life. Moreover, we cannot overlook the fact that ... the study of English is, and will remain for some time to come a *sine qua non*. The study of English, to a limited extent, is also necessary for the preachers of the Vedic *Dharma*, who have not infrequently to preach to the English educated classes".[41] It was, however, decided to introduce, English in the ninth form. Gurukul Kangri, which developed into a full-fledged university in 1921, was increasingly accepted as an alternative form of schooling and at the end of five years the number of its students rose to 159. The Kangri Gurukul was followed by a number of other Gurukuls for boys, the prominent ones being, Gurukul Mahavidyalaya, Jwalapur and Brindaban Gurukul.

Mahatma Munshiram spearheaded the campaign for Kanya Gurukul in 1889 in his series of articles, *Adhura Insaf*. He, also, put forward the suggestion that Putri Pathshala of Ferozepur could be expanded into a Kanya Gurukul.[42] This suggestion was however never implemented. In 1891, when Kanya Pathshala was set up in Jullunder, Munshiram wanted it to adopt the Gurukul system of education. He said, 'If the officials of the school construct a house two to three miles away from the city and convert it into an *ashram* for Kanya Mahavidyalaya and after duly segregating unmarried girls from married girls and widows, replace all male teachers by female teachers, this can be considered as the first step towards the transformation of Kanya Mahavidyalaya into Putri Gurukul".[43] Since the very beginning, the *Niyamavali* of Gurukul Kangri had a note that as soon as there were enough resources, a Gurukul for girls would also be established.[44] Shraddhanand's preoccupation with the boys' Gurukul however left him with insufficient time and resources for the Kanya Gurukul.

The first Gurukul for girls was started at Hathras in 1910 but it had to be closed due to functional problems and want of resources.[45] In 1916, Swami Shraddhanand reiterated the demand for a Kanya Gurukul through the columns of his journal, *Saddharmapracharak*. He argued that a Gurukul for girls could be more meaningful since the major criticism against education of boys in Gurukuls was that it was not employment-oriented. This kind of disapproval was not applicable to girls' Gurukuls, for they were not required to enter into any profession.[46] The establishment of Kanya Gurukul, Indraprastha in 1923 marks the beginning of a new trend in women's education. The Gurukul was affiliated to Gurukul Kangri. While the physical arrangements were the same, substantial changes were made in the curriculum, to make it more suitable for the specific functions and roles of women. Instead of an exhaustive study of all the four *Vedas*, only 100 *mantras* of *Rig Veda*, 50 *mantras* of *Yajur Veda* and 150 *mantras* of *Atharva Veda* were to be mastered to become a *Snatika*. Chemistry, Physics and Engineering were replaced by training in child rearing. Mathematics was replaced by simple Arithmetic and Book-keeping to enable women to maintain household accounts. Six systems of philosophy were considered to be unnecessary for women. Therefore, only *Prashastpadbhashya* was included in the syllabus. Similarly, *Ashthadhyayi Sampurna Shanka-Samadhan* and *Mahabhashya Nawahink*, which were taught in the boys Gurukul were replaced by simple grammar. Indian history was also taught to the girls. In 1930, medical science and physics were also included in the curriculum. In addition to these, girls were also trained in such arts as sewing, knitting, embroidery, cookery and music. Sanskrit was introduced in the college section. This syllabus covered a period of 11 years. The Gurukul was started with five classes of the school section and later on increased to its full course of 11 years; eight classes in the school section and three in the college section.[47] It attracted students from Punjab, Bihar, Bengal, Karnataka, Fiji and Eastern Africa. By 1941, there were three Gurukuls for women at Dehradun, Hathras and Porbander. At present, there are innumerable Gurukuls for women, notable among them being at Dehradun, Hardwar, Porbander, Kankhal, Rohtak, Itola, Jamnagar, Baroda, Sonepat, Varanasi and Narela.[48]

The Gurukul system of education became a subject of criticism by both, Samajists and non-Samajists. Henry W. Nevinson, after visiting the Gurukul Kangri, in the first decade of the nineteenth century wrote, "such isolation in the midst of our common and intermingled world is, perhaps, dangerous. It comes too near the inhuman monotony of workhouse schools. It is likely to exaggerate the desires and curiosity of growing men, or to produce the hesitation of bashful and secluded lives when confronted with the need for action ... even if we grant that most parents are unfit to bring up children, sixteen years, seems too long for any boy to remain in the same place, with the same teachers and the same companions"[49].

Lala Lajpat Rai, too, condemned the isolation of the students from actual conditions of life in the Gurukul system of education. He remarked, "The new idea is to let the boys and girls be surrounded by the conditions of life in which they have to move and which they have to meet in later life". Moreover, he felt that the personal relationship of *Guru* and *Shishya* had crippling effects on the development of a pupil's individuality. He wrote, 'The aim of every parent and teacher should be to enable the children and pupils to be greater and better persons than mere copies of themselves".[50] Despite these variegated limitations, it must be admitted that Gurukul system of education forms one of the most distinctive and original contribution of Arya Samaj to the evolution of national education in India.

Besides Kanya Mahavidyalaya, Kanya Pathshalas and Kanya Gurukuls, Samajist experimented with numerous alternatives in women's education to reach out to larger number of women. Lucknow Stree Samaj started Arya Stri Shikshalaya in December, 1915, for those women, who were either housewives or those who observed strict *purda* could not attend the existing schools for girls. The classes were held once in a week. Twenty *purda* women attended the classes.[51] Arya Samaj of Lyallpur ran a school of vocational training for women under its auspices called the League of Women. The League enabled women to earn their own livelihood or supplement the meagre incomes of their families.[52]

Arya Samaj established a wide network of schools for girls. By 1912, Arya Samajists had established over 100 schools. Even distant regions like Bengal, Hyderabad and Sind did not remain untouched.[53] The phenomenal success of the Arya Samaj evoked mixed feelings of appreciation and fear even amongst the colonial officials. Lt Governor of Punjab admitted in 1893, "In the matter of female education, we are deplorably backward. Not one girl in a thousand receives any education. The Arya Samaj has been displaying commendable zeal in this direction and under their auspices there are many well-connected schools in the province".[54] Butler expressed his apprehension regarding the Samaj's tremendous success in this direction, thus, "If the government is not quick it will find the women of India educated by Arya Samajists ... our position in the country will be almost hopeless, if the women are trained up in hostility to us."[55] The most favourable outcome of the Samajist campaign for women's education was that it led Sanatan Dharm Sabha, the leading body of conservative Hindus, to establish schools for girls in Punjab. This was, perhaps, the most significant outcome because the initiative of the Sabha went a long way in mitigating the resistance from caste orthodoxy and dissolution of traditional social prejudices against women's education.

Girls' schools under the auspices of Arya Samaj added distinctive dimensions to women's education. The imparting of education through the medium of Hindi and strong religious and moral content of the curriculum not only reinforced cultural roots but went a long way in assuaging the fears of the community regarding cultural alienation of women. Women had been considered as repositories of culture and tradition and it was feared that exposure to modern western education would distance them from their cultural tradition and conventional roles. The leaders of the Arya Samaj had aimed at the all-round development of personalities of the girl-students. The curriculum was designed to facilitate moral, intellectual and aesthetic faculties of the students. The Samajist leaders, however, did not consider women's employment outside homes as appropriate and necessary. They, instead, sought to relate education to women's roles as wives and mothers. Mahatma Hansraj, while emphasizing the different spheres of work of men and women, wrote, "Necessarily, this difference demands a difference in the scheme of students. Women exist to make a heaven of this earth and if the education they receive does not help them to make heaven of their homes, it stands self condemned".[56] In an article, '*Striyan aur Vakalat*', Swami Shraddhanand categorically ruled out those careers which had traditionally been considered the preserve of men. He remarked, "God has provided for a lot of difference between the functions of men and women. In its place, this difference is beneficial. Without the courage of men and modesty of women, social cycle would not run smoothly. The functions which belong to a woman's sphere cannot be performed by men, while those belonging to a man's sphere should remain their special preserve. Two wheels of the chariot should remain in their proper places, then only can the chariot move".[57] The Mahatma section felt that those women who wished to devote themselves to the highest service of humanity by remaining single may opt for any career but women as wives and mothers have special duties and their education must correspond to those duties.

Leading Samajist women like Satyavati, Kalavati and Vidyavati Seth, too, attached priority to women's roles as wives and mothers.[58] Kalavati felt that those women who wished to pursue higher echelons of knowledge and opt for a career should remain *Brahmcharinis*. Therefore, they advocated that women should be kept free from an educational system that was burdensome and, instead, be trained in household accomplishments. While Samajists were not against women's participation in public life, they feared that social stability would be disturbed if women indulged in multiple functions.

Keeping in view the limited purpose of women's education 'masculine' subjects like Mathematics, Geography, Economics,

Philosophy, Physics, Chemistry and Engineering were substituted by 'feminine' subjects like simple Arithmetic, Home Science, Book-Keeping, a little bit of Medical Science required for child bearing, rearing etc. sewing, culinary arts and embroidery. In the curriculum of the boys' schools their role as bread earners remained a major consideration. This attitude came in for sharp criticism from some Samajist leaders like Lala Lajpat Rai who outrightly rejected the idea of different educational requirements of men and women. He felt that it would be highly detrimental if 'education of girls was primarily meant to instill in them the ideals of motherhood'. "We certainly want more affectionate wives and good fathers but women are more than that just as men are more than affectionate husbands and good fathers."[59] Bhimsen Vidyalankar (Mantri, Arya Pratinidhi Sabha, Punjab) remarked, women is, no doubt, a mother, but apart from that she can be anything according to her *varna*, a teacher, a preacher, judge, commander-in-chief, soldier, a trader and a professional. After reading Dayanand's *Bhashyas*, it seems that there is no accomplishment, which women cannot acquire … . This dream of Dayanand is incomprehensible even to his followers."[60] In fact, the Arya Samajists digressed from Dayanand's concept of women's education that had not linked acquisition of learning to the social functions and roles of women.

Segregated educational institutions for girls and boys formed yet another significant attribute of Samajist educational institutions. According to Chamupati, a prominent member of the Mahatma section, "Apart from moral considerations, which should dominate, in decisions of matters involving cultural accompaniment of the sexes, there are also educational and economic drawbacks in a system yoking persons of different sexes together … . Providence it appears has assigned the winning of bread to men and management of household to women. Such being their respective parts in the economy of both, the community and the household, it is but necessary that their training for these parts be different".[61] Apart from highlighting the basic differences between the role and functions of men and women, mixed education was rejected since it was considered to have been the cause of keen rivalry and bitter resentment between the opposite sexes for social and political rights and also led to the 'unsexing process'.

Lajpat Rai, leader of the College section, displayed a more rational attitude on the subject. He found the concept of limited education for women in separate educational institutions detrimental to both the sexes. He advocated combined education to render a more harmonious intermingling of the two sexes. He was strongly against the conservative attitudes of compartmentalizing the students into two different segments. Nevertheless, in an era when social prejudices against institutional and formal schooling for girls were deeply entrenched, co-educational institutions would have caused enormous trepidation.

The Arya Samaj refrained from introducing radical measures that would have discouraged people from sending girls to school. Their interventions, like separate institutions and different curriculum for girls, were devised in deference to popular feelings. They incorporated diverse subjects for holistic development of the students. Quite significantly, the emphasis on moral and religious content of education was the most decisive factor that produced social sanction for Arya Samajist educational institutions for girls. Moreover, the most remarkable outcome of their efforts for diffusion of education among girls was the stimulation of similar endeavours among the conservative Hindus, spearheaded by their leading organization, the Sanatan Hindu Mahasabha. The contribution of Arya Samaj to the growth of education and diffusion of learning among boys and girls has received universal appreciation. Nevertheless, it was the Samaj's dedication to the cause of women's education that has been upheld as historic, incredible and truly groundbreaking. Despite their multifaceted approach to the widow's question, they could not achieve social acceptance for widow remarriage but they were able to gain a significant breakthrough as far as education for girls was concerned. It required the zeal, passion and resolute determination of the Samajists to transform social attitudes towards women's education. Unfortunately, too much emphasis on the communal nature of Arya Samaj due to its proselyting activities, resulting in its direct confrontation with extremist Muslim organizations, has overshadowed its seminal contribution towards women's education.

Notes

1. Veena Mazumdar, The Social Reform Movement in India, from Ranade to Nehru, in B.R. Nanda (ed.), *Indian Women: From Purdah to Modernity*, p. 48.
2. Malavika Karlekar, Women's Nature and Access to Education, in Karuna Chanana (ed.), *Socialisation, Education and Women*, pp. 136–137.
3. D.K. Karve, *Looking Back*, p. 97.
4. *Collected Works of Vivekanand*, Vol. VII, p. 217.
5. L.V. Kaikini (ed.), *Speeches and Writings of N.G. Chandavarkar*, p. 37.
6. Aparna Basu, A Century's Journey: Women's Education in Western India, 1820–1920, in Karuna Chanana, op. cit., p. 74; Pandita Ramabai, *The High Caste Hindu Woman*, p. 57.
7. In 1891, the *Bangabasi*, a journal of Hindu orthodoxy accused Kadambini of being a whore. According to Malvika Karlekar, 'In calling Kadambini a whore the *Bangabasi* was externalizing the male fear of a competitive and competent woman.' Malavika Karlekar, *Voices from Within: Early Personal Narratives of Bengali Women*.
8. Gopal Ganesh Agarkar, 'Common Curriculum for Boys and Girls' Mathreyi Krishnaraj, *Remaking Society for Women: Visions, Past and Present*, pp. 27–28.
9. R. Nathan, Progress of Education in India: 1897–98, 1901–1902, Vol. I, *Fourth Quinquennial Review*, p. 258.
10. Karuna Chanana (ed.), *Socialisation, Education and Women*, p. 101.
11. K.W. Jones, *Arya Dharma*, p. 19.
12. Shyamla Bhatia, *Social Change and Politics in Punjab, 1898–1910*, p. 128.
13. Shri Ram Sharma (ed.), *Our Education Mission, An Account of Education Work of the Arya Samajes under the Arya Pradeshik Pratinidhi Sabha*, The Dayanand Anglo Vedic College, Lahore, pp. 7–9.
14. *Proceedings*, Dayanand Anglo-Vedic College, 1911–1915, June 7, 1914, cited from, K.W. Jones, op. cit., p. 226.
15. *Tribune*, January 15, 1893.
16. K.W. Jones, op. cit., p. 77 and *Punjabee*, 3.4.1907 in Shyamla Bhatia, op. cit., p. 130.
17. For Shraddhanand's views, see, Swami Shraddhanand, 'Stri Shiksha', in Rajendra Jigyasu (ed.), op. cit., pp. 9–17. And also, 'Adhura Insaf', in *Kalyan Marg Ka Pathik*, (An Autobiography of Swami Shraddhanand) in B.L. Bhartiya (ed.), *Swami Shraddhanand Granthavali*, Vol. I, p. 189.
18. Stri Shiksha, *Anath Rakshak*, September, 1919, pp. 6–8.
19. 'Female Education', *Tribune*, May 9, 1894, p. 5, cited from, K.W. Jones, op. cit., p. 108.
20. Lala Devraj, *Ek Anpad Stri Ki Yatra*, Source: Shrimati Paropkarini Sabha, Ajmer.

21. The girls' school at Ferozepur formed one of the earliest attempts at imparting education to women in Punjab. The school, therefore, found frequent mention in the education reports of the province of Punjab. The Education Report of the year 1888–89 commended the institution thus, "A Boarding House is attached also to the girls' school and orphanage maintained by the Arya Samaj at Ferozepur. The arrangements could appear to be satisfactory. A rich shawl merchant of Amritsar, who now carries on business at Cuttack and is a member of the Arya Samaj has allowed his two daughters to live in the Boarding House". Education in the Punjab, *Tribune*, March 8, 1890.
22. Bhimsen Vidyalankar, *Arya Pratinidhi Sabha, Punjab Ka Sachitra Itihas*, p. 91; Swami Shraddhanand, 'Stri Shiksha', in Rajendra Jigayasu (ed.), op. cit., p. 14; Jordens, *Swami Shraddhanand*, p. 26; K.W. Jones, op. cit., p. 103.
23. The incident that has become integral to the Arya Samajist lore is that Munshi Ram decided to set up a girls' school when he heard his daughter Ved Kumari reciting Isa Mera Ram Ramaiya, Isa Mera Krishna Kanhaiya. This episode caused immense consternation among the Arya Samajists. The proselyting activities of the missionary schools were a well-known fact. The *Tribune* in an article 'Female Education in Punjab' referred to this, The girls' schools maintained by Christian missionaries cannot be very popular. The mission of these institutions is not purely educational and managers and teachers in their enthusiasm resort to practices, which are simply revolting. *Tribune*, March 7, 1904.
24. *Digest of the Kanya Mahavidyalaya Reports*, cited in, K.W. Jones, op. cit., p. 105.
25. Jones, op. cit., p. 215.
26. For the debate and disagreements among the Arya Samajists refer, *Dayanand Anglo Vedic College Samachar*, February, 1894, p. 5, cited in, Vidyalankar Bhimsen, op. cit., p. 98; *Tribune*, March 28, 1894, p. 5, cited in, K.W. Jones, op. cit, p. 106; Jordens, op. cit., p. 40.
27. *Tribune*, March 7, 1904. Also 'Female Education in the Punjab', *Tribune*, November 28, 1906.
28. *Panchal Pandita*, November, 1900.
29. *Tribune*, March 7, 1904 and November 28, 1906.
30. Ram Chandra Javed, *Punjab Ka Arya Samaj*, p. 17.
31. Details regarding Kanya Pathshala have been cited from Shadiram Joshi, Kanya Mahavidyalaya, Jullunder, p. 109; Satyaketu Vidyalankar, *Arya Samaj Ka Itihas*, Vol. III, pp. 244–245 and K.W. Jones, op. cit., p. 186; Satyadev Vidyalankar, *Lala Devrajji*, p. 49; K.W. Jones, *Arya Samaj in Punjab: A Study of Social Reform and Religious Revivalism*, (Unpublished Ph.D. thesis), p. 253.
32. *Arya Patrika*, December 24, 1896, cited from, Bhimsen Vidyalankar, op. cit., p. 101.
33. Durga Das, *India: From Curzon to Nehru and After*, pp. 34–35.

34. For details of the school see, *The 28th and 31st Annual Reports of Mathura Prasad Gulab Devi Arya Kanya Pathshala, Ajmer and Smarika, Shradheya Chachiji*, p. 9.
35. The 28th Annual Report of the School prided itself on the fact that the students of the Pathshala have turned out to be remarkable and amiable housewives. Even in today's quarrelsome atmosphere of mutual bickering in the family they preserve a peaceful environment in their homes. *28th Annual Report of Mathura Prasad Gulab Devi Arya Kanya Pathshala*, p. 6; J. Mitra, Assistant Superintendent of Female Education, Delhi, Ajmer-Merwara, remarked, "This is a private school. The individual effort of a wonderfully inspired woman named Gulab Devi, whose desire is to teach girls to be simple good women filling in their rightful place in their homes as good mothers". *The 31st Annual Report of Mathura Prasad Gulab Devi Arya Kanya Pathshala, Ajmer*, p. 11.
36. *Arya Stree Samaj, Ajmer Ka Vivran, 1906–1913 AD*, p. 7.
37. *Arya Directory*, 1941, p. 179.
38. Swami Shraddhanand, *Autobiography*, M.R. Jambhunathan (ed.), p. 38.
39. Lala Lajpat Rai, *A History of Arya Samaj*, p. 144.
40. *Arya Patrika*, cited from, K.W. Jones, *Arya Samaj in the Punjab: A Study in Social Reform and Religious Revivalism*, p. 267.
41. J.T.F. Jordens, *Swami Shraddhanand*, p. 57.
42. Swami Shraddhanand, *Kalyan Marg Ka Pathik*, (Autobiography), p. 176.
43. *Saddharmapracharak*, December 11, 1903, cited from, Bhimsen Vidyalankar, op. cit., p. 394. Mahatama Munshiram had extended his full cooperation to Lala Devraj in the establishment of Kanya Pathshala and Kanya Mahavidyalaya. Later on, however, the two developed serious differences over Kanya Mahavidyalaya, Jullunder, which led to a split between the two friends. Differences perhaps, commenced on the issue of converting the Mahavidyalaya into a Gurukul. Without giving any inkling of the exact cause of the divide between the two, it has been referred to in Munshiram's biographies and letters. See, Indra Vidyavachaspati, *Mere Pita, Sansmaran*, pp. 95–96; J.T.F. Jordens, *Swami Shraddhanand*, p. 54; *Indra Vidyavachaspati Collection*, Correspondence between Sumitra and Munshiram, Group 1(b).
44. Bhimsen Vidyalankar, op. cit., p. 394.
45. *Kanya Gurukul Ki Kahani*, in Hari Shankar Sharma (ed.), *Lakshmi Devi Abhinandan Granth*, pp. 5–6.
46. *Saddharmapracharak*, May 6, 1917 and August 4, 1917.
47. Satyaketu Vidyalankar, op. cit., pp. 467–470.
48. K.S. Arya, *Hundred Years of D.A.V. Movement*, pp. 72–90.
49. N.W. Newinson, *The New Spirit in India*, p. 307.
50. Lala Lajpat Rai, *Problem of National Education in India*, p. 30.

51. *Saddharmapracharak*, January, 1916.
52. Article of P. Seshadri in H.B. Sarda (ed.), *Dayanand Commemoration Volume*, p. 42.
53. In 1941, the Samaj had established 100 girls' schools in Punjab, 67 in the United Provinces, 14 in Bihar, 7 in Rajasthan, 2 in Madhya Pradesh, 3 in Calcutta, 4 in Hyderabad, and 1 in Sind. V.L Shastri, op. cit., p. 96 and *Arya Directory*, 1941, pp. 155–184.
54. *Tribune*, December 20, 1893, cited from, Shiv Dayal Gupta, *British Attitude and Policy Towards Arya Samaj*, p. 71.
55. Martin Gilbert, *Servant of India* (*Dunlop Smith Diary*) dated 1–12–1907, cited from, Shyamla Bhatia, op. cit., p. 132.
56. Sri Ram Sharma, *Mahatma Hans Raj: Maker of the Modern Punjab*, p. 78.
57. *Saddharmapracharak*, July 7, 1917. For views of the Mahatma section refer, Prof. Sudhakar, Co-education, *The Vedic Magazine and Gurukul Samachar*, April-May, 1916, pp. 1061–1062.
58. For their views refer, Kalavati, *Bhartiya Mahilaon ke Liye Uchit Shiksha Kram*; Vidyavati, "Striyon ke Liye Uchit Shiksha Kram", *Saddharmapracharak*, August 4, 1917.
59. Lala Lajpat Rai, *Writings and Speeches*, Vol. I, p. 381, cited from, Shamanand Shahi, *Lala Lajpat Rai*, p. 229.
60. Bhimsen Vidyalankar, op. cit., p. 92.
61. Chamupati, *Glimpses of Dayanand*, p. 85. In the nineteenth and early twentieth centuries, the traditional distinction of sex schools was common. Co-educational schools were, however, not altogether absent. In 1901–02, there were 1,98,000 girls under instruction in boys' schools and 17,000 boys in girls' schools. R. Nathan, op. cit., p. 319.

‖Chapter 8‖

Conclusion

The Arya Samaj movement made a critical contribution towards liberalization of social norms in the Hindu society. Dayanand and later the Samajist leaders instead of visualizing piecemeal reforms sought to restructure some of the basic institutions of the Hindu society, particularly caste and marriage. At the same time, the tireless efforts of the Samajists led to wider diffusion of education among boys and girls. These reforms, apart from modernizing the Hindu social structure, were motivated with a view to redeem the status and position of women. While dealing with a gamut of social reform issues, they brought about substantive changes in the status of women. The preceding chapters underscore their concern for upliftment of women's condition that was pre-eminently exemplified in their tenacious efforts and dogged determination in the spheres of widow remarriage and women's education.

Ironically, the dominant image of Arya Samaj that has survived in popular memory, British official records and even in historical writings is one of communal organization and a movement that took its role as defender of the faith too seriously. In fact, Arya Samaj has been held responsible for the worsening of inter-communal relations. Nonetheless, Arya Samaj added a new and extremely significant dimension to Hinduism. It became a forceful religion, a *pracharak dharm* and a converting religion "with a capacity for defence and offence". The revivalist nature of the movement has been another stereotype that has become integral to the image of Dayanand and Arya Samaj. This was probably because Dayanand while exploring the basis of an Aryan identity projected the *Vedas* as a unified source of Hinduism and prime determinant of the cultural ethos. The urgency to assert the supremacy of Hinduism, unfortunately, led to his aggressive, parochial and intolerant posturing towards other religions.

This overriding discourse regarding the Samaj has eclipsed a significant strand of the movement, i.e., its persevering endeavours for social and religious reform. It clearly emerges from the study that for Dayanand, resurgent Hinduism had to be a reformed Hinduism. The preceding chapters prove beyond doubt that the real impact of Arya Samaj was as a dynamic movement combatting superstition, challenging the caste system, championing the cause of women, pleading for liberalization of marriage. The reformer put forth a comprehensive programme of social reform – firstly, to prevent the missionaries from luring the disadvantaged communities into their fold and, secondly, to vindicate his vociferous assertions regarding the superiority of Hindu religion and society. Dayanand was apparently intimidated by the missionaries' enthusiasm and rigour in reaching out to the people through a wide network of schools, orphanages, medical missions, *zenana* missions and work among untouchables.

Dayanand Saraswati's conceptualization of regenerated Hinduism and his approach to social reformation distinguished him from other exponents of the Golden Age theory, articulated during the nineteenth century. For the regeneration of the Aryan race, he carved out a grandiose blueprint of socio-religious and political structure through a painstaking reinterpretation of the *Vedas*. Dayanand's primary agenda was creation of physically robust, morally upright, intellectually enlightened and culturally proud Hindu race. Women, therefore, had a vital role to play in reproducing and nurturing a healthy race. Dayanand's construction of an alternative model of womanhood was not merely an exercise in the creation of a new self-image in which fellow Indians could take pride, nor did he use fragments of the past for imparting legitimacy to isolated women's issues such as *sati*, polygamy, widow remarriage etc. Instead, he wished to recreate the idyllic conditions of the Vedic Age, characterized by equality between men and women in the spheres of education, religion and marriage. Dayanand's inclination to actualize his version of reformed Hinduism and counteract the colonial critique led him to deal with women's issues in a comprehensive manner.

It emerges quite clearly that Dayanand was deeply concerned by the decadent nature of the institutions of caste and marriage. While apparently upholding the scriptural basis of caste, Dayanand advocated a fundamental revision of caste system by shifting its basis from birth to *guna*, *karma* and *svabhava*. He also pleaded for a healthier institution of marriage when he laid stress on compatibility and companionship in marriage. To achieve this objective, he suggested marriages between individuals corresponding to each other in *guna*, *karma* and *svabhava*, rather than abiding by the boundaries of castes and sub-castes. His passion for equal marriages found its most vehement expression in the advocacy of a single status for women rather than marry a person unsuitable for her. Although espousal of an unusually advanced marriageable age for men and women and the doctrine of *niyoga* are some of the aberrations in the otherwise rational thinking of the reformer, yet in totality Dayanand articulated a comprehensive and a progressive outlook on women's issues.

The foregoing chapters bring out the tenacity, consistency and commitment of Arya Samaj in actualizing the vision of its founder for socio-religious resurgence of Hinduism. Its indisputable contribution towards betterment of women's status in the early decades of the twentieth century needs to be particularly commended on account of two factors – firstly, these were the years when the hegemony of the nationalist struggle had considerably weakened the cause of social reform; secondly, numerous organizations which had been striving for social betterment in the nineteenth century had been drawn by the irresistible pull of the political agitation. Consequently, this period saw the gradual politicization of the majority of associations and groups.[1] Arya Samaj, however, assiduously remained engaged in its efforts to bring about progressive changes in the social fabric and herein lay the historic role of the movement. Moreover, the Samaj was able to impart critical importance and urgency to women's issues which no earlier or contemporary movement could accomplish.

The death of the founder was followed by a brief period of indolence and internal dissensions. However, soon after their crusade for social reform gained momentum when both the groups within the Samaj – the College faction and the Mahatma faction – dedicated themselves towards realization of the founder's ideology for resurgence of Hindu social structure. Nevertheless, it was the Mahatma or Gurukul faction under the leadership of Samajist stalwarts Lala Munshiram and Lala Devraj that launched a multifaceted programme for women's upliftment laying special emphasis on rehabilitation of widows, dissemination of education, promotion of equal marriage, liberalization of caste system and simplification of marriage rituals.

The domain in which Samajist success was most appreciable was their exceptional commitment towards rehabilitation of widows. These exertions deserve particular appreciation particularly when they are adjudged in the backdrop of the failure of the earlier movements. The sluggish progress of early years was replaced by a more meaningful, structured and concerted programme for bringing reprieve, dignity and self-sufficiency for the miserable widow. Quite significantly, the Samajists were able to make a dent in the extremely rigid postures in the realm of widow remarriages. In the year 1924, they were able to arrange 892 widow remarriages and by 1931, the number registered a steep rise to a phenomenal 5,484. The establishment of the Vidhwa Vivah Sahayak Sabha with the primary objective of promoting widow remarriages, the incorporation of the widow remarriage movement within the larger movement of *Hindu Sanghathan*, the intensive instructive propaganda and the establishment of widow homes, were measures that contributed to the success of the movement. The most critical intervention was, however, the strategic move whereby the widow remarriage movement was positioned within the *Hindu Sanghathan*. It certainly gave a new lease of life to the failing widow remarriage movement. Quite pertinently, it had the effect of softening the trenchant opposition of the orthodox Hindus whose hostility had hitherto remained the major stumbling block in the widow remarriage movement.

The sphere in which the Samajists triumphed over entrenched social mindset was women's education. Their dogged perseverance not only led to a higher literacy rate amongst the Arya Samajist women but it produced widespread social sanction for women's education when it was able to stimulate a similar movement amongst the Sanatanists. The success of Arya Samaj in this particular direction was ensured by the numerous dimensions they imparted to women's education. Quite pertinently, they chose Hindi as the medium of education and painstakingly composed text books with intellectual content that did not alienate women from their cultural moorings. They were able to mitigate the fears of the conservative sections regarding exposure of women to westernization. The major contribution of the Samajists in the sphere of education was to evolve an alternative system of education with an accent on formation of character, inculcation of moral values, revival of *Brahmcharya* and study of ancient scriptures. Gurukul system of education is particularly pertinent to the present times when youth is being driven by consumer culture or the market culture and crass materialism.

A comprehensive system of education coupled with increasing involvement of women in Samaj activities and emergence of Stree Samajes were enabling measures for women's participation in the national movement. Lala Devraj, the pioneer of women's education and founder of the renowned Kanya Mahavidyalaya observed with extreme satisfaction on the active participation of women in the Civil Disobedience Movement (1931–32), "Whether India attains *Swarajya* or not, [but] the mission of my life is fulfilled. The dream of Indian women's awakening which I had nurtured has come true".[2]

The efforts to liberalize and simplify the institution of marriage surfaces as yet another critical area where the Samajists tried to make inroads. These were aimed at strengthening the institution of marriage and also for creating favourable conditions for women. The introduction of simple Vedic ceremonies, as also rejection of the custom of dowry and other festivities, was indeed a contrast to the complex rituals and prolonged celebrations that characterized traditional Hindu weddings. The quintessential Arya Samajist marriage has emerged as an embodiment of simplicity and dignity. Sadly, people have remained largely indifferent to the dignified marriage ceremonies evolved by the Arya Samaj. Indian marriages continue to be ostentatious, extravagant and comprise of prolonged pre-wedding and post-wedding ceremonies marked by pomp and grandeur.

Quite pertinently, the Samajist endeavour for a more companionate conjugal relationship by arranging marriages on the basis of compatibility between *guna*, *karma* and *svabhava*, irrespective of the rules and regulations of the caste, too received a gloomy response. Such an approach towards settlement of marriages was considered extremely radical in a social milieu fettered by the rigours of the caste system. The Samajists themselves could not sever their links with the larger society and hence, did not pursue these reforms resolutely. The emergence of radical groups within the Mahatma section of the Samaj did provide a fillip to the cause in the first two decades of the twentieth century. The whole subject of caste reform also received attention with the onset of propaganda regarding *Hindu Sanghthan* and the imminent threat to the survival of Hinduism. The formation of *Jat Pat Todak Mandal* in the 1920s by the College faction also testifies to the sincerity of the Samaj leaders towards liberalization of caste rules. Nevertheless, caste reforms could create a dent only on the enlightened sections of society and were more or less restricted to the leaders of the Samaj.

The most notable outcome of the Arya Samaj movement was the stirrings of reform that it could induce among the conservative Hindus, i.e., the Sanatanis. Quite incredibly, the Sanatani Hindus and their premier organization, Sanatan Dharma Sabha, started pursuing a liberal agenda on women's issues, most notably women's education and widow remarriage. They joined hands with the Samajists on these issues and promoted the same from their own platforms. Following the lead of the Samaj, the Sanatan Dharm Sabha also encouraged women to take part in public activities for women. In 1917, for the first time women delegates had a special session for themselves during the anniversary session of the Sanatan Dharma Sabha in Patiala.

The convergence between the two movements that had been adversaries, as far as their socio-religious creed was concerned, was affected due to various factors. The intensive propaganda of the Samajist leaders regarding a steady decline in the numerical strength of the Hindus, as compared to other religions and their appeal for Hindu solidarity, engendered a favourable reaction from the conservative sections. Henceforth, the orthodox sections in order to stem the tide of conversions from Hinduism adopted a sympathetic stance towards widows' rehabilitation, women's education and the issue of untouchability. Moreover, the Sanatanists apprehended that popularity of the doctrines of the Samaj might culminate in their large scale acceptance. Perhaps, this was a major consideration when the Sanatanists liberalized their stand on issues which it had earlier denounced as contravention of the creed of Hinduism.

There were other factors that explain the association between the orthodox and liberal streams. Some programmes of Arya Samaj like

Shuddhi, orphan relief and *Go-Raksha* struck a sympathetic chord amongst the Sanatani Hindus.[3] Moreover, increasing tensions between Muslims and Hindus during this period led to narrowing of differences between the Samajists and the Sanatanists. J. Ried Graham has found an explanation in the changing nature of the second and third generations of Arya Samajists. The later generations were not willing to rouse the ire of the Sanatanists by proposing measures of reform that were absolutely unacceptable to the latter. They were, therefore, willing to compromise on most issues which did not infringe upon their fundamental doctrines. Lala Lajpat Rai had noted with extreme satisfaction the collaboration between Arya Samaj and Sanatanis but, at the same time, apprehended the danger to the future of Arya Samaj moving closer to orthodox Hinduism. He remarked, "In this increasing friendliness with orthodox Hindus lies the strength of Arya Samaj, therein lurks the danger of a lowering of standards of reform. We desire the Arya Samaj to serve Hindu community ... but we should not like the Arya Samaj to be lost in the sea of Hinduism."[4] While it is true that the Sanatanists could not be brought completely within the reformist ethos, nonetheless the mitigation of their rigid stances on issues like widow remarriage and women's education signified a triumph for the Samaj.

The role of Arya Samaj in weakening the centuries old prejudices had been universally appreciated. The movement definitely had a wider appeal than the earlier movements for socio-religious resurgence of the Indian society. Dayanand and Arya Samaj did succeed in creating urgency for women's issues. Their holistic perspective, multi-pronged strategies and whole-hearted enthusiasm for issues like women's education and widow remarriage ultimately triumphed over the unyielding and hardened attitudes of the people. It is rarely recognized that Arya Samaj's herculean efforts to diffuse education amongst women prepared the milieu for women's participation in the freedom movement and the subsequent emergence of the women's movement. They affected a paradigm shift in the widow remarriage movement in the sense that so far humanitarian concerns and sympathy for the forlorn widow had dominated the discourse on widows. The concern for widows was now translated into the larger concern for saving the Hindu religion from extinction. By arousing a sense of urgency, Arya Samaj was able to elicit support and sympathy from Sanatani Hindus, thus affecting the lives of a larger number of widows. Despite the fact that the movement derived inspiration from ancient tradition, their perspective and efforts, with regard to women's education and widow remarriage were clearly a sincere struggle for gender equality and social resurgence. Significantly, contemporary Indian society and policy makers are still grappling with these challenges. Female illiteracy, caste rigidity and strict control over female sexuality continue to keep women in a subordinate, powerless and marginalized position.

Notes

1. Punjab Hindu Sabha was one such example. While the Sabha was formed with the objective of social, religious and cultural advancement of the Hindus, it became completely political in nature by the 1920s. The *Parkash* carried the following news item, 'Punjab Hindu Sabha and the work before it'. The Sabha professes to aim at rendering social service to Hindus but social differences between the various sections of the Hindus are so great that no society can render such service to the Hindu community. It is only in regard to politics that Hindus of all persuasions can stand on a common platform and this renders it necessary for the Sabha to take up the work of safeguarding the political rights and interests of the Hindus. *Parkash*, Lahore, October 8, 1912, *Selections from Indian Newspapers published in the Punjab*, for the week ending October 19, 1912, *GI Proceedings*, Home Poll (B), November, 1912, S. No. 59.
2. Satyadev Vidyalankar, *Lala Devrajji*, p. 54.
3. J. Ried Graham, *Arya Samaj as a Reformation in Hinduism*, p. 436.
4. Lala Lajpat Rai, *History of Arya Samaj*, p. 185. Apart from Lala Lajpat Rai and J. Ried Graham, many historians have commented on the increasing proximity between the Sanatanists and the Arya Samajists. For details, refer, Umakant Upadhyaya, *Calcutta Arya Samaj ka Itihas*, pp. 119–132; Bhai Parmanand, *Hindu Sanghthan and Arya Samaj*, p. 164; *Saddharmapracharak*, May 13, 1916; K.W. Jones, *Arya Dharm*, pp. 235–252; Sri Ram Sharma, *Our Education Mission*, p. 22; Indra Vidyavachaspati, *Arya Samaj ka Itihas*, Vol. I, p. 217.

Bibliography

Dayanand Saraswati's Writings

Saraswati, Dayanand, *Aryabhivinay*, Vedic Yantralaya, Ajmer, 1987.

——, *Autobiography of Swami Dayanand Saraswati*, K.C. Yadav (ed.), Manohar, New Delhi, 1978.

——, *Dayanand Granthavali*, 2 Vols., Nirvan Shatabdi Sanskaran, Shrimati Paropkarini Sabha, Ajmer, 1983.

——, *Dayanand Pravachan Sangrah, Arthat Poona Bombay Pravachan.* Y. Mimansak (ed.), Ramlal Kapur Trust, Bhagalgarh, 1982.

——, *Dayanand Shastrarth Sangrah*, B.L. Bhartiya (ed.), Ram Lal Kapur Trust, Bhagalgarh, 1982.

——, *Maharishi Dayanand Dwara Teen Baar Mein Kaha aur Likhaya Gaya Apna Jiwan Charitra*, Adityapal Singh Arya and Vedvrata Alok (eds.), Aditi Prakashan, New Delhi, 1987.

——, *Maharishi Dayanand ke Sarvshreshtha Bhashan*, Rajdhani Granthagar, New Delhi, 1986.

——, *Rig Veda Bhashya*, Dayanand Sansthan, New Delhi.

——, *Rig Vedadi Bhashya Bhumika*, Sarvadeshik Arya Pratinidhi Sabha, New Delhi, 1982.

——, *Rishi Dayanand Swarachit, Likhit va Kathit, Janmcharit*, Bhagwat Dutt (ed.), Ramlal Kapur Trust, Amritsar.

——, *Sanskar Vidhi*, (English Translation by A. Vaidya Nath Shastri), Sarvadeshik Arya Pratinidhi Sabha, New Delhi, 1985.

——, *Satyarth Prakash*, Arsha Sahitya Prachar Trust, New Delhi, 1986 (33rd Edition), Also available in English, (Translated by Chiranjiv Bhardwaj), Sarvdeshik Arya Pratinidhi Sabha, New Delhi, 1989.

——, *Swami Dayanand ke Patra aur Vijnapan*, Vols. I and II, Y. Mimansak and Pt Bhagwat Dutt (eds.), Ramlal Kapur Trust, Bhagalgarh, 1981.

——, *Swami Dayanand ko Likhe Patra aur Vijnapan*, Vols. I and II, Y. Mimansak and Pt Bhagwat Dutt (eds.), Ramlal Kapur Trust, Bhagalgarh, 1982.

——, *Updesh Manjari* (*Poona Pravachan*), Raghuvir Singh Shastri (ed.), Arsha Sahitya Prachar Trust, Delhi, 1984.

——, *Vyavahar Bhanu*, (English Translation by R.B. Ratan Lal), Paropkarini Sabha, Ajmer (n.d.).

Tracts and Pamphlets

Aryopdeshak, Lakshman, *Niyoga Praman, Arya Musafir Granth Mala I*, 1900.

Ayurvedacharya, Harinandan, *Vidhwa Vivah Vichar*, Arya Samaj, Bikaner, 1929.

Devraj, Lala, *Ek Anpad Stree ki Yatra*, Shrimati Paropkarini Sabha, Ajmer, 1900.

Dubey, Harishankar, *Vidhwodvah Vivek*, Mahesh Pustakalaya, Ajmer, 1928.

Gupta, Ghanshyam Singh, *Arya Vivah Act: Vistrit Vyakhya, Sankshipt Itihas*, Sarvdeshik Arya Pratinidhi Sabha, Delhi, 1946.

Kavyatirth, J.P. Choudhary, *Vidhwa Vivah Prashnotri*, Tract Pracharak Mandal, Kashi, 1927.

Kavyatirth, Shyamji, *Kya Vidhwa Vivah Adharma Hai?*, Sudhar Granth Mala No. I, Shahabad, 1940.

Lala Khanulal, *Strisudhar*, published by Hussainwala, 1883.

Mimansak, Yudhishthir, *Kanyopnayan Vidhi*, Ram Lal Kapur Trust, Bhagalgarh, 1983.

Niyog Nirnaya, Sarvdeshik Arya Pratinidhi Sabha, New Delhi, 1920.

Saraswati, Swami Karmanand, *Nari Punarvivah Mimansa*, Arya Samaj, Hyderabad.

Sathe, Triyambak Rao, *Vidhwa Vivah Samvad*, published by Shrotiya Shankar Dutt (editor of *Akalhitkarak*), Bijnore, 1901.

Sharda, Kunwar Chand Karan, *College Hostel*, Vedic Yantralaya, Ajmer, 1923.

——, *Sharda Act Arthat Bal Vivah Nishedhak Kanoon*, Vedic Yantralaya, Ajmer, 1938.

——, *Vidhwa Vivah Karo*, Vedic Yantralaya, Ajmer, 1924.

Sharma, Akhilananda, *Vaidhwya Vidhwansan Champu*, Sarvdeshik Arya Pratinidhi Sabha, New Delhi, 1910.

Sharma, Bhumitra, *Niyoga Mardan ka Vimardan*, published by Raghuvir Saran Dublis (ed.), *Bhaskar*, 1920.

Swami, Pandit Chuttanlal, *Vivah Vayo Vichar*, Swami Machine Yantralaya, Meerut, 1927.

Upadhyaya, Ganga Prasad (ed.), *Dahej*, Tract No. 9, *Arya Tract Mala II*, Arya Samaj, Allahabad, 1935 (Reprint).

——, *Dukhadai Durvyasan*, Tract No. 10, *Arya Tract Mala II*, Arya Samaj, Allahabad, 1936 (Reprint).

——, *Ghar ki Devi*, *Arya Tract Mala I*, Arya Samaj, Allahabad, 1932 (Reprint).

——, *Hindu Dharma ka Nash*, Tract No. 5, *Arya Tract Mala II*, Arya Samaj, Allahabad, 1937 (Reprint).

——, *Hindu Jati ki Raksha ke Upaya*, Tract No. 6, *Arya Tract Mala II*, Arya Samaj, Allahabad, 1936 (Reprint).

——, *Hindu Strion ki Loot ke Karan*, Tract No. 3, *Arya Tract Mala II*, Arya Samaj, Allahabad, 1936 (Reprint).

——, *Hinduon Jago*, Tract No. 4, *Arya Tract Mala II*, Arya Samaj, Allahabad, 1938 (Reprint).

——, *Sharda Act Kya Hai*, Tract No. 18, *Arya Tract Mala II*, Arya Samaj, Allahabad, 1937 (Reprint).

——, *Shri Swami Shraddhanandji ka Balidan*, Tract No. 14, *Arya Tract Mala II*, Arya Samaj, Allahabad, 1938 (Reprint).

——, *Vidhwa Vivah Mimansa*, Sarvdeshik Arya Pratinidhi Sabha, New Delhi, 1930.

——, *Vidhwaen aur Desh ka Nash*, Tract No. 8, *Arya Tract Mala II*, Arya Samaj, Allahabad, 1938 (Reprint).

Vedopdeshak, Ganpati, *Vidhwa Vivah Apaddharma Hai*, Govindram Hasanand, Vedic Press, Delhi, 1928.

Vidhwa Insaf, Sarvdeshik Arya Pratinidhi Sabha, New Delhi, 1924.

Smarikas

Arya Samaj Shatabdi Samaroh, Arya Pratinidhi Sabha, Kanpur: Uttar Pradesh, 1974.

Sharma, Harishankar (ed.), *Lakshmi Devi Abhinandan Granth*, Snatika Mandal, Kanya Gurukul Mahavidyalaya, Hathras, October, 1955.

Smarika, Antarrashtriya Arya Samaj Sthapna Shatabdi Samraoh, New Delhi, December, 1975.

Smarika, Arya Samaj Shatabdi Samaroh, Amritsar, Arya Pradeshik Sabha, Amritsar, 1973.

Smarika, Shraddheya Chachiji ke Ek Sau Gyarven Janmotsav par Samarpit, Shri Mathura Prasad Gulab Devi Arya Kanya Pathshala, Ajmer, 1986.

Swarn Jayanti Smarika, Arya Samaj, Lallapura, Varanasi, 1985.

Reports

Annual Reports of Mathura Prasad Gulab Devi Arya Kanya Pathshala, Ajmer.

Annual Reports of Rajasthan Vanita Ashram, Ajmer.

Annual Reports of Shrimaddayanand Orphanage, Ajmer.

Annual Reports of Vidhwa Vivah Sahayak Sabha, Lahore.

Census Reports, Punjab, United Provinces and Bombay Presidency, 1891–1931.

Nathan, R. Progress of Education in India, 1897–98 and 1901–1902, Vol. I, Quinquennial Review, Calcutta, 1905.

Sands, E.W., Arya Samaj in the United Provinces, Allahabad, 1910.

Selections from Records, No. LIV, 'Note on the State of Education in India 1865–1866', by A.M. Monoleath, Calcutta, 1867.

Towards Equality: Report of the Committee on the Status of Women in India, Government of India, Department of Social Welfare, New Delhi, 1974.

Newspapers and Journals

Anath Rakshak, monthly journal of Srimaddayanand Orphanage, Ajmer

Arya Magazine, journal of Arya Samaj, Lahore.

Arya Martand, journal of Arya Samaj, Ajmer.

Arya Mitra, journal of Arya Samaj, Lucknow.

Arya Prakash.

Arya, monthly journal of Arya Pratinidhi Sabha, Punjab.

Gurukul Samachar and Vedic Magazine, journal of Gurukul Kangri, Haridwar.

Panchal Pandita, journal of Kanya Mahavidyalaya, Jullunder.

Prabhat.

Punjab, Past and Present.

Regenerator of Arya Varta.

Saddharmapracharak, journal of Gurukul section.

Selections from Vernacular Newspapers published in the Punjab.

Tribune.

Vidhwa Bandhu, journal of Vidhwa Vivah Sahayak Sabha.

Archival Records

Government of India, Proceedings, Home Department, Poll (B) (Confidential) November, 1912, Nos. 59–68; December, 1912, Nos. 102–112; November, 1912, Nos. 53–58; May, 1912, No. 44.

Indra Vidyavachaspati Collection, (Private Papers of Swami Shraddhanand), National Archives of India, New Delhi.

Mahakma Khas Records, Marriage Legislation File C/5/1 Volume 5, 1940; C/5/1 Volume 5, 1946; C/2/11 Volume I, Welfare Works, 1930.

Proceedings, D.A.V. College Management Committee:

(a) Papers and Correspondence relating to the award of prizes to Arya Samaj Girls School, Lahore.

(b) Private Records of Sushila Devi and Shanti Gupta.

Unpublished Works on Dayanand and Arya Samaj

Arya, K.S., Hundred Years of D.A.V. Movement (to be published).

Arya, Puran Singh, The Contribution of Arya Samaj to Education in Haryana, Dissertation for Master of Education, Kurukshetra University, 1968.

Gupta, Shashi Bala, A Survey of Gurukul System of Education in Haryana, Ph.D. Thesis, Department of Education, Kurukshetra University, 1973.

Gupta, Shiv Kumar, British Attitude and Policy towards Arya Samaj, 1875–1920, Ph.D. Thesis, Maharshi Dayanand University, Rohtak, 1981.

Jain, Pratibha, Liberation of Women: A Case Study of Jaipur Arya Samaj, Centre for Women's Studies, University of Rajasthan, Jaipur.

Jones, K.W., The Arya Samaj in Punjab: A Study of Social Reform and Religious Revivalism, 1877–1902, Ph.D. Dissertation, University of California, Berkeley, 1966.

Mittal, Chiranjeet Kumar, Development of Arya Samaj in the Punjab, Ph.D. Thesis, Punjab University, Patiala, 1978–1979.

Ried, Graham J., Arya Samaj as a Reformation in Hinduism, with special reference to Caste, Yale University, Ph.D. Dissertation, 1943.

Singh, Nagendra Prasad, Bihar Mein Arya Samaj ka Shaikshnik Yogdan, Bihar University, Muzaffarnagar.

Books on Swami Dayanand and Arya Samaj

Arya Directory, Sarvdeshik Arya Pratinidhi Sabha, New Delhi, 1941.

Arya Directory Part I and II, Sarvdeshik Arya Pratinidhi Sabha, New Delhi, 1977.

Arya Directory: *A Guide to Educational Institutions under Arya Samaj in India and Abroad,* 1983.

Arya Samaj ke Niyam aur Up-Niyam, Sarvdeshik Arya Pratinidhi Sabha, New Delhi, 1967.

Arya Stree Samaj, Ajmer ka Vivran, 1906–1913, Shrimati Paropkarini Sabha, Ajmer.

Aurobindo, Sri, *Bankim-Tilak-Dayanand*, Sarvdeshik Arya Pratinidhi Sabha, New Delhi, 1984.

Bhartiya, B.L., *Maharishi Dayanand aur Maharishi Vivekanand*, Vedic Yantralaya, Ajmer, 1975.

——, *Maharishi Dayanand aur Raja Ram Mohan Roy ke Tulnatmak Vichar*, Arya Pracharak Pustakalaya, Agra, 1955.

——, *Navjagran ke Purodha, Dayanand Saraswati*, Vedic Pustakalaya, Ajmer, 1983.

Bhartiya, Bhawani Lal and Rajendra Jigyasu (eds.), *Swami Shraddhanand Granthavali*, Vols. I to XI, Govindram Hasanand, Delhi, 1987.

Chamupati, M.A., *Glimpses of Swami Dayanand*, Sharda Mandir Limited, Delhi, 1937.

Devbala, Shanti, *Maharishi Dayanand aur Nari ki Samajik Tatha Rajnaitik Chetna*, Dr Ratna Kumari Svadhyaya Kendra, Allahabad, 1984.

Diwedi, Kapildev and Bhartendu Diwedi, *Vedamritam: Vedon Mein Nari*, Vishwabharti Anusandhan Parishad, Gyanpur (Varanasi), 1986.

Durrani, F.C. Khan, *Swami Dayanand: A Critical Study of His Life and Teachings, Lahore, 1929.*

Ghasiram, *Maharishi Dayanand Saraswati ka Jiwan Charit*, Vol. I, Arsha Sahitya Mandal Limited, Ajmer, 1950.

——, *Maharishi Dayanand Saraswati ka Jivan Charit*, Vol. II, Arsha Sahitya Mandal Limited, Ajmer, 1961.

Javed, Ram Chandra, *Punjab ka Arya Samaj*, Arya Pratinidhi Sabha, Punjab, Jullunder, 1964.

Jones, Kenneth W., *Arya Dharam: Hindu Consciousness in the Nineteenth Century Punjab*, Manohar, New Delhi, 1976.

Jordens, J.T.F., *Dayanand Saraswati: His Life and Ideas*, Oxford University Press, Delhi, Bombay, Calcutta, Madras, 1978.

——, *Swami Shraddhanand: His Life and Causes*, Oxford University Press, Delhi, New York, 1981.

Joshi, Shadiram, *Kanya Mahavidyalaya: Uttar Pashchimi Bharat Mein Shakti Jagran ka Moort Roop*, published by Ram Chandra Javed (Mantri), Kanya Mahavidyalaya, Jullunder, 1982.

Kulyar, S.P., *Swami Dayanand Saraswati: His Life and Teachings*, Sharma and Kulyar, Patna, 1938.

Lekhram, Pt, *Maharishi Dayanand ka Jivan Charitra*, (Hindi Translation by Kaviraj Abhinandan Nirmal), Harish Chandra Vidyalankar (ed.), Arya Samaj, Nayabans, Delhi, 1971.

Lakshmi, Manjulika, *Maharishi Dayanand aur Bhartiya Nari*, Dr Ratna Kumari Svadhyaya Sansthan, Allahabad, 1983.

Mal, Bahadur, *Dayanand: A Study in Hinduism*, Hoshiarpur, 1962.

Mimansak, Yuddhishthir, *Rishi Dayanand ke Granthon ka Itihas*, Dayanand Balidan Shatabdi Sanskaran, Ram Lal Kapur Trust, Bahalgarh, 1983.

Pandit, Saraswati, *A Critical Study of the Contribution of Arya Samaj to Indian Education*, Sarvdeshik Arya Pratinidhi Sabha, New Delhi, 1975.

Pareek, Radhey Shyam, *Contribution of Arya Samaj in the Making of Modern India*, Sarvdeshik Arya Pratinidhi Sabha, New Delhi, 1973.

Parmanandji, Bhai, *Hindu Sanghathan and Arya Samaj*, Central Hindu Yuvak Sabha, Lahore, 1936.

Prakash, Dev and Lala Jagat Ramji, *Arya Samaj ke Mahapurushon ke Jivan tatha Karya*, Amritsar (n.d.).

Rai, Lala Lajpat, *A History of the Arya Samaj: An Account of Its Origin, Doctrines and Activities with a Sketch of the Founder*, (Revised by Sri Ram Sharma), Orient Longmans, Bombay, Calcutta, Madras, New Delhi, 1967.

Rama and Others, *General Survey of Life and Teachings of Swami Dayanand*, L. Nand Kishore, Lahore, 1925.

Sarda, Har Bilas (ed.), *Dayanand Commemoration Volume*, Vedic Yantralaya, Ajmer, 1934.

——, *Life of Dayanand Saraswati*, Vedic Pustakalaya, Ajmer, 1968.

——, *Speeches and Writings*, Vedic Yantralaya, Ajmer, 1935.

Saraswati, Swami Satya Prakash, *A Critical Study of Philosophy of Dayanand*, Arya Pratinidhi Sabha, Rajasthan and Malwa, Ajmer, 1938.

——, *Dayanand and His Mission*, Paropkarini Sabha, Ajmer, 1983.

——, *Speeches, Writings and Addresses*, Vols. I, II and III, Dr Ratna Kumari Svadhyaya Sansthan, Allahabad, 1985.

Sarvdeshik Arya Pratinidhi Sabha ki Uplabdhiyan: Ek Drishti Mein, Sarvdeshik Arya Pratinidhi Sabha, New Delhi, 1974.

Shahi, Shamanand, *Lala Lajpat Rai: His Life and Thought*, Chanakya Publishers, Delhi, 1986.

Sharma, Sri Ram, *Arya Samaj and its Impact on Contemporary India* (in the nineteenth century), Institute of Public Administration, Una (n.d.).

——, *Mahatma Hans Raj: Maker of the Modern Punjab*, Institute of Public Administration, Una, 1941.

——, (ed.), *Our Education Mission: An Account of the Educational Work of the Arya Samajes under the Arya Pradeshik Pratinidhi Sabha*, The Dayanand Anglo-Vedic College, Lahore, Arya Pradeshik Sabha, Lahore, 1925.

Shastri, Acharya Vaidyanath, *The Arya Samaj: Its Cult and Creed*, Sarvdeshik Arya Pratinidhi Sabha, New Delhi, 1967.

Shastri, Raghuvir, *Arya Mahasammelanon ke Adhyakshiya Bhashan*, Sarvdeshik Arya Pratinidhi Sabha, New Delhi, 1961.

——, *Arya Mahasammelanon ke Prastav, 1908–1960*, Sarvdeshik Arya Pratinidhi Sabha, New Delhi, 1965.

——, *Arya Mahasammelanon ke Prastav, 1961–1977*, Sarvdeshik Arya Pratinidhi Sabha, New Delhi, 1977.

Shastri, Vishnu Lal, *Handbook of Arya Samaj*, Tract Department of the Pratinidhi Sabha, United Provinces, 1912.

Shraddhanand, Swami, *An Autobiography*, M.R. Jambunathan (ed.), Bhartiya Vidya Bhavan, Bombay, 1961.

——, *Hindu Sanghathan: Saviour of the Dying Race*, 1926.

——, *Kalyan Marg ka Pathik* (Autobiography), Sarvdeshik Arya Pratinidhi Sabha, New Delhi, 1978.

Shrimaddayanand Vidhwa Ashram ke Niyam, Dayanand Orphange, Ajmer (n.d.).

Singh, Bawa Chhajju, *Life and Teachings of Swami Dayanand*, Jan Gyan Prakashan, New Delhi, 1971.

Upadhyaya, G.P., *Landmarks of Swami Dayannand's Teachings*, Kala Press, Allahabad, 1947.

——, *Origin, Scope and Mission of Arya Samaj*, Kala Press, Allahabad, 1940.

——, *Raja Ram Mohan Roy, Keshav Chandra Sen, Dayanand*, Kala Press, Prayag, 1954.

Vidyalankar, Bhimsen, *Arya Pratinidhi Sabha Punjab ka Sachitra Itihas*, Arya Pratinidhi Sabha, Punjab, 1936.

——, *Maharishi Dayanand Saraswati*, Sarvdeshik Prakashan Limited, Rishibodh, Delhi, 2007.

Vidyalankar, Satyadev, *Lala Devrajji*, Saraswati Sadan, Mussoorie, 1935.

Vidyalankar, Satyaketu and Haridutt Vedalankar, *Arya Samaj ka Itihas*, Vols. I-V, Arya Svadhyaya Kendra, New Delhi, 1983.

Vidyarthi, Jagdish, *Amar Senani: Swami Shraddhanand*, Arya Kumar Sabha, Delhi, 1969.

Vidyavachaspati, Indra, *Arya Samaj ka Itihas*, 2 Vols., Sarvdeshik Arya Pratinidhi Sabha, New Delhi, 1957.

——, *Swami Shraddhanand, Mere Pita: Sansmaran*, Saraswati Vihar, New Delhi, 1957.

What is Arya Samaj? A member of the Arya Samaj, Ajmer. Printed at the Rajputana Mission Press, Ajmer, 1890.

General Works

Agnes, Flavia, *Women and Law*, Oxford University Press, New Delhi, 2004.

Agnihotri, Satish Balram, *Sex Ratio Patterns in the Indian Population: A Fresh Exploration*, Sage, New Delhi, 2000.

Altekar, A.S., *Position of Women in Hindu Civilization*, Motilal Banarasidas, Delhi, Varanasi, Patna, 1973.

Bader, Clarisse, *Women in Ancient India*, Anmol Publications, Delhi, 1988.

Basu, Krishna and Others, *Role and Status of Women in India*, Firma K.L. Mukhopadhyaya (P) Ltd., Calcutta, 1978.

Bhatia, Shyamla, *Social Change and Politics in Punjab, 1898–1910*, Enkay Publishers Pvt. Ltd., New Delhi, 1987.

Bose, P.N., *A History of Hindu Civilization during British Rule*, Vols. I, II and III, Asian Publication Services, New Delhi, India, 1978 (Reprint).

Brown, J.C., *Indian Infanticide: Its Origin, Progress and Suppression*, W.N. Allen & Co., London, 1857.

Butalia, Urvashi and Tanika Sarkar (eds.), *Women and the Hindu Right*, Kali for Women, New Delhi, 1995.

Butler, Clementia, *Pandita Ramabai Saraswati: Pioneer in the Movement for Education of Child Widow of India*, Fleming H. Revell Company, New York, Chicago, London, Edinburgh, 1922.

Carolla, Theodora Foster, *Women, Religion and the Third World*, Praeger Special Studies, Praeger Scientific, New York, Philadelphia, Eastbourner, U.K., Toronto, Hong Kong, Tokyo, Sydney (n.d.).

Chanana, Karuna (ed.), *Socialisation, Education and Women: Explorations in Gender Identity*, Orient Longman Limited, New Delhi, 1988.

Chandavarkar, G.L., *A Wrestling Soul: Story of the Life of Sir Narayan Chandavarkar*, Popular Book Depot, Bombay, 1955.

——, *Maharishi Karve*, Popular Book Depot, Bombay, 1958.

Chandavarkar, N.G., *Speeches and Writings of N.G. Chandavarkar*, L.V. Kaikini (ed.), Manoranjan Granth Prasarak Mandali, Bombay, 1911.

Chattopadhyaya, Kamla Devi, *Indian Women's Battle for Freedom*, Abhinav Publications, Delhi, 1983.

Chintamani, C.Y., *Indian Social Reform*, Thompson & Co., Popham's Broadway, Madras, 1901.

Dahiwale, S.M., *Understanding Indian Society: The Non Brahmanic Perspective*, Rawat Publications, Jaipur, 2006.

Das, S., *Purdah: The Status of Indian Women*, Ess Ess Publications, New Delhi, 1979.

Datta, V.N., *Sati: A Historical, Social and Philosophical Enquiry into Hindu Rite of Widow Burning*, Manohar Publications, New Delhi, 1988.

Desai, Neera and Mathreyi Krishnaraj, *Women and Society in India*, Ajanta Publications, Delhi, 1987.

Dharampal, *The Beautiful Tree: Indigenous Indian Education in the Nineteenth Century*, Biblia Impex Private Limited, New Delhi, 1983.

Dua, Shiva S., *Society and Culture in Northern India, 1850–1900*, Indian Publishers Bureau and Balaji Enterprises, Delhi, 1985.

Dubois, J.A., *Hindu Manners, Customs and Ceremonies,* (Translated into English by Henry Beauchaump), Oxford Clarendon Press, Oxford, 1953 (Third Edition).

Das, Durga, *India: From Curzon to Nehru and After*, Collins, London, 1969.

Dyer, Helen S., *Pandita Rambai: The Story of Her Life*, Organ and Scott, London (n.d.).

Farquhar, J.N., *The Crown of Hinduism*, Oriental Books of Corporation, New Delhi (Reprint 1971).

Gatwood, Lynn E., *Devi and the Spouse Goddess*, Manohar, New Delhi, 1985.

Gedge, E.C. and M.C. Choksey (eds.), *Women in Modern India*, Kitab Mahal, Bombay, 1921.

Ghosh, Vinay, *Ishwarchandra Vidyasagar*, (Hindi Translation by Devi Shankar Avasthi), Publication Division, Government of India, New Delhi, 1959.

Ghurye, G.S., *Caste and Race in India*, Trubner and Co. Ltd., London (n.d.).

Gidumal, Dayaram, *Behramji M. Malabari: A Sketch*, T. Fisher Unwin, London, 1892.

——, *Status of Woman in India*, Ford Printing Press, Bombay, 1959.

Gupta, Atul Chandra (ed.), *Studies in Bengal Renaissance*, National Council of Education, Jadavpur, 1958.

Habib, Irfan and Vijay Kumar Thakur, *The Vedic Age and the Coming of Iron c.1500–700 BC*, Aligarh Historians Society, Tulika Books, 1952.

Hiemsath, C.H., *Indian Nationalism and Hindu Social Reform*, Oxford University Press, Bombay, 1964.

Indra, *The Status of Women in Ancient India*, Minerva Bookshop, Lahore, 1940.

Jain, Pratibha, *Gandhian Ideas, Social Movements and Creativity*, Rawat Publications, Jaipur, 1985.

Jain, Pratibha and Rajan Mahan (eds.), *Women's Images*, Rawat Publications, Jaipur, 1996.

Jain, Pratibha and Sangeeta Sharma (eds.), *Bhartiya Stree*, Rawat Publications, Jaipur, 1998.

Jagirdar, P.J., *Mahadev Govind Ranade*, (Hindi Translation by Shakuntala Mathur), Builders of Modern India Series, Publication Division, New Delhi, 1981.

Jayvardhane, Kumari, *History of Women's Movement: A Lecture Series*, Part II, Institute of Social Studies, The Hague, 1982.

Joardar, B., *Prostitution in the Nineteenth and Early Twentieth Centuries*, Inter India Publications, New Delhi, 1985.

Karlekar, Malvika, *Voices from Within: Early Personal Narratives of Bengali Women*, Oxford University Press, Delhi, 1993.

Karve, D.K., *Looking Back*, Hindu Widows Home Association, Poona, 1936.

Kopf, David, *British Orientalism and the Bengal Renaissance*, Firma K.L. Mukhopadhyaya, Calcutta, 1969.

Krishnaraj, Mathreyi, *Remaking Society for Women: Visions, Past and Present*, Indian Association for Women's Studies, 1995.

Kujur, Scholistika, *Vedic Evam Dharmshastriya Sahitya Mein Nari*, Vishwavidyalaya Prakashan, Varanasi, 1982.

Kumar, Radha, *History of Doing*, Kali for Women, New Delhi, 1993.

Liddle, Joanne and Rama Joshi, *Daughters of Independence: Gender, Class and Caste in India*, Kali for Women, Delhi, 1986.

Macnicol, Nicol, *Pandita Ramabai*, Association Press (Y.M.C.A.), Calcutta, 1926.

Mali, M.G., *Krantijyoti Savitribai Phule*, Publication Department, Government of India, New Delhi, 1986.

Malik, S.C. (ed.), *Dissent, Protest and Reform in Indian Civilization*, Studies in Indian and Asian Civilization, Indian Institute of Advanced Studies, Simla, 1977.

Mehta, V.R., *Foundations of Indian Political Thought*, Manohar, New Delhi, 1996.

Menon, Nivedita (ed.), *Gender and Politics in India*, Oxford University Press, New Delhi (Reprint 2001).

Mukherjee, Prabhati, *Hindu Women: Normative Models*, Orient Longman Limited, New Delhi, 1978.

Nanda, B.R. (ed.), *Indian Women: From Purdah to Modernity*, Vikas Publishing House, Delhi, Bombay, Bangalore, Calcutta, Kanpur, 1976.

Natrajan, S., *A Century of Social Reform in India*, Asia Publishing House, Bombay, Calcutta, Madras, New Delhi, 1959.

Nehru, Shyam Kumari (ed.), *Our Case: A Symposium by Indian Women*, Kitabistan, Allahabad (n.d.).

Newinson, Henry W., *The New Spirit in India*, Metropolitan Book Company Pvt. Ltd., Delhi, 1975.

O'Malley, L.S. (ed.), *Modern India and the West*, Oxford University Press, London, New York, 1941.

Oman, J.C., *Cults, Customs and Superstitions of India*, Vishal Publishers, Delhi, 1972.

Parvate, T.N., *Mahadev Govind Ranade: A Biography*, Asia Publishing House, Bombay, Calcutta, New Delhi, Madras, Lucknow, London, New York, 1963.

Phadke, Y.D., *Social Reformers of Maharashtra*, Maharashtra Information Centre, Bombay, 1985.

Pinkham, M.W., *Women in the Sacred Scriptures of Hinduism*, Columbia University Press, New York, 1941.

Prasad, Bisheshwar (ed.), *Ideas in History: Proceedings of a Seminar on ideas motivating social and religious movements and political and economic policies during the eighteenth and the nineteenth centuries in India*, Asia Publishing House, Bombay, 1968.

Radice, William, *Swami Vivekananda and the Modernization of Hinduism*, Oxford University Press, Delhi, 1998.

Raghuvanshi, V.P.S., *Indian Society in the Eighteenth Century*, Associated Publishing House, New Delhi, 1969.

Rai, Lala Lajpat, *Problem of National Education in India*, Publication Division, New Delhi, 1966.

Ramabai, Pandita, *The High Caste Hindu Woman*, Maharashtra State Board for Literature and Culture, Mantralaya, Bombay, 1981.

Ranade, M.G., *Miscellaneous Writings of Justice M.G. Ranade*, Published by Mrs Ramabai, Bombay, 1915.

Ranade, Ramabai, *Ranade: His Wife's Reminiscences,* (English Translation by Kusumvati Deshpande), Publications Division, Government of India, New Delhi, 1968.

Robertson, Bruce Carlisle (ed.), *The Essential Writings of Raja Rammohan Roy*, Oxford University Press, Delhi, 1999.

Roy, Kumkum (ed.), *Women in Early Indian Societies*, Manohar, New Delhi, 2001.

Said, Edward, *Orientalism*, Penguin Books, England, 1991.

Sangari, Kumkum and Sudesh Vaid (ed.), *Recasting Women: Essays in Colonial History*, Kali for Women, New Delhi, 1993.

Sarma, D.S., *Hinduism through the Ages*, Bhartiya Vidya Bhavan, Bombay, 1952.

Saxena, R.K., *Education and Social Amelioration of Women* (A Study of Rajasthan), Sanghi Prakashan, Jaipur, Udaipur, 1978.

Sen, Amiya P. (ed.), *Social and Religious Reform: The Hindus of British India*, Oxford University Press, New Delhi, 2003.

——, *Swami Vivekanand*, Oxford University Press, New Delhi, 2000.

Sharma, Tripat, *Women in Ancient India*, Ess Ess Publications, New Delhi, 1988.

Shastri, Shakuntala Rao, *Women in the Vedic Age*, Bhartiya Vidya Bhavan, Bombay, 1952.

Singh, Sardar Jogindar, *B.M. Malabari: Rambles with the Pilgrim Reformer*, G'Bell & Sons, New Delhi, 1914.

Singh, S.R., *Nationalism and Social Reform in India*, Ranjit Printers & Publishers, Delhi, 1968.

Sinha, Pradeep, *Nineteenth Century Bengal: Aspects of Social History*, Firma K.L. Mukhopadhyaya, Calcutta, 1965.

Singh, Yogendra, *Modernization of Indian Tradition*, Thomson Press, Delhi, 1973.

Sriniwas, M.N., *Social Change in Modern India*, Allied Publishers, New Delhi, Calcutta, Madras, 1972.

——, *Caste: Its Twentieth Century Avatar*, Viking Penguin India, New Delhi, 1996.

Tandon, Prakash, *Punjabi Century, 1857–1947*, Chatto and Windus, London, 1963.

Thomas, P., *Indian Women through the Ages*, Asia Publishing House, Bombay, Calcutta, New Delhi, Lucknow, London, New York, 1964.

Tyagi, Anil Kumar, *Women Workers in Ancient India*, Radha Publications, New Delhi, 1994.

Upadhyaya, B.S., *Women in Rig Veda*, S. Chand & Co., New Delhi, Jullunder, Lucknow, Bombay, Calcutta, Madras, Hyderabad, Patna, 1974.

Vedalankar, Ramnath, *Vedic Nari*, Samarpan Shod Sansthan, New Delhi, 1984.

Vivekanand, Swami, *Collected Works of Vivekanand*, Advaita Ashram, Pithoragarh, 1963 (Tenth Edition).

——, *Letters of Swami Vivekanand*, Advaita Ashram, Calcutta, 1981.

Vidyasagar, Ishwarchandra, *Marriage of Hindu Widows*, K.P. Bagchi & Company, Calcutta, 1976.

Vyas, K.C., *The Social Renaissance in India*, Vora & Co., Bombay, 1957.

Yadav, Santosh, *Unnisvin Aur Biswin Shatabdi Mein Strion ki Stithi*, Printwell Publishers, Jaipur, 1987.

Index